THUNDER
IN THE
DESERT

THUNDER IN THE DESERT

THE STRATEGY AND TACTICS OF THE PERSIAN GULF WAR

James Blackwell

BANTAM BOOKS

NEW YORK · TORONTO · LONDON · SYDNEY · AUCKLAND

Thunder in the Desert

A Bantam Book / October 1991

Library of Congress Cataloging-in-Publication Data

Blackwell, James.
    Thunder in the desert : the strategy and tactics of the Persian
Gulf War / James Blackwell.
    p.   cm.
Includes index.
ISBN 0-553-35124-9
    1. Persian Gulf War, 1991.   I. Title.
DS79.72.B56   1991   91-17173
956.704′3—dc20   CIP

Published simultaneously in the United States and Canada

PRINTED IN THE UNITED STATES OF AMERICA

RRH   0   9   8   7   6   5   4   3   2   1

This book is dedicated to the memory of those who lost their lives in the line of duty as a result of hostile fire in the Persian Gulf War. May their sacrifice serve as a perpetual reminder of the cost of liberty. Let us renew our commitment to restore peace to the region so their deaths will not be in vain. May God comfort those who mourn their loss.

Contents

ACKNOWLEDGMENTS

A NUMBER OF people deserve mention for their help in preparing this book. Dr. William J. Taylor, Jr., Center for Strategic and International Studies (CSIS) Vice President for International Security Programs, not only suffered the war without the full-time attention of his deputy program director, he also made available the limitless intellectual resources of the CSIS Political Military Program Staff in the preparation of this book. He did so under the able leadership of CSIS President Ambassador David M. Abshire, who consented to place me on "loan" to CNN for the duration of the war. I am ever grateful to them both for mentoring me over the years and for giving me the opportunity to write this book.

Cable News Network was of course instrumental in providing me a unique perspective on the war. Gail Evans was enough of a risk taker to hire me in the first place, for which I am indeed grateful. The production staff in the Washington Bureau, under Bill Headline's competent leadership, was superb in providing me the opportunity to help with their understanding of the military side of things as well as in providing me with an education in broadcast journalism I doubt anyone else has ever had the opportunity to acquire. Special thanks go to Rick Davis, Tom Farmer, David Grossman, Tammy Haddad, Pam Hill, Peter Kendall, Sol Levine, Fran Lewine, Jill Neff, Pat Reap, Dan Silva, Tom Dunlavey, Jim Barnett, and Peter Tedeschi. I gained new respect for the abilities of a television news anchor through many hours on the set in Washington with Reid Collins, Bernard Shaw, and David French, who collectively have probably forgotten more history than I will ever be able to understand and who individually coached me and taught me. They helped me to bring the jumble of technical military jargon racing around inside my brain into common-sense understanding accessible to millions of viewers around the world.

Carol Blackwell has been my cartographer for the entire book. She is a uniquely talented person who has provided insight and understanding to complex military operations with her common-sense approach to presenting so much data in such highly efficient maps. Jeff Shaffer provided the same kind of enthusiastic aptitude in his preparation of the other diagrams, sketches, and drawings. Several members of the research staff at CSIS provided invaluable help too many times to number, but those persons who deserve individual mention include Don Snider, Mike Mazarr, Greg Grant, Robin Niblett, Matt Culinan, Erv Massenga, Eric Greenwald, Michelle Wolpert, Bob Schneider, and Bob McGahan. The Center's Military Fellows for 1990–1991 were real heroes who provided counsel throughout the process and deserve my many thanks: U.S. Army Colonel Bill Flavin, U.S. Navy Commander Al Myers, U.S. Marine Corps Colonel Mike Ennis, U.S. Air Force Lieutenant Colonel Hans Stoll, and National Guard Fellows Ron Tipa and Don Bills.

This is my first single-author book. I could not have done it without the help of those who know the business far better than I, including Ed Novak and Nancy Eddy. Special thanks go to Larry King, who provided experienced personal advice at a critical point in my decision to attempt to write this book. An author is only as good as his editor and I had the best. Tom Dyja would no doubt have done well as a First Sergeant, but Bantam got him before the Army discovered him. It was my privilege to have worked with Tom, and I hope to do it again.

At root I am a family man. This book was a team effort of my family. My mother faithfully videotaped nearly every appearance I made during the war; my oldest son Joshua helped with the historical analysis; my middle son Jonathan faithfully checked on my health every day; and my kindergarten daughter Elizabeth helped me keep the project in perspective by being thoroughly unimpressed by it all. But above all, I owe my inspiration to my wife Rosalie, who encouraged me every moment and made sure my customary household responsibilities did not stand in the way of completing this project.

A NOTE ABOUT SOURCES

THIS BOOK IS a first draft of history. It is not the final word on what happened in the great Persian Gulf War of 1991. But the art of writing history has undergone profound change in the electronic media age. The written word has not lost its importance, just its immediacy. We no longer have the luxury of waiting for years before attempting to identify and synthesize the views of events and then to draft an integrative interpretation of those accounts.

In another time, the views of a battlefield took years to assemble because it took so long simply to track down those who were there and to collect their stories. Today the camera is there in so many places simultaneously that the video account has become an equal partner in catching history as it happens. The immediacy of the electronic account demands an equally immediate written interpretation.

My primary source for this book has been my own collection of experiences and images from my service as CNN's military analyst during the Persian Gulf War. I worked on the set of CNN's Washington bureau an average of twelve hours a day during the war. My notes of every day of that experience provided my first source of accounting for the events of the war. Videotapes of the stories prepared by the CNN news staff were an invaluable archive in that regard. Every press conference during the war was transcribed and filed at CNN. Those transcripts provided useful supplements to my notes.

The military provided an unusually robust collection of field notes available for historical work on the Persian Gulf War. Dozens of reporters were assigned by military authorities to all the services involved in Desert Shield and Desert Storm. Their reports were shared by all and are on file at the Public Affairs Branch of the Department of Defense; the Pentagon made those reports available to me in my research. The most useful reports were those filed by the staff of the *Army Times*, which covered every major unit involved in the ground war. These reports are a rich source, which has yet to be thoroughly plumbed by historians.

The Center for Strategic and International Studies has been a global resource for this kind of work. The center has conducted an ongoing program in political-military studies, which has provided the basis for my understanding of the Persian Gulf War. Specifically, CSIS has held a series of off-the-record, not-for-attribution meetings in the past year, which have been an inimitable resource. We have had speakers from each of the military service staffs, the joint staff, Central Command, industry, and warriors who fought in the war, all of whom provided valuable documentary and personal accounts, which must remain unmentioned.

Just after the war concluded, I was invited by Army Chief of Staff General Carl E. Vuono to accompany him and his staff as a guest journalist on a trip to the war zone as he conducted a personal assessment of the war from the viewpoints of his commanders and their soldiers. The ground rules of the trip (and of the CSIS sessions) were such that I cannot name names or attribute information to specific sources, and I will not violate that confidence. Suffice it to say that I was granted unparalleled access to commanders at several levels and to enlisted personnel who actually engaged the enemy in mortal battle. In the course of this visit, I was able to gain information from accounts given to military officials by Iraqi military personnel as well.

These personal accounts were supplemented by official accounts that are now virtually complete. The Air Force has an official briefing that summarizes the air war. Each division and corps for the Army units has compiled an official after-action report, and most of those were made available to me soon after they were compiled. The Marines have done likewise.

Much of the technical information in this book comes from publicly available, although in many cases obscure, sources. The U.S. Air Force staff compiled a "Quick Reference Guide, Aircraft & Weapons," which was the principal source for data on aircraft equipment, while the Army's version is simply titled "Weapons Systems 1991."

A few unclassified intelligence documents were extremely useful, specifically, "How They Fight: Desert Shield Order of Battle Handbook," and "How They Fight: Desert Shield Order of Battle Handbook, Friendly Forces," both of which addressed air, land, and naval forces and were made available by the U.S. Army Intelligence and Threat Analysis Center. A particularly thorough source is *The Iraqi Army: Organization and Tactics*, National Training Center Handbook 100–91, January 1991, a copy of which was made available during the conflict.

The discussions of the more general related topics were compiled from various public accounts, primarily the series of public hearings held by the Senate Armed Services Committee, the House Armed Services Committee, and the Senate Foreign Relations Committee during the crisis. Of particular value was the series of public discussions organized in December 1990 by House Armed Services Committee Chairman Les Aspin. The most useful document on the historical development of Iraq is the State Department's *Area Handbook for Iraq*, last revised in 1990.

Where specific attribution is needed it appears on the text. I have tried to remain faithful to the accounts as presented in the various sources, but in the end only one person can author this book and that is James Blackwell. I remain fully responsible for the conclusions as to fact as I have presented them and believe this book is the best possible synthesis of the information thus far available on the war in the Persian Gulf.

TABLE OF MILITARY SYMBOLS

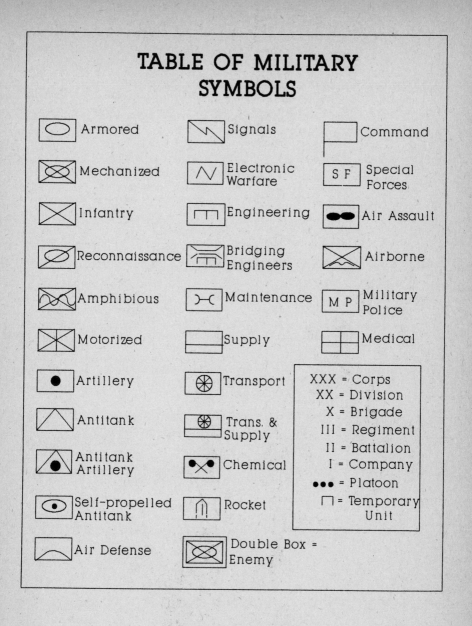

Armored

Mechanized

Infantry

Reconnaissance

Amphibious

Motorized

Artillery

Antitank

Antitank Artillery

Self-propelled Antitank

Air Defense

Signals

Electronic Warfare

Engineering

Bridging Engineers

Maintenance

Supply

Transport

Trans. & Supply

Chemical

Rocket

Double Box = Enemy

Command

S F Special Forces

Air Assault

Airborne

M P Military Police

Medical

XXX = Corps
XX = Division
X = Brigade
III = Regiment
II = Battalion
I = Company
●●● = Platoon
⊓ = Temporary Unit

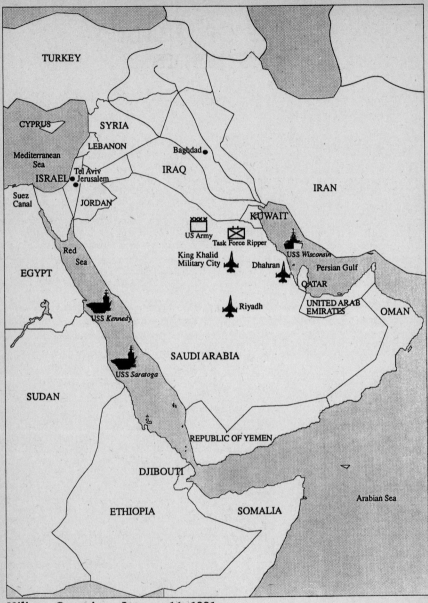

Military Operations, January 16, 1991

INTRODUCTION

The Liberation of Kuwait Has Begun

The next few days will set the course of the world for decades to come. If we must fight, we will. If we can restore freedom to Kuwait without a fight, we will. For you and I, the choice is not ours to make. If the call to fight is sounded, I am confident in your abilities, your courage, and your stamina. We are joined by professional, talented allies with impressive skills, courage, and dedication. We are not alone. Now is the time to ensure that the final checks are made. Reach inside and put all the normal fear to bed and replace it with calm, cool, collected thought. War is won by those who can think best and make the fewest mistakes. There is a marvelous line from the book Bridge of Toko-Ri, *"Where did we get such men!" Where indeed. I am proud of each of you. Good hunting and God-speed.*

—Message to the Fleet from VICE ADMIRAL STANLEY P. ARTHUR, Commander of Naval Forces in the Persian Gulf, sometime in the afternoon, January 16, 1991

ABOARD THE USS *WISCONSIN*, SOMEWHERE AT SEA IN THE PERSIAN GULF, JANUARY 16, 1991

For weeks the team of mission planners had been working in secret, preparing the target data packages to be sent to the *Wisconsin's* thirty-two TLAMs (Tomahawk Land Attack Missiles). They had come out of the best staffs from Headquarters, U.S. Central Command, the Navy, and Joint Staffs in the Pentagon and included technical experts from the manufacturers of the TLAM. Precise flight instructions were converted to bit streams of computerized targeting data that would guide the missiles to Baghdad and other points deep inside Iraq. Downloading guidance data can be done in a couple of hours, but the preparation is tedious. In theory the entire process can be done remotely by satellite downlink; in practice it can sometimes take days to prepare and enter into the missiles' computers the point-by-point instructions to get to a specific building on a particular block within the designated ground zero.

Captain David Bill, the *Wisconsin*'s skipper, had spent five grueling months at sea preparing his complement of over 1,500 men for this moment. It had not been easy. A few months before the deployment to the Persian Gulf, his ship had been designated for retirement for a third time since it was first commissioned in 1944. Now it was again in the middle of a real shooting war. The drills were tiresome but vital, made even more difficult by new systems such as the Tomahawk, and the new potential combat environment of chemical warfare.

Just a few days earlier, high seas and bad weather had conspired to produce a less than satisfactory performance on a routine general quarters drill. The crew had fallen just fifteen seconds short of the minimum eleven-minute standard to close off all watertight compartments and to man all battle stations, and far short of the objective of eight minutes. By the morning of the sixteenth they had gotten the drill down to a more proficient eight minutes, thirteen seconds. Now there was a new sense of urgency about their business.

Upon completion of the general quarters drill, Captain Bill addressed the entire crew:

> Gents, from all indications that I am getting, we have a very large potential to go to war this evening. That order has not been given. But barring any last-minute breaks in the diplomatic scene, which I do not expect, my best guess is that we will launch Tomahawk missiles north towards Iraq on the midwatch tonight. Again, that is speculation. And again, I repeat, we have not received the formal order. But all the cards are falling into place. What I want you to do

now, having gone through our last drill, is to get some rest and be ready. I expect to go to general quarters about thirty to forty-five minutes before we shoot and then remain at general quarters until the tactical situation clarifies. We need to respond to whatever happens. Gentlemen, we are ready. I have no doubt of that. And I have no doubt that you are on the winning team. . . . So gents, we'll stand by to stand by. But . . . every expectation I have [is that] we'll go to war tonight. That is all.

The entire crew let out a cheer.

At 0140 hours Gulf time on the seventeenth, the *Wisconsin*'s Fire Control Officer, Petty Officer First Class Todd Brannan, who had helped install the Tomahawk launch system on the *Wisconsin*, pushed the execute button, and the opening shots of Desert Storm were on their way. One of the first Tomahawk Land Attack Missiles ever fired in anger blasted out of its armored box launcher, propelled by an explosive charge. Its rocket motor ignited, propelling the missile downrange to its cruise altitude, where its jet engine cut in after the rocket motor burned out. Brannan said afterward, "I never thought I'd actually fire a missile. . . . I didn't realize that they were so big." A few hours later it would ruin someone's night somewhere in Iraq.

The cruise missile is one of America's technological marvels of warfare. It is so effective that the Russians agreed with the United States in 1987 to ban one version—the ground-launched cruise missile, or GLCM—from production entirely. The Soviet government agreed to the ban not so much because of its heartfelt desire for peace and stability in Europe as from its fear of the tremendous scientific lead the United States has in the development and application of the technology.

The cruise missile is essentially a sophisticated drone. It flies at about the speed of a commercial airliner, and some can reach out to ranges of over 1,500 miles—a Tomahawk launched from Los Angeles, California, could fly into City Hall in Kansas City, Missouri. Its on-board computers store three kinds of guidance data. Inertial guidance systems record the starting point for the missile wherever it is when launched and keep track of how far away from the launch point the missile is at any given moment.

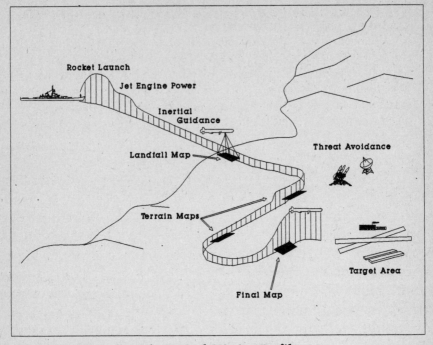

Tomahawk Cruise Missile Typical Mission Profile

Along the flight path the missile's sensors look downward and instantly construct a map of what they "see." The missile compares this real-time map to maps loaded into the computer by the target planners, and the Tomahawk is steered over a predesignated route of flight along a recognizable feature on the ground. A favorite landmark used in the attacks on Baghdad was the main six-lane highway leading into the city.

Along the way the missile also looks at more detailed maps at specific critical places to make twists and turns for navigational purposes or to avoid known enemy defenses. Once in the target area the computer tells the missile to look for an object that matches a photograph loaded into the computer's memory; when the target is recognized, the missile flies itself to its objective. The missile can carry a nuclear warhead, but the versions used against Iraq were conventional, carrying 1,000 pounds of high explosives, or hundreds of bomblets to destroy multiple targets in the impact area.

Cruise missiles had been tested extensively during the 1970s and 1980s. Critics had alleged that they would never work in combat. Now the world was about to witness, live by satellite, just how wrong those critics were. Brannan pressed the execute button again.

AT AN AIR BASE IN CENTRAL SAUDI ARABIA, JANUARY 16, 1991

The F-15Es of the U.S. Air Force 4th Tactical Fighter Wing had been in Saudi Arabia since the tenth of August, when they were the first fighters to arrive capable of launching ground strikes. It had been "hurry up and wait" ever since then, but now the waiting was over. Today's Air Tasking Order had brought the coded instruction "Execute Operation Desert Storm," and the war was on. The wing's Maintenance Officer, Colonel Ray Davies, could only find words in cliché: "This is history in the making. . . . It's absolutely awesome." For National Guard pilot Thorne Ambrose, it was combat of another kind; formerly a pilot for Eastern Airlines, he remarked, "Working for Frank Lorenzo kind of got me used to working in a war zone." Even a truck on the flight line seemed to have the élan of the fighter pilots it supported; the truck carried its own message for the enemy, written on a side panel: "Don't run, Saddam, you'll only die tired."

At another base in southwestern Saudi Arabia, the Air Force's 35th Tactical Fighter Wing and the 3rd Marine Air Wing prepared to launch their birds by putting on their bullet- and shrapnel-proof shields, known as flak vests, and taking their anti–nerve agent pills. All outgoing telephone calls from the base stopped at 7:30 that evening. The 35th's Wing Commander, Colonel Ron Karp, had no dramatic speech for sending his men off, only a fighter jock's euphoric overstatement: "This is the most powerful air armada ever formed. . . . I know they'll make us proud."

His lead pilot, Colonel George "John Boy" Walton, had prayed and emptied his pockets of personal effects in the age-old pilot's ritual intended to keep the enemy from knowing anything more about him than his dogtags indicated, although Walton had no intention of getting shot down that night. As he strapped himself into the cockpit of his F-4G fighter jet, Colonel Karp yelled to his Electronic Weapons Officer, Captain Buddy Redmond, "Hey, Budman, hit 'em hard!" Redmond answered, "Yes, sir, I'll kick their ass," and raised his fist with a thumbs up. At 0125 hours on the seventeenth, Walton and Redmond were airborne, on their way toward Iraq.

The Air Force's F-4G Wild Weasel aircraft, Vietnam era gas-guzzlers used to snuff out antiaircraft ground radar, had been loaded with High-Speed Anti-Radiation Missiles (HARMs). A receiver on the F-4G picks up enemy radar beams, and the pilot presses a button to transfer data to the missile for the target he wants to hit. Each HARM picks up an enemy ground-based radar and automatically homes in on its source on the ground. The 35th Wings missile flew right into the radar dishes from over ten miles away and destroyed several installations with 800 pounds of high explosives.

A few minutes later the Marine Air Wing's aircraft were launched in the same fashion; over thirty F/A-18 and Navy A-6E fighters roared into the night sky. It took nearly an hour to get them all aloft. The A-6E is another Vietnam veteran still in service. The Intruder, as it is called, has been upgraded and remains the world's best all-weather precision bomber. The "E" model had proven its capabilities in the raid on Libya in 1986, when a flight of fifteen A-6Es evaded over a hundred of Qaddafi's modern Russian-made surface-to-air missiles.

Guns, bombs, and missiles are not the only weapons of war. Some aircraft carry only electrons to do their business. And on this night, American electrons totally overwhelmed Iraqi electrons. Many were fired by the EF-111 Raven aircraft flown by the 390th Electronic Combat Squadron. The mission of the EF-111 is

to jam enemy radar with powerful signals that cause the operator's screen to "white out," as if it were breaking down. By the
time they realize it is an American jamming signal, it's too late. It
can also create on enemy radar screens phantom false targets,
many of which might have been the intended targets of all the
seemingly aimless antiaircraft fire over Baghdad that night.

Squadron Commander Lieutenant Colonel Dennis Hardziej
and his Electronic Warfare Officer Captain Tom Mahoney told of
a greeting party of Iraqi MiG-29s and -25s that came up to meet
them that night. But the EF-111's superior dash speed at low
level—supersonic at 200 feet above the ground—made escape
possible with a quick maneuver as the enemy's missiles impacted
on the ground.

While F-4s, A-6s, and F-111s are all combat veterans of previous
wars, the Air Force's newest fighter received its baptism by fire as
the liberation of Kuwait began. Existence of the supersecret
Stealth fighter, the F-117, was not even acknowledged by the Air
Force until 1989. It had seen experimental use against a very
limited threat in Panama in December 1989, but it was present in
strength in Saudi Arabia. At about 0300 hours on the seventeenth, the 37th Tactical Fighter Wing's F-117s, under the command of Colonel Al Whitley, struck several key targets in
Baghdad and elsewhere in Iraq.

Colonel Whitley's wing had studied for weeks, going over specific targets including floor plans and photographs. Their handi-
work was dramatically revealed at a Riyadh briefing a few days
after the attack, when videotapes from the aircraft showed laser-
guided bombs from the F-117s flying down a skylight on the roof
of the presidential bunker and down the air shaft of the AT&T
communications central building. Colonel Whitley seemed to
echo Luke Skywalker's attitude on gunnery when he later said,
"You pick precisely which target you want. You can want the
men's room or you can want the ladies' room."

These stories and more were repeated throughout that first
night as 1,000 pilots completed their first missions of the air
campaign. Apache helicopters from the Army conducted a bold
raid deep into Iraqi territory to knock out a key antiaircraft radar

site, creating an air corridor for many jets to penetrate Iraqi airspace. A-10 Thunderbolt aircraft searched out and destroyed several known Scud missile sites, and F-111B bombers dropped 2,000-pound laser-guided bombs on key targets as well. Some did not return: An American F/A-18 and an F-15E were shot down, as were two British, one Italian, and one Kuwaiti aircraft.

At least one Iraqi pilot secured his heavenly reward, too. U.S. Air Force F-15 pilot Captain Steve Tate had taken off at 0130 to fly high cover over Baghdad for the bombers flying in at medium altitude. At about 0315 he scored the first air-to-air kill of the war as an Iraqi F-1 (an advanced French-made fighter known as the Mirage) came up to take on one of Tate's colleagues in the flight of four F-15s. Alerted by the Airborne Warning and Control System (AWACS) aircraft, a sophisticated Boeing 707 outfitted with a dazzling array of radars, computers, and communications devices, Tate locked onto the "bogie" and launched a single Sparrow radar-guided missile with hypersonic speed and a twenty-five-mile range. The Mirage tried to turn and run but could not outdistance the Sparrow. The resulting impact caused a brilliant fireball. Thus Captain Tate's 1st Tactical Fighter Wing kept intact the motto it earned after scoring the first aerial kills of World War I and World War II: "The First is the first."

SOMEWHERE IN THE RED SEA, ABOARD THE CARRIER USS *JOHN F. KENNEDY*, JANUARY 16, 1991

The headline on the ship's newspaper, *The Bird Farm Bulletin*, the day before had quoted Army General George S. Patton, Jr., on the essential matter of combat: "To use the means at hand to inflict the maximum amount of wounds, death, and destruction on the enemy, in a minimum amount of time." The Navy was not normally so enamored of Army theories about warfare, but the only other real news of the day was that it was payday, as the 5,500 men of the supercarrier began their sixth month at sea since the fifteenth of August deployment from their home port of Norfolk,

Virginia. Earlier in the day, on the sixteenth in the Gulf, as the U.N. deadline for Iraq to withdraw from Kuwait had passed, the ship's skipper, Vietnam veteran Captain John P. Gay, had told his men not to be afraid of combat, that their apprehensions were normal and would pass as they got through the first one or two missions.

As the day wore on and it was revealed that the attack would begin after midnight, preparations began in earnest. The ship's lunch menu even included a listing for Iraq's next meal, courtesy of the U.S. Navy: LGBs, CBUs, and HARMs (LGB stands for Laser-Guided Bomb, CBU is Cluster Bomb Unit). Ordnance was brought out and gas masks were kept near as the Red Sea Fleet Commander, Admiral Riley D. Mixson, spoke words of encouragement over the ship's loudspeaker system: "You have trained hard, you're ready. Now let's execute. . . . I wish you good hunting and Godspeed. God bless us all."

The ship's Catholic chaplain, Lieutenant Commander John Kaul, had noted the men's increased interest in religious faith each time they came close to the war zone: His chapel filled with sailors whenever they entered the Red Sea. He called it "Red Sea religion." At 2200 hours that night he led the entire ship's company in prayer as they steeled themselves for the launch of the *Kennedy*'s forty-one combat aircraft designated for the assault on Iraq:

An evil man is loose, O Lord. Argument and reason have failed us. As much as what we must do now is the right thing, we know you are with us. We do not abandon our prayer for peace. We now pray that it come as soon as possible. As our families and friends hear the news, we pray that you support them in their anxiety.

Belowdecks the men expressed relief that the long wait was soon to be over. At precisely 0120 hours Gulf time on the seventeenth, launch operations commenced with the catapult of an A-7 attack fighter. It took over an hour to get all forty-one birds into the air. Another seventeen A-7 Corsairs followed the first plane, then six A-6 Intruders, four F-14 Tomcats, four EA6-B Prowlers, one E-2C Hawkeye, four more F-14s, and four refueling tanker aircraft, each pilot calling back to the air boss with the message that he was successfully airborne. The sequence was repeated on five other U.S. carriers that night in the war zone. Their targets were near Baghdad and western Iraq, air bases, communications centers, air defense emplacements, and Scud missile sites.

WITH THE U.S. MARINES OF TASK FORCE RIPPER, NEAR THE SAUDI-KUWAITI BORDER, JANUARY 16, 1991

The passing of the U.N. deadline earlier in the day was noted with the discontented ambivalence that only an American grunt can express. "This war sucks," said one Marine back in the supply dump. Sergeant Alvin Grimes had been a little more articulate yet uncannily prophetic a few days earlier when he said, "I want to see those bombs and missiles come down so hard that by the time we get to them Iraqis all we see is a bunch of waving white flags." But there were no white flags this day as the Marines watched and heard the Allied air armada thunder over their heads into Kuwait and Iraq. Lance Corporal Everett Eason scratched out the word "Peace" he had penned on his helmet to make the inscription read, "Pray for Victory."

The Marines had been deploying and organizing themselves since arriving in force early in August. Much of the work involved activating and bringing in reserve forces from the States and incorporating them with their full-time-duty counterparts. Some had time to train on new equipment as some Marine tank units traded in their older M-60 tanks for brand-new M1A1s with help from Army trainers and prime contractor General Dynamics Corporation technicians. One reservist, Sergeant Bernard Castro, had been activated just two weeks before his final exams at the University of Houston. He told a reporter, "I wasn't doing too well anyway."

Much of the effort was devoted to establishing the huge logistics apparatus that would be needed to provide the food, fuel, ammunition, and equipment they would need for a land campaign. Earlier in January the Marines had intercepted a phantom Iraqi helicopter formation supposedly penetrating Saudi airspace to defect. Officials said that early reports by forward sentries of approaching helicopters were mistaken. It turned out that they had been American special operating forces helicopters, commandos disguised as Iraqis, sneaking back across friendly lines. They had fooled the Iraqis but not the Marines.

Task Force Ripper was a combined arms force including infantry, tanks, amphibious assault vehicles, artillery, engineers, and special intelligence troops trained and equipped for deception operations. The commander, Colonel Carl Fulford, watched the aircraft overhead and yelled, "Go Air Force!" He had led his troops through months of hard training to prepare to launch their part of the war. Only a few days ago the weather had been the worst in fifty years on the Arabian Peninsula. His troops were cold and very wet after being drenched with over half of Saudi Arabia's average annual rainfall in just thirty-six hours. But his troops' spirits were high. Lieutenant Robert Stuart said, "Mud and rain doesn't bother Marines, rotten conditions just inspire us to more articulate gripes." Watching the air war pass over them, they knew their ticket home, through Kuwait, was near.

Their job for the moment was to sit tight until they received the order to attack. Most of Task Force Ripper's Marines were ready to do just that. After hearing the news that the air war had begun, many just turned over in their sleeping bags and went back to sleep, eager only to get their fair share before their shift on duty began. For some the sixteenth was simply another payday with nowhere to spend their money. It turned out that the Iraqis did have a response to the Allied air campaign, but the response was aimed at the grunts rather than the aviators.

At 0500 hours an Iraqi artillery battery opened fire on Task Force Ripper's positions, using 155mm howitzers and rockets. While not as accurate as American artillery in general, the Iraqis' best 155mm gun had a range of up to twenty-four miles, about eight miles farther than the Marines' own 155mm howitzers firing standard ammunition. The Marines of Task Force Ripper would have a hard time responding to the attack in kind.

Instead, the task force called on its close air support, consisting of four AH-1W Cobra attack helicopters and four AV-8B Harrier jump jet attack fighters. The Cobras were also sent to look for reported enemy tanks in the area, but finding none, concentrated on destroying the Iraqis' observation post with TOW missiles. The Harriers dropped four tons of bombs on the Iraqi artillery battery, silencing all six guns. Iraqi ground forces had fired anti-aircraft guns at the AV-8Bs, but not a single round hit the British-designed, McDonnell Douglas–built fighters. No count of Iraqi casualties could be made, but a Navy medical corpsman and two Marines were wounded. They became the first to receive the Purple Heart, America's medal for those who receive wounds in battle.

For the hundreds of thousands of U.S. Army soldiers in Saudi Arabia, the first day of the war was much like the previous four months. Other than the Apaches that flew in support of the air campaign and commandos operating behind Iraqi lines, the Army's VII and XVIII corps continued to deploy more forces into the theater of war, and those already there continued to train and organize for the beginning of the anticipated ground campaign.

Much new equipment was being integrated, including the newest tank, the M1A1 with its 120mm gun, the most powerful tank in the world. One Apache helicopter pilot with the 82nd Airborne Division, Chief Warrant Officer Cleveland Simmons, had spent his second Christmas in a combat zone away from home, having fought with his helicopter in Panama in 1989–90; now he was preparing to fly into battle against Iraqi forces facing the coalition. For one soldier in the 37th Engineers, the months of waiting had stretched on so long he told a reporter, "It seems like I was born here." Major John Chapman, Executive Officer for the 1st Armored Division's 1st Battalion, 35th Armor, had only recently arrived with his unit from Germany but was confident his Abrams tanks would be instrumental in the defeat of Iraq: "We want to show up where the Iraqis can't believe we could possibly be." He would have to wait another four weeks, but he would get his chance to do just that.

CNN WASHINGTON BUREAU, 6:30 P.M. EASTERN STANDARD TIME, JANUARY 16, 1991

It was beginning to be a weird evening at CNN Washington. David French was filling in for Bernard Shaw as anchor. Bernie had gone to Baghdad to get the prize, an interview with Saddam Hussein. Shaw had gotten the interview, but it was almost anti-climactic. Saddam had only rhetoric in answer to Bernie's pointed questions about Iraq's intentions; the President's answers sounded more like a Gorbachev speech to the Soviet Agriculture Ministry than a tyrant wanting to send a message to the world.

Then there was the eerie atmosphere around the White House. CNN's White House correspondent, Frank Sesno, had observed that it reminded him of the day in December 1989 before the President had ordered U.S. forces into Panama. Then as now, President Bush seemed unusually subdued yet confident; the "wimp factor" and the "vision thing" had vanished.

On the set, the director had just checked the "four wire," the unique telecommunications link CNN had smuggled into Baghdad that provided several simultaneous links for pictures and voice over telephone, satellite, and microwave transmission systems to the global news network. Shaw, veteran war correspondent Peter Arnett, and junior reporter John Holliman were wired up and ready to go for their next segment. Atlanta Executive Producer Bob Furnad was his usual fiery self, insisting on perfection in every detail of his prime-time news show. From time to time the world could hear on the air his terse commands to his team—instructions normally carried only internally to CNN staff.

Bernard Shaw was just completing his checkout with the director when Shaw said, "Wait a minute, something's happening outside. . . ." What happened that night is etched indelibly in all our minds. Shaw, Arnett, and Holliman made journalistic history in providing the first live coverage from the target area of the beginning of a surprise war.

When I saw the pictures they were sending on the monitor in our office area at CSIS, my first thought was that we were seeing only trigger-happy Iraqi gunners firing perhaps at birds that might appear to be airplanes in the gloomy darkness of the night. Having spent many a long, lonely night waiting for ducks or deer to approach my hunting blind in darkness, I knew how deceptive a still, dark, moonless night could be. I could imagine how nervous you must be if you were worried that your prey could shoot back at you. But it quickly became clear that whatever the Iraqi gunners were shooting at was causing all kinds of havoc on the ground in and around Baghdad. They were scared, all right—and they had good reason to be.

The war was on, and CNN had captured it live from the target area. The coverage was so timely, even the supersecret Defense Intelligence Agency, monitoring the nation's sophisticated spy network around the world, had every analyst's desktop television monitor tuned in to CNN to catch the live reports from Baghdad—it was the only human intelligence available. I had but a few minutes earlier signed an exclusive contract to provide CNN's military analysis for the war and was on my way to the Washington bureau to get introduced to the production staff and to familiarize myself with the inner workings of a world-class network news operation. I left quickly for the studio at 111 Massachusetts Avenue, a block from the Capitol building, while Marlin Fitzwater made a terse announcement at the White House: "The liberation of Kuwait has begun."

The CNN control room was so much like my Army command post at division headquarters it was scary. I almost expected incoming artillery or chemical-attack alerts to sound, and I wondered as I stared at these strangers if any of them knew how to put on a gas mask. I stood just beside the producer's seat at the control room watching a scene that might have appeared to be pandemonium had I not seen so many tactical operations centers work just like this one.

It was not my first live appearance on CNN; I had been on the *Larry King Live* show in August, when Iraq invaded Kuwait and the United States had deployed a few ground brigades from the

Army and the Marines, four wings of fighters, and a carrier to the Gulf. I had predicted then that Saddam Hussein would move into the northern and eastern oil fields of Saudi Arabia because neither the Saudis nor the meager U.S. forces could defend the area for more than a few days. If he did not attack soon, Saddam would lose the opportunity he had created for himself and apparently was intent on exploiting as additional, more powerful U.S. forces were brought to bear. The prospect of controlling as much as half the world's oil reserves must have been his reason for attacking in the first place, it seemed to me. I was wrong, but CNN hired me anyway.

It was clear from the reporting by our boys in Baghdad that the aerial strikes were going in with great precision. As John Holliman and Peter Arnett described bombs going off at an oil refinery, then the presidential office building, then the communications center at the AT&T building, Bernard Shaw concluded, "Gentlemen, we are witnessing a surgical strike." You could place the strikes on the studio map with exactitude from their descriptions. They were serving as effectively as any scouts I had had in my command in the armored cavalry when reconnaissance was my primary mission.

The attack caught the Iraqis totally by surprise. That their command and control system had been seriously disrupted became evident when John Holliman described the last block of lights blinking out in the city, in accordance with air-raid procedures, a full hour after the first strikes went in. In a drill held just a few days earlier, the city had blacked itself out in fifteen minutes. At one point Bernard Shaw could hear the sound of helicopters going by but could see no lights on the dim outline of the two craft as they sped past their hotel window. It was highly unlikely that it was an Iraqi helicopter—their pilots do not have night-vision goggles for flying while blacked out and do not like flying in darkness even with lights on, especially at low altitude in an urban environment. This was more likely an Allied helicopter flight, perhaps on a commando mission. In another moment Bernie remarked, "Just one comment: Clearly I've never been there, but this looks like the center of Hell." Later he told of a solitary rooster crowing in the darkness below, a surreal sound he said he would remember for the rest of his life.

Then the President spoke to Americans directly, promising them that the liberation of Kuwait would not become another Vietnam. He reassured the public that he had not tied the hands of the military leadership in carrying out the war and that he believed it would not be long nor would casualties be high. Bush declared that Iraq would comply with all the resolutions passed by the U.N. Security Council, and he spoke of the unspeakable atrocities Saddam's forces had committed in occupied Kuwait. He promised, "Our goal is not to conquer Iraq, it is to liberate Kuwait."

At 9:30 P.M. Secretary of Defense Richard Cheney and Joint Chiefs Chairman General Colin Powell briefed the waiting press on the operation. They reported that four Allied air forces had taken part in the first night's attacks: U.S., British, Saudi, and Kuwaiti pilots had all reached their targets. The objectives were military, but the Pentagon was going to limit the amount and kind of information they would release. They indicated that preliminary reports were encouraging but that the operation was likely to run for a long time. At the end of the briefing, Secretary Cheney remarked that his best reports on what was happening in Baghdad were indeed from CNN. At that comment the entire Washington bureau broke into loud cheers and applause.

The United States had undertaken a war of vast proportions. This was bigger than Vietnam at its peak, there were more tanks in the theater of operations than in the largest tank battles of World War II, and the technologies present were far more advanced even than those in the Arab-Israeli War of 1973. The expectations were for many casualties; but times had changed, and the mood of the country was remarkably supportive, even considering the normal tendency early in a crisis to support the President and the troops in the field. There was a sense that the liberation of Kuwait had liberated us from the ghost of Vietnam that had haunted previous military operations in the 1970s and 1980s and that this time we would do it right.

And we did do it right. From the moment Iraqi troops stepped across the Kuwaiti border, the United States realized that the world was facing a fundamental crisis in the world order. Given Iraq's heritage, the character of Saddam's regime, and the incredible military machine the Iraqis had perfected in defeating the Iranians, most Americans sensed that the world faced a clear and present danger. The embargo, the vast deployment of troops and equipment, and the domestic and international politics of the crisis were all driven by George Bush toward the purposes he set out in early August. The air and land campaigns were the culmination of a decade of reform and rebuilding of the American military, and the final win in Kuwait was a triumph of America's new role as the only superpower in the world capable of building a coalition against a threat to international security.

THUNDER IN THE DESERT

CHAPTER ONE

By the Waters of Babylon

MODERN-DAY IRAQ occupies the region of the world where civilization was born. The human race could have prospered there, but in just about every century since the emergence of civilization there have been wars and rumors of wars in Iraq, with thousands to hundreds of thousands of people killed in each conflagration. The history of Iraq is very much a history of warfare. When ancient people of the region eventually built a city to enshrine the art of war, they built it in Iraq. It was called Babylon. Before his defeat in the Persian Gulf War of 1991, Saddam Hussein had set out to rebuild Babylon in all its splendor and brutality. His ambition was ultimately to rule the world from his throne in the rebuilt Babylon.

From the earliest recorded times, the human race had lived in the fertile basin between the Tigris and Euphrates rivers in this region. The plentiful water supply from the two rivers provided an abundance of natural resources for Stone Age *Homo sapiens*, although frequent flooding made life there a risky proposition sometimes. Compared to the surrounding deserts and mountains, however, it had been a life-giving, prosperous area for millennia.

Its agrarian culture was from time to time threatened by those less fortunate tribes on the periphery, whose grass was always less green. To defend his people, the ancient Urukain tribal chief Habuba el-Kabira built a fort 1,100 yards long in 3300 B.C. in a

1

part of the region now in Syrian territory. Within the confines of this fruitful watershed an advanced culture developed among the Sumerian inhabitants.

Iraq's Ancient Martial Heritage

The Sumerians were an industrious people who invented the art of making bricks. They applied their craft in constructing the Ziggurat of Ur, still the world's oldest continuously standing man-made structure. Saddam Hussein's defiant pretensions to greatness were revealed to the world when American satellite reconnaissance photos disclosed two MiG-29s the dictator had parked in front of the ziggurat in mock portrayal of the bronze lions that had once stood guard at the entrance to the ancient temple tower. Saddam, of course, had no cultural advancement in mind; he simply counted on the Allies' magnanimity to keep them from dropping bombs close to one of the world's most treasured archaeological sites.

The Sumerians invented bronze when they discovered that melting tin and copper together produces an even harder metal. They used it not only for fine artistic creations but also for weapons, namely, to shape sharp tips for their spears and arrows. They invented the chariot, precursor of the twentieth-century main battle tank. In order to record their exploits the Sumerians were the first culture to organize the shaping of forms to represent words for communicating. They even developed a body of epic literature to pass on the history of their martial exploits. The first classic in this genre—the story of the Sumerian warrior king Gilgamesh—preceded the better-known Greek stories of Homer by centuries.

From 3360 to 2334 B.C. the Sumerians ruled the region from the northwesternmost reach of the Persian Gulf to the place where the Tigris and Euphrates make their closest approach to each other, a few dozen miles south of present-day Baghdad. But in their success they sowed the seeds of their own demise. Rival city-states grew around the main population centers, and in 2334 B.C., Sargon I of Akkad, from the one-third of Mesopotamia centered on present-day Baghdad, conquered the Sumerians. Though he subjugated them, Sargon I held the Sumerians in a position of honor in the larger society he was building across the Middle East.

Sargon united the region and spread his rule out to Egypt and Ethiopia. He, too, was a military innovator of substantial achievement, establishing the world's first conscripted army. His martial craftsmen created the first composite material when they pressed strips of wood and horn together to manufacture a much more resilient bow. Sargon's grandson Naram-Sin completed the establishment of the Akkadian kingdom with the decisive defeat of the city-state of Ebla, in modern-day Turkey, in a classic battle of annihilation and utter destruction in 2250 B.C. Saddam Hussein had designs on forging his own empire reaching at least as far as that of the Akkadians.

Naram-Sin did not have his grandfather's wisdom and soon was eclipsed by the Amorites from the east, who invaded Mesopotamia and built the great Iraqi city of Babylon on the banks of the Euphrates. Hammurabi, the Amorite king, was the first ruler to codify his rules and judgments to provide consistency in his governance. The Code of Hammurabi consists of 282 laws literally carved in stone and preserved on a large stele now displayed in the Field Museum in Chicago. Saddam fashioned himself as a modern-day Hammurabi, a benevolent ruler who could both rule with a firm hand and display respect for the children of his enemies.

Saddam's ancient alter ego was overtaken by Hittites from the northwest, historical forerunners of the twentieth-century Kurds. The Hittites had mastered the art of iron forging to make weapons superior to any the Amorites could field. In turn, the region was dominated in the last millennium before Christ by the Assyrians. From 883 to 612 B.C. the Assyrians threatened to subjugate the entire Mesopotamian basin under a savage rule of successive dictators.

In 853 B.C. the onward march of the brutal Assyrian conquerors caused the ancient ancestors of modern-day Iraq to form an unholy alliance to resist defeat by the dreaded Shalmaneser III. At the Battle of Qarqar, the Hittites threw their lot to a coalition with Hadadezer of Damascus and Ahab of Israel. The combined army deployed over 62,000 infantry, nearly 4,000 chariots, and 2,900 cavalry mounted on horses or camels. They won the day, but by the next generation of Assyrian rulers, control of Babylon had changed hands once again.

Assyrian King Tiglath-Pileser III took Babylon and moved his throne there, declaring himself ruler of all Mesopotamia. He created the world's first permanent standing army and built himself a new capital city in the northern region, at Nineveh. When it was completed, he moved his throne there and destroyed Babylon. He also sent an army into Judah and conquered that growing nation.

In 701 B.C. the Assyrian King Sennacherib sent an army to take Jerusalem by storm. They surrounded the city and demanded a ransom and surrender. Judah's King Hezekiah refused to capitulate. The Old Testament records the ensuing battle:

> That night the angel of the Lord went out and put to death a hundred and eighty-five thousand men in the Assyrian camp. When the people got up the next morning—there were all the dead bodies! So Sennacherib, King of Assyria, broke camp and withdrew. He returned to Nineveh and stayed there.
>
> [II Kings 19:35–36]

The picture that comes to mind here is that of Kuwait's "Highway of Death" as the Iraqi army, suffering from perhaps tens of thousands of casualties from Allied night bombing runs, fled in the face of death from the sky, never knowing what hit them.

In the next century the Chaldeans became heirs to the Assyrian Empire in a great battle. In 606 B.C. Chaldean Crown Prince Nebuchadnezzar defeated an Egyptian army at Carchemish, a city on the northern reaches of the Euphrates River, and claimed control of Syria, Palestine, and the Lower Mesopotamian Valley. Again, the Israelis had helped by causing serious delays through skirmishes and intrigues at Megiddo and Riblah in front of the Egyptian advance. The fighting between the Chaldeans and the Egyptians was brutally personal, even hand-to-hand, at Carchemish; in the end the Egyptians were annihilated, never again to become a great power.

In victory, Nebuchadnezzar set out systematically to destroy all vestiges of Assyrian culture, obliterating Nineveh and moving the capital back to Babylon. Later, Nebuchadnezzar defeated the city of Jerusalem in 586 B.C. and deported most of the population to Babylon. There he built the famous hanging gardens and sought, as did Saddam Hussein in the twentieth century, to build a new glory in the city of war. But the glory was short-lived as Babylon fell in 539 B.C. to Cyrus the Great of Persia, the land we call Iran.

The Persians, first under Cyrus, then Darius, brought a measure of stability to the area for over 200 years. A transportation network was built around the world's first good road system. The rivers were tamed by rudimentary flood-control techniques, and a government structure brought prosperity to the citizenry. When the great Persian leaders died off without leaving successors who were their equal, a period of decline set in, leading to the economic demise of the region.

By 331 B.C. Mesopotamia was vulnerable to attack, and the Macedonian conqueror Alexander the Great took Babylon in that year. The Persian Empire did not collapse, though; it merely consolidated its hold on a smaller area. Babylon and the Lower Mesopotamian Valley became a Greek outpost that prospered at the crossroads of the world until later in the century, when the focus of economic activity took on a more maritime character, with the most important commerce along the Mediterranean coasts rather than the interior lands. Iraq was then a skirmish line along the perimeter of the Greek Empire, more valuable to its rulers as a buffer than for any intrinsic reason. Alexander himself died in Babylon after a particularly nasty excursion into India.

The glory of Babylon was never to return. After the Macedonians came, in rapid succession followed the Parthians, the

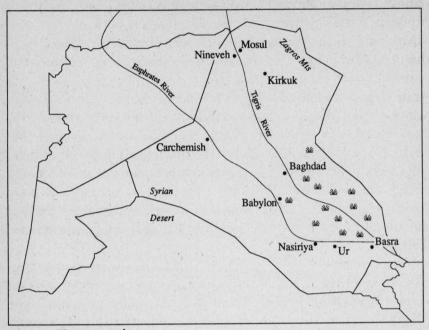

Ancient Mesopotamia

Romans, and the Sassanids, all conquering, none building. Over a half dozen centuries Mesopotamia lost all its glamour and became a pallid, diseased wasteland of utter despair. Its peoples lost their cultural identities, the land became sterile; no one wanted to conquer it anymore because there was nothing worth taking. Most of the tribes had been Christianized by the time followers of the Prophet Muhammad in the seventh century A.D. brought his divine revelations to Mesopotamia.

The great Muslim warrior General Khalid ibn al-Walid, "The Sword of Islam," brought the Prophet's claims to Iraq under the secular direction of Muhammad's successor, the Caliph Abu Bakr. General Khalid's inspiration was Allah, his instrument was the sword. In 634, at the ensuing Battle of the Chains—so called because the Sassanid defenders chained themselves together to prevent mass flight from the battlefield—General Khalid's 18,000 warriors encircled their prey and extended the mother of all ultimatums: "Accept the faith and you are safe; otherwise pay tribute. If you refuse to do either, you have only yourself to blame. A people is already upon you, loving death as you love life."

Most of the local tribes accepted his offer to be extorted, but the ruling Persians tried to fight on. They counterattacked west of the Euphrates River at Al-Hirah but lost summarily. In 635 the Arabs again attacked, this time at Buwayb, farther north, and again trounced the Sassanid army. The final battle happened at al-Qadisiyah, just outside modern-day Baghdad, and from there the Arabs pushed far to the north, to Madain, on the Tigris. The conquering Arab army quickly spread its control over the region, establishing its faith as the glue that would hold the diverse conquered peoples together and building a number of forts to provide for the defense of the new kingdom. Basra was created as a fortified city to guard the approaches to the new empire.

It worked for a time. The caliphs had fought under religious law a holy war, or *jihad,* which demanded the building of a new society, not through indiscriminate killing and plundering, but through respect for human life and industriousness in economic activity. But ideological differences in the faith soon caused a split among factions with rival claims to legitimacy. Bloody infighting ensued among adherents to the Islamic faith, with leaders dealing with each other through treachery or misunderstanding, the perspective shifting depending on which side the issues were viewed from. Rival army factions faced each other, awaiting the outcome of the succession struggle. Bloody battles resulted that involved internal betrayal as much as warring among the factions. The Sunnis eventually wrested control of secular and religious power, but the south remained a Shia stronghold. The burial sites of Shia leaders at Karbala and An Najaf have become holy places that many of the faithful consider to be equal in status to Mecca.

These disputes caused a schism in the Islamic faith that lives to this day in the form of rival Sunni and Shia branches of Islam. Arabic culture developed over the centuries and was firmly in control when the Christian Crusaders invaded from Europe. The warrior tradition continued in the person of Salah al-Din, "Saladin," the Kurdish Muslim general who led the fight against the Crusades in capturing the Kingdom of Jerusalem in 1187. It would not be until the thirteenth century, out of the Far East, that the first real threat to Arab rule over Iraq would come.

In the thirteenth century the infamous Genghis Khan, arising out of China, conquered much of the world, reaching as far as present-day Iran. His grandson Hulagu Khan seized Iraq, taking Baghdad and killing the last of the caliphs. Hulagu Khan utterly destroyed Iraqi culture, killing the elite class and building a pyramid of skulls as a monument to his own cruelty. When the Mongols left in the fourteenth century, rival tribes fought with each other for a couple of decades until the last Mongol ruler, Tamerlane, attempting to reestablish the empire in 1401, again ravaged Baghdad and built himself a tower of skulls. This time the last vestiges of Iraqi culture were eliminated, bringing on a great dark age that was to last for over a hundred years.

Rival Islamic political centers in the north, the Sunni Ottomans, and in the south, the Shia Safavids, vied for control over the strategic region between their domains, now central Iraq, with Baghdad the midpoint between the two sides. By 1638 the Ottomans gained the upper hand and ruled the entire region from the Danube Valley in the north to the Persian Gulf and Red Sea coasts in the south, although significant opposition to their rule came from Kurdish tribesmen in the mountains of northern Iraq and from the entrenched and distant Shias in southern Iraq, around Basra.

The ruling Ottoman Mamluks of the nineteenth century built an extensive transportation system and reformed their army. The Ottoman Empire exerted less rigid control over the area than many previous conquerors had, permitting many holders of local power to retain some measure of influence in spite of their lack of independent political authority. By the time of the downfall of the Empire, Iraq had developed an intelligentsia that had effectively resisted attempts in the late nineteenth and early twentieth centuries by the Turkish rulers to tighten their control over the region.

Iraq's ancient history is thus one of frequent and devastating wars. Many of the peoples who inhabited the region were innovators, bringing new military technologies into the world for the first time. Many were innovators only in butchery, creating new ways of ravaging the human race. Iraq's next set of outside occupiers got an unpleasant taste of Iraqi brutality themselves as the defeat of the Ottoman Empire in World War I shifted Iraq's political orientation to the West for the first time since the rule of Alexander the Great.

The Baghdad Campaign of World War I

World War I brought the British Empire into conflict with the Ottoman Empire in 1914. The main theater of the war was in Europe, but the British were concerned with the protection of their interests in the Persian Gulf region. Mesopotamia of 1914 was a particularly dreadful place, especially in the hot months. Because flood control had deteriorated, countless infectious diseases infested the area. The British might well have simply avoided the region altogether considering its limited value to the Empire. Nevertheless, the campaign that ensued between October 1914 and November 1918 was in many ways a harbinger of the 1991 Persian Gulf campaign.

There were some British interests in the area during World War I. In the northern reaches of the Persian Gulf there was a strategic pipeline that ran from an oil spring at Maidan-I-Naftun in Iran to Al Faw and Abadan Island on the Shatt-al-Arab that was vital to resupply British ships maintaining control of the seas. The British also tried to stir up long-standing Arab animosities toward the ruling Turks, hoping to create enough trouble to force the Ottomans to divert significant military forces away from Europe and into the Mesopotamian region.

Britain dispatched a single reinforced infantry brigade (5,000 men, but little in the way of artillery) from India to the Persian Gulf region in October 1914. When Britain formally declared war on Turkey, the brigade landed at Al Faw. The defending Turkish garrison offered little resistance and mounted an ineffectual counterattack. When the remainder of the British 6th Indian Division landed on November 15, the Turks withdrew to Basra.

The British force moved farther north up the Shatt and met the Turks again in a major skirmish on November 17. The Turks began to reinforce by bringing three divisions into the theater, with one in Baghdad, one at Nasiriya, and the third at Kut-al-Amara. The British formed a corps by adding another division and a reinforced brigade. By the summer of 1914, the British commander, General Sir John E. Nixon, achieved his initial objective, after several pitched battles, by capturing the cities of Amara and Nasiriya. The oil line was safe for the time being.

The British commander was not content with the positions he had taken and convinced his political superiors to allow him to undertake a further advance to the north. He decided to take on the entrenched Turkish army defending at Kut on the Tigris. His plan was to deceive the Turks into concluding that his main

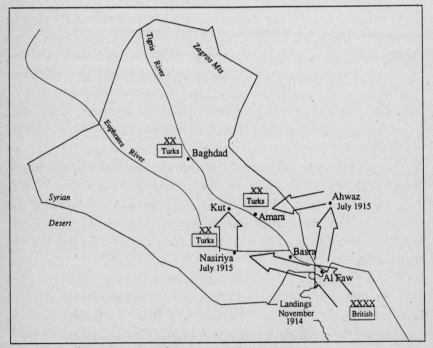

The Battles for Kut, September 1915, February 1917

attack would come right up the valley into the Turkish trench lines. In fact the main attack was to swing around to the right in a great turning movement.

The attacking British division succeeded in this effort, aided by aerial reconnaissance that revealed that the Turks' reserve would have to cross the river at a bridge five miles away to stop the outflanking maneuver. By the time the Turks realized what the British were doing, it was too late. But instead of cutting off and killing the defenders, the British attackers ran out of vigor and stopped short, allowing the Turks to beat a hasty retreat back to a defensible position outside Baghdad. The British pursued until October 5, when they halted twenty-five miles away. The British then mustered their strength for a final attack on November 19, 1915, but were repulsed by November 22. The British withdrew to Kut but were surrounded. Forced to surrender in late April 1916, the British lost 40,000 men in the ill-fated campaign.

A new commander was brought in, General Sir Stanley Maude, who set about rebuilding the force, especially its logistics apparatus. Maude launched his campaign in February 1917, and as did his predecessor, began his attack on Kut, with secondary attacks toward the Turkish center, followed by a flanking movement, this time around the Turks' left flank. This operation was successful and the Turks fell back closer to Baghdad, while Maude pursued only as far as Aziziya, thirty-five miles away, for logistical refit. He continued the advance in March and entered Baghdad on February 11.

The Turks continued to fall back along the Tigris and Euphrates, fighting a delaying action designed to allow them to focus on the Russian threat farther to the north, which was then more serious. During the summer of 1917, both sides continued to build supplies, no easy task given the great distances involved in the hot summer, with no rail transportation available.

In November 1917 a third British commander, General Sir William R. Marshall, initiated an advance on Mosul in the north. By October 1918 Marshall secured the final surrender of the Turkish army in Mesopotamia after a rout north of Tikrit. The next day Turkey signed an armistice agreement with Britain,

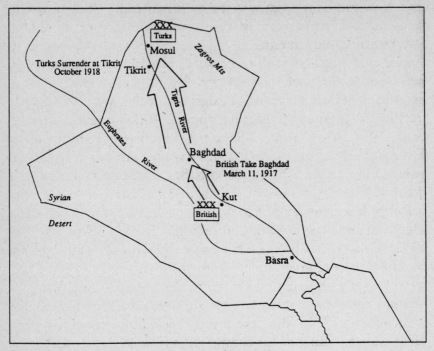

Turkish Retreat, March 1917 to October 1918

ending hostilities. In the end Britain had spent 92,501 lives to protect an oil pipeline. The postwar treaties gave Britain the mandate to rule Iraq.

In 1932 Britain established Iraq as the first sovereign state in its Arab mandate territory. There had been much unrest under its rule after the war, and sovereignty was aimed at appeasing the populace while affording British forces continued access to the region. The British tried to implant a constitutional monarchy, but it lasted in name only until 1958, when the regime was overthrown in a military coup. That coup occurred in part because of animosity engendered by British support for the United Nations' partitioning of Palestine after World War II and in part because of the poor performance by the 10,000 troops Iraq sent to aid the Palestinian armed resistance against the creation of Israel in 1948.

In the 1973 Arab-Israeli war, Iraq sent two mechanized divisions to fight alongside the Syrians on the Golan Heights. When the Israelis turned the tide and began to push the combined Arab forces back toward Damascus, the Iraqis were tasked to cover the withdrawal of the other Arab forces. The Iraqis took heavy losses, suffering 125 soldiers killed and 278 wounded, captured, or missing, for a total of thirteen percent of its force. They also lost eighty of four hundred tanks (twenty percent) and twenty-one of sixty of their fighter aircraft (thirty-five percent) committed to the war. Military historian Trevor Dupuy rates the Iraqi armed forces as the least effective of all the Arab forces ever to fight the Israelis.

Although he was by 1973 a member of the ruling triumvirate of the governing Ba'ath party, Saddam had nothing to do with the military operations against Israel, nor had he played a role in the skirmishes Iraq had with Kuwait in March 1973 over the approaches to the new Soviet-built Iraqi naval base in the Shatt-al-Arab at Umm Qasr. In fact Saddam had no military experience whatsoever, and certainly, as General Schwarzkopf so eloquently put it at a briefing during Desert Storm, "He is no general."

Saddam Hussein

Clearly Iraq has a long and sometimes glorious, sometimes inglorious, military history. It has had its share of martial heroes, reaching back far into ancient history to Gilgamesh, as well as its share of tyrants such as Tamerlane. Saddam considers himself in the tradition of Nebuchadnezzar. But he has established his own peculiarly brutal brand of Mesopotamian despotism that has no precedent.

Saddam Hussein is from a rural area near Tikrit, north of Baghdad. His youthful years were evidently made harsh by a cruel stepfather. In adolescence he was raised by a concerned uncle, who not only provided for Saddam's education but also introduced him to politics. As a young man he developed a passion for intrigue, participating in at least one conspiracy against the Iraqi monarchy in the early 1950s. He joined the radical Ba'ath party in 1957. A non-Ba'ath coup succeeded in getting rid of the king in 1958, and Saddam drew his first blood as a member of an assassination squad sent by the Ba'ath to kill the leader of the coup in an attempt to steal the government for the Ba'athists. The attempt failed, and Saddam injured himself while escaping, but he had established his Ba'athist credentials.

In 1963 the party executed its own coup, and Saddam, who had been away at the time in Egypt to finish school, returned to Baghdad to take part in the new government. He had married a distant cousin by then, and other relatives also took favor with him, cementing family ties in what was becoming a Tikriti Mafia. He was put in charge of the new regime's torture chamber. Later that year the army took power away from the Ba'athists, but Saddam remained in the country and rose to become deputy party leader by 1965. He was an enforcer of party discipline as head of security and when another coup brought the Ba'ath party back to power in 1968, Saddam was one of three who controlled the reins of government.

One of Saddam's heroes, besides Adolf Hitler, is supposedly the character Don Corleone from the motion picture *The Godfather*. It is reportedly his favorite movie, with its depiction of loyalty to the clan at all costs and ruthlessness in enforcing the discipline of the family. Similarly he has built his network of terror and control over all aspects of the Iraqi government mainly through control over the army, the police, and the state security organizations. No aspect of life in Iraq escapes his purview. Iraq is the ultimate totalitarian state; wherever two or more people are gathered, at least one is an informer.

Beginning in 1976, Saddam consolidated his rule over the country and began to exploit it for his own macabre purposes. To deal with the ongoing problem of Kurdish unrest in the north, he alternately offered appeasement and threats to various Kurdish factions. What he achieved was the effective splitting of the Kurds so that they would be so preoccupied with each other that they could not pose a threat to his own regime. He undertook an economic reform program to rebuild the country, but he turned out to be more interested in consuming the nation's wealth in a military buildup than in the advancing of the population's own prosperity.

By 1979 Saddam had used his control over the secret police to dominate the other two Iraqi leaders. The nominal president of the republic, Ahmad Hassan al-Bakr, had been negotiating with Syria for the unification of the two Ba'athist countries. Saddam feared that the merging of the two governments would dissipate his own power. In the summer of 1979, he persuaded the aging Bakr to hand over the presidency to him, at which point Saddam nullified the unification process. Saddam immediately purged the party and the military, killing dozens, perhaps hundreds, and placing his own loyalists in key positions to solidify his grip on power.

Psychologist Gerald Post has suggested that Saddam Hussein suffers from a psychological disorder known as narcissistic megalomania. The megalomaniac suffers from delusions of grandeur and power and has a passion for doing great things. Basic narcissism is characterized by excessive concern for one's own importance. It is believed by many to occur in those who stopped development at the first stage of sexual progression at which the self is the sole object of pleasure. When the two disorders are present in the same individual, you have an explosive combination that becomes quite unpredictable in its outward manifestations.

An individual suffering from this complex disorder perceives all negative inputs as direct threats to himself and often strikes out aggressively as a preemptive defense mechanism. He would rather attack someone first than wait to let the attacker get the first blow. When everyone seems to be an attacker, it can be dangerous being anywhere near such a person.

Post suggests that there is no treatment for the narcissistic megalomaniac. He may be constrained and taught, but in the end must be restrained if therapy does not work. Ultimately he must not only be protected from his own unwitting self-destruction but also must be restrained from causing harm to others with whom he comes into contact. On one CNN appearance soon after the Iraqi invasion of Kuwait, Dr. Post suggested that the only way to deal with Saddam Hussein was with a straitjacket.

Few professional psychologists would probably classify Saddam Hussein as psychotic, though most would agree with Post that he is disturbed. As president of the republic, he has adopted the cause of Pan-Arabism. He fully believes that the rightful place of Arabs in the world needs to be restored and that he is the one best placed in modern times to do so. In this regard he sees both Israel and Iran as modern versions of the ancient Jewish and Persian threats to the Arab peoples. He is capable of manipulating alliances with the outside world, including the superpowers, in his attempt to secure the larger Arab place in the modern world. He aspires to be a modern Saladin.

He can be quite flexible in his relations with other Arabs and with religious factions within Islam, alternating tactics of alliance with betrayal as he deems it convenient for the purpose of forging a larger Arab universe. Since he sees his own security and power as essential to that end, he has no hesitation at using ruthless force to make sure he is the only claimant to Pan-Arab leadership. He showed just how ruthless he could be shortly after taking power in 1979 by attacking Iran.

CHAPTER TWO

The Iran-Iraq War

THE ANIMOSITIES BETWEEN Iran and Iraq are ancient, as we have seen. Saddam Hussein did not suddenly discover some new bone of contention when he invaded Iran in a surprise attack on September 17, 1980. He used one of many that had existed for centuries to start a war of aggression designed to bring about the downfall of the new fundamentalist Islamic regime in Iran under Ayatollah Khomeini.

The pretense for the initiation of hostilities was an ancient dispute between Iran and Iraq over the appropriate border along the Shatt-al-Arab. The Shatt is a fairly wide expanse of a tidewater channel where the Tigris and Euphrates rivers meet to flow to the Persian Gulf. It is particularly valuable for shipping because it is navigable all the way north to Basra. It controls an approach to Iran, and it is the only outlet Iraq has to the sea.

At issue in the dispute was where in the Shatt the boundary line should be. Iran believed that the border should be along a line running down the middle of the waterway. But Iraq always claimed the entire channel, including the opposite bank. Several treaties had been arranged to settle the dispute, but a satisfactory permanent settlement was never found. The latest one was signed in 1975, when the late Shah of Iran agreed to stop supporting Kurdish insurgents in their fight against the central government in Baghdad, while Iraq for its part abandoned its claim to control the entire Shatt. As soon as the Shah was deposed and summarily exiled, Saddam repudiated the 1975 treaty and demanded restoration of Iraq's "rightful" ownership of the entire channel.

There was more to the fight than the pretense of a border disagreement. Of course the dispute was very real, but it had been in contention for years, indeed for centuries; there were larger strategic issues between Iran and Iraq in 1979.

Iraq was ruled by people of the Sunni faction of the Islamic faith. The Tikriti Mafia was, however, only nominally faithful, and its rule was eminently secular. It had much to fear from Islamic fundamentalism, with its call to allegiance to a higher power even unto death, and the Shiite-dominated Islamic revolution under way in Iran could rapidly spread to Iraq's Shias as well. The danger to Saddam's regime was that Iraq's Shias were the majority sect in the country. If they were to catch the revolutionary fever, Saddam's regime would have a huge problem on its hands.

Iraq's ruling Ba'ath party had not helped its prospects of resisting the spread of fundamentalism by expelling Ayatollah Khomeini from their country after a period of sheltering him in Iraq during his exile by the Shah. Khomeini had taken refuge in France until his return to Iran in 1979 as political and spiritual ruler.

Thus, beginning in 1979, Saddam put his security apparatus to work undermining the control of the Khomeini regime in Iran. He stirred up disputes among Iranian Sunnis and encouraged the Kurds to resist the regime. Meanwhile, in secret he planned a surprise attack to defeat the weakened Iranian military. The boundary dispute was a carefully premeditated pretense designed to weaken Iran's power so that fundamentalist fervor would pose no real threat to Saddam's personal control over his countrymen.

Saddam's attempt to defeat Iran was bold and risky. The Shah, with American assistance, had built the strongest military organization in the region. The U.S. policy of support for the Shah was rooted in the belief that it was necessary to balance Soviet designs on the region. Iranian oil revenues had given its well-educated military elite the ability to buy the best in weapons and equipment.

But America was the symbol of everything wrong in Iran to the revolutionaries, and once the revolution toppled the Shah they quickly set out to dismantle the military machine he had built. The officer corps was purged of most of its senior leadership. Many were executed. In cutting off all ties to the United States, the Iranian regime had stopped the flow of spare parts and training assistance vital to keeping a modern military structure operating. Much of Iran's high-technology equipment was no longer useable.

The professional people in the Iranian armed services were replaced with popular volunteers. Their only qualification for being in the military was their enthusiasm for the cause—they had little training or experience. On paper the Iranian military was impressive, with over 1,700 modern tanks of U.S. and British manufacture; 459 combat aircraft of the latest design, including seventy-seven U.S.-made F-14s; and a navy of over thirty combatant ships, with several large U.S.-made frigates (more advanced than those built for the U.S. Navy) on order. In reality the Iranian military was much weaker than the numbers indicated.

The Iraqi military, in contrast, had reached a new peak of effectiveness. The Iraqis carefully studied their failures in the Arab-Israeli wars and set out to redress fundamental problems. They reequipped themselves with the most modern Soviet-made tanks, artillery, and aircraft. They organized themselves along Soviet lines and trained in modern combined-arms tactics. Soviet advisers provided the latest in support and innovations. In most categories of measure Iraq was at least equal to Iran. Considering the intangibles of military effectiveness such as morale, leadership, and training, the Iraqis believed they could win big in a fight with Iran.

So Saddam and his generals put together a bold plan on the gamble that the time to strike a preemptive blow was sooner rather than later. They believed that the correlation of forces, a Soviet concept of looking at the flow of military, economic, and political power in all dimensions, was in Iraq's favor but was shifting to Iran. They had seen how a well-placed preemptive blow could quickly overwhelm an opposing threat when the Israelis pulled it off so effectively in 1967. The Iraqis put together their own attack designed to end the Iranian threat before it got too large.

The attack opened with air strikes by Iraqi fighters on Iranian airfields and air defense radar sites early on September 22, 1980. The attack was not effective, and the Iranian air force escaped serious damage by hiding in reinforced concrete shelters built under the Shah. Iranian counterstrikes were much more effective because the American-built planes carried considerably larger bomb loads.

On the ground, Iraq launched a four-axis attack with six of its twelve divisions. Its objectives were Qasr-Shirin, Khorramshahr, Ahu, Susangard, and Dehloran. All objectives were taken in rapid order, and within days the Iraqis had seized a piece of Iran thirty miles wide along the border. But the Iranians did not collapse as Saddam had calculated. Instead they fell back and regrouped to wage a defensive fight to give them time to develop a counter-

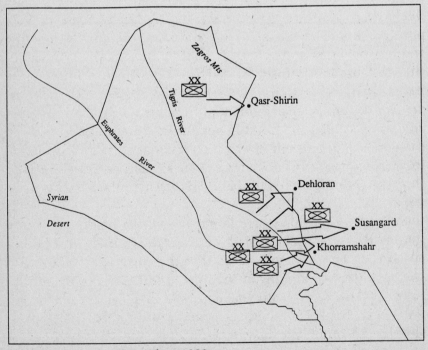

Iraq Attacks Iran, September, 1980

strategy. Thus most of 1981 saw a war of attrition characterized by limited air and ground engagements.

In the summer of 1982 Iran launched its counterattack, employing an equally bold strategy. In July the Iranian military opened an offensive of its own known as Operation Ramadan. In it, human waves of holy warriors known as the Pasdaran lurched forward right into the Iraqi lines. Old men and boys walked through Iraqi obstacle emplacements, clearing minefields and drawing artillery fire. Casualties were in the tens of thousands, but the Iranian soldiers drove on. Ultimately they broke through in a number of places, but the integrity of the Iraqi lines held. The Iranian assault was exhausted after a few weeks, and both sides settled into sporadic raids and bombardments as they prepared for the next offensive.

The Iraqis used the time to their advantage. They developed their defensive positions along Soviet lines, which the USSR had developed over numerous campaigns against Germany in World War II. This defensive doctrine emphasized fortifications, minefields, and obstacles woven together to force an attacker into predetermined killing zones, where the defending force concentrates its tank and artillery fire. Once the attacker is mired in the web of obstacles, the defender unleashes the full fury of its firepower on the helplessly immobilized enemy. It is designed to create a battle of annihilation.

In February 1983 the Iranians gave the new Iraqi defenses their first real test in launching another massive offensive all along the front, but concentrating on a thirty-mile sector near Amara, on the approaches to Baghdad. It broke the Iraqi defense, and the Iranians committed their reserves to exploit the moment, but by then they had exhausted themselves and had to stop to recover. Iraq seized the lull and began hitting Iranian positions with massive air strikes. In April Iran resumed the attack toward Baghdad, but this time the Iraqis were able to maneuver their own armored reserves to blunt the Iranian attacks. All told, in the 1983 offensives, Iran had lost 150,000 killed or taken prisoner, while Iraqi casualties were about 75,000. Although Iraq was holding its own, at those attrition rates Iran was bound to prevail eventually by sheer weight of numbers. The Iraqis could not afford to win even when they took half the casualties that the Iranians suffered, since the Iranian population, at nearly fifty million, could support an army three or four times that of Iraq's fourteen million people. Iraq set out to find a better strategy.

Before Iraq could begin to execute what was to become an attrition strategy of a different kind, Iran again struck at Iraq in the spring of 1984. Operation Dawn V took the Iranian human wave strategy a step further. The Iranians found a weak point in Iraqi lines and struck with over 500,000 troops on February 27. The attack was aimed at Basra and was directed across the swampy plains north of the city. They never quite reached the road that links Basra to Baghdad, so they made their next move farther to the northeast, in the open desert. But an Iraqi counterattack repulsed the Iranian move on terrain more suitable to the developing Iraqi style of armored warfare.

Then the Iraqi strategy began to take form. Late in February 1983 Iraq opened an air campaign aimed at hitting Iran's economic lifeline, its oil infrastructure, with an attack on the main Iranian Persian Gulf terminal on Kharg Island. This operation led to the tanker war in which Iraq attacked any oil vessel shipping to or from Iran. By 1985 Kharg Island had been rendered virtually useless and thirty-five tankers had been destroyed or rendered inoperable. The tanker war eventually threatened Western interests and brought about the first involvement of the United States and many of its European allies. It also caused other Arab states to move closer to the United States militarily, as they became concerned for their own oil shipping. As a result, Saudi Arabia purchased several Airborne Warning and Control Systems (AWACS), manned in part by Americans for technical assistance, for their own integrated air defense. This limited American military presence opened the door for a later widening of U.S. military force involvement toward the end of the war and paved the way for the rapid reintroduction of U.S. military forces early in the war in Kuwait.

In March 1984 the Iranians again struck out across the marshes, this time much farther north, near Qurnah. Iraqi commandos were able to helicopter up to the Iranian positions and destroy the Iranian infantry in a battle at Majnoon. In response, the Iranians employed a particularly brutal approach, reminiscent of the ancient Sassanid Battle of the Chains tactic, by roping together 10,000 children, according to eyewitnesses, and sending them ahead of an assault into Iraqi minefields as a human wave. The Iraqi response was to fire mustard gas into the Iranian attackers. These actions failed to resolve the conflict, and once again both sides settled into a battle of attrition.

The war reached a turning point in 1986, although at the time they probably did not realize which way it had turned. In February of that year the Iranians attacked far to the south, crossing the Shatt-al-Arab, and retook the Faw Peninsula. The Iraqis had been caught by surprise, and when they sent the elite Republican Guard division to restore the situation, the Iranians simply outmaneuvered and outfought the best force the Iraqis could bring to bear. The Iranians got so close to the border with Kuwait that Kuwait and Saudi Arabia heightened their alert status.

To the north, the Iranians again attacked outside the area of current operations by striking deep into Iraqi Kurdestan, toward the vital oil infrastructure centered at Kirkuk. For the second time that can be verified, the Iraqis used chemical agents, this time using nerve gas as well as mustard gas against the Iranians. The year 1986 ended with substantial Iranian forces deep inside Iraq, and Saddam's position was very much in question. Offensives in 1987 were not of significant consequence, although the casualty rate continued to mount.

The ground war was eclipsed by the May 1987 incident in which an Iraqi fighter struck an American destroyer, the USS *Stark*, with a French-made Exocet antiship missile. The Iraqis claimed it was an accident, and while the U.S. government officially accepted the explanation, on the same day a Soviet ship hit an Iranian mine in the Gulf. Eventually the United States took a fundamental turn in its policy toward this war in the Gulf when it decided to reflag several Kuwaiti oil tankers to U.S. registry to legitimize providing armed escort for oil leaving the Gulf. These escort operations provided the rationale for a substantial increase in the number of

U.S. warships in the region, with the total reaching over twenty in an increasingly crowded Persian Gulf. European Allies were also in the Gulf in force to participate in the protection of the West's oil lifeline, particularly with minesweepers.

On April 14, 1988, the USS *Samuel B. Roberts*, while escorting a Kuwaiti tanker under the U.S. flag, struck a mine near the Emirate of Qatar. U.S. President Reagan and his national security advisers decided that this time the United States could not afford to let the combatants get away with such a challenge to the U.S. policy of maintaining access to the Gulf. They put into effect Operation Praying Mantis, which involved retaliation against Iran for placing mines in the Gulf so indiscriminately. In an operation involving a combined raid by secret Army helicopters, Marine raiding parties, naval gunfire, and air strikes, the American force hit several Iranian oil facilities that also sheltered military command and control operations.

In response, the Iranian navy offered battle to the assembled U.S. naval surface combatants. It remains a mystery why the hopelessly outclassed Iranian navy came out to attack the American fleet. The Iranians had allowed their once-impressive navy to degenerate to a second-rate force of only four effective combatant ships and a few fast patrol boats. In the end, in less than ten hours the Iranian navy lost three of its four main ships, and the fourth was severely damaged as it steamed away. The speedboats attempted to make a lightning strike on the larger American ships but were intercepted and routed before they could cause any serious damage. It was a total loss for the Iranians. The effect was to bring the Americans into the Gulf as a balance to the expected Iranian victory on land and was the crucial factor that led to Iran's surprise final defeat on the battlefield.

The year 1988 also marked a change in the approach to the war of attrition between the two sides. Iran and Iraq had purchased Scud medium-range ballistic missiles from the Soviet Union. Both sides adapted those missiles for their particular aims in the war. These missiles offered a way of striking at each other's strategic centers without risking loss of the precious few remaining pilots and aircraft over the opponent's air defenses.

In the Battle of the Cities, Iran fired more than sixty missiles into Iraq, while Iraq launched over two hundred. These were mostly aimed at each other's capital city, and although terribly inaccurate, they terrorized the urban populations. Iraq learned through this effort that the political value of ballistic missiles in a war far outweighed the military value. It was to use this lesson to great effect in the Gulf War in 1991.

The dramatic end to the war between Iran and Iraq, however, was not the result of Iran's loss to the Americans at sea nor to its fewer numbers of launches in the missile war. The demise of Iran in this war came at the hands of the ground forces in a campaign the Iraqis called "Tawakalna Ala Allah."

After the disaster at Al Faw in 1986 and the subsequent defeat of the Republican Guard near Basra, Saddam Hussein relieved many of his commanders and set out to build a new army. He used the Republican Guard, a division that had grown out of the Presidential Guard garrison protection force in Baghdad, as the core of a new elite force. He recruited to its ranks the best of Iraq's younger generation, who had been exempted from war service in order to continue schooling and to hold key occupations in the economic infrastructure. The Republican Guard Force, as it came to be called, grew to over 100,000 in strength and was officered by the best-qualified, most loyal followers of Saddam Hussein. It was equipped with the very latest Soviet tanks, artillery, and infantry fighting vehicles. At the same time, the regular army was professionalized and refitted with better Soviet equipment as well, although not with the newer models the Republican Guard had. Even the popular forces in the reserves received new emphasis for unit training, and elaborate mobilization plans were put into effect to draw on those manpower reserves quickly. The Iraqi air force was reequipped with late-model French aircraft, and the Iraqis purchased some high-technology precision-guided bombs and missiles as well. By the beginning of 1988 Iraq had over a million men under arms and could call up another 850,000 if necessary.

Iraq launched this force in a final offensive on the ground on April 17, 1988. The first battle was an attack down the Shatt-al-

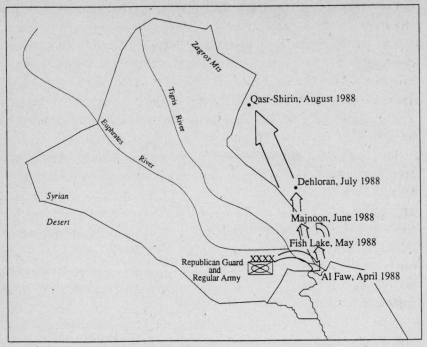

Iraq Defeats Iran, 1988 Campaign

Arab to retake the Faw Peninsula. This was a tremendously complex operation involving armor, infantry, artillery, and helicopters in a combined-arms offensive approximating that of Western forces. It was extremely well executed and included two corps-size formations attacking abreast from north to south down the peninsula. It was accompanied by an amphibious assault that crossed the Shatt, landed behind the Iranian defenders, and disrupted their rear-area operations with great impact. The 15,000 Iranian defenders were totally surprised and overwhelmed by the size, violence, and speed of the 200,000 Iraqis descending on them. Apparently the Iraqi attack had been well rehearsed, and when the Iranian defenders fled, the Iraqi commanders left one bridge open to allow for their escape, which they then videotaped and showed across Iraq to boost morale.

The Iraqis spent the next three weeks consolidating their gains and preparing for the next phase. On May 25 the Iraqi forces launched a frontal assault to the north on Iranian positions near the so-called Fish Lake, after a massive artillery preparation that again overwhelmed the Iranian defenders. This frontal assault demonstrated an operational flexibility that the Iraqi army had not shown before. In these two short, decisive battles, the Iraqi army quickly gained a reputation for being on a level of tactical and operational proficiency equal to that of the best Western armies.

The third major fight showed even more creativity in the Iraqi approach. In a battle farther north, near the Majnoon Islands, the Republican Guard led a classic envelopment maneuver that got around and behind the Iranians occupying Iraqi territory, cut them off, and began to kill them systematically. Thousands of Iranians were encircled and captured. By the time the Iraqi forces pushed north to Dehloran and deep into Iran near Kermanshah, it was clear that this was a very different Iraqi army than the one that had launched the war in 1980.

In four short months and five quick, decisive battles the Iraqi army had marched over 700 miles from south to north, routed a large Iranian army, and penetrated deep into Iranian territory. Combined with the effects of the tanker war and the disenchantment of the population with the Battle of the Cities, after eight years of war the two sides called a truce and sat down to talk out their differences. Iran still held portions of Iraqi territory, and their revolution was intact. But after nearly losing it all in 1986, the Iraqis demonstrated a remarkable ability to recover and rebuild from adversity, and they reestablished an uneasy balance of power between the two giants of the Persian Gulf.

At war's end in 1988 that balance was fairly even and the war ended in a stalemate. But where Iran was exhausted after a wrenching revolution and eight years of attritive warfare, Iraq had discovered a way in which a smaller power could take on a larger one and prevail. It meant taking risks, but Saddam was now a thug who had learned how to play for high stakes. The important lesson he learned was how to recover from a big loss and turn it into a big win. He set out to create a set of circumstances that would allow him to turn his attention to his other neighbors in the region.

By the end of the war the military balance in the Middle East had tipped decisively in Iraq's favor. The amassing of tanks, artillery, and aircraft with a large number of men under arms created for Saddam Hussein the largest military in the region. To balance him militarily, his neighbors would have to maintain a coalition of three or more out of the five that had sufficiently large military establishments to form such an offsetting military coalition: Israel, Egypt, Syria, Turkey, and Iran. Iran was not likely to be interested in taking on Iraq again soon, and the other Islamic states were not likely to consider Israel a potential ally, so Saddam could calculate that all he had to do was keep Egypt, Syria, and Turkey from forming an alliance against him and he could have his way in the Persian Gulf. He set out to exploit that favorable position by initiating another massive military rebuilding campaign aimed at preparing himself for his next target: the Arabian Peninsula.

CHAPTER THREE

The Iraqi Military and the Invasion of Kuwait

SADDAM HUSSEIN STARTED the war with Iran hoping for a quick victory, but not only did he almost lose the war, he nearly lost his country as well. In the end, he avoided stalemate by adeptly changing his objectives and reforming his military machine. In sheer numbers, the Iraqi military had grown by immense proportions during the war with Iran. In every category of weapon, Saddam bought in quantities far exceeding those needed for defense against a prostrate Iran. After the war he continued the relentless buildup; by 1990 Iraq had the fourth-largest army in the world, an extensive air-defense network fashioned after the Soviet model, and one of the most powerful air forces in the region. He had changed the basic character of the force as well, making it one of the most modern and effective in the world.

His program for stockpiling weapons of mass destruction included nuclear devices and chemical weapons. He is the only leader we know since World War I to have ordered the use of lethal gas in war. He had used chemical weapons both against his own Kurdish population and against the Iranians, in the latter part of the 1980s war. He even had his scientists research biological weapons, instruments of terror that all other technologically advanced military powers have abandoned as too unstable to be

29

useful as military weapons. By 1990, this buildup had caused many of Iraq's neighbors to become very worried about Saddam's intentions.

The quality of Iraq's force grew as well during this period, with many technological advancements being incorporated into the tanks, planes, and ships the Iraqis used. Saddam also modified the organizational structure of the force and created new elite units to build on the success of the Republican Guard during the war with Iran. Most important, he instituted a procedure for changing his armed forces as new developments occurred and as battle experience presented new lessons from warfare. This is the mark of a truly professional military force, one that few armies in history have achieved. The Iraqi military institutionalized a process of self-examination that allowed it to recover from defeat and to exploit new applications of technology. It could change its tactics and operations and rapidly train the force to fight in new ways. When new, advanced weapons became available, the Iraqi armed forces quickly assimilated them into their inventory. And if defeat showed that a particular way of organizing the force did not work, Saddam's generals reorganized and started over again with new force structures.

The Iraqi military that emerged from the war against Iran was a most dangerous military force indeed, and Saddam turned that force on his smallest neighbor, Kuwait, in a lightning strike that gave new meaning to the term "blitzkrieg." This chapter will examine the buildup, elements, and doctrines of the Iraqi military and their applications in the seizure of Kuwait.

The Iraqi Military Machine

Weapons of mass destruction. Saddam Hussein's nuclear-weapons program was perhaps the most threatening aspect of the Iraqi military buildup. His previous efforts at developing a nuclear device included the purchase of a research reactor. Installed at Osirak, its purpose was the production of enriched uranium.

Though the Iraqis claimed it was for generating electrical power, the enriched uranium could be used only to build a nuclear bomb. The Iranians, fearing an Iraqi nuclear strike to end their Islamic revolution, tried to destroy the reactor in an air strike in September 1980, but the attempt failed.

In 1981 the Iraqis purchased excessive amounts of uranium ore from Brazil, Portugal, Nigeria, and Italy, raw material that could serve only as the core for enrichment to be used for an atomic weapon. The Israelis launched a preemptive air strike on the reactor site on June 7, 1981, successfully destroying the facility but not eliminating the enriched uranium itself. Iraq claimed the raid was the product of an Iranian-Israeli conspiracy. This raid set back Iraq's nuclear-weapons development program but did not end it. By the time of the invasion of Kuwait, many analysts had concluded that Iraq could have been within a year of deploying a crude nuclear device. When the Gulf War broke out, President Bush claimed that the Iraqis were within months of deploying at least one nuclear device. The facilities where the research and development were conducted had been dispersed since the Osirak raid, and those sites were the highest priority for U.S. air strikes when Desert Storm began. Those targets included facilities near Mosul, Baghdad, Qaim, Tawaitha, and Ibril.

Iraq had developed its nuclear-weapons capability through every possible means. It did not really need nuclear energy to meet its electrical-power distribution requirements, but it exploited this excuse to secure internationally sanctioned, and well-monitored, nuclear power plants from France and the Soviet Union. In the mid-1980s Iraq purchased nuclear fuel on the legitimate and controlled international market, but it also tried smuggling additional fuel from other sources. Iraq had technical help in this effort from several European corporations. Other firms, from Brazil, Pakistan, and China, reportedly had also been providing help to Iraq's nuclear weapons program. Many of Iraq's purchases were made by a network of dummy corporations that Saddam had created and financed with millions of dollars from revenues realized during the oil price increases following the 1979 oil price shock.

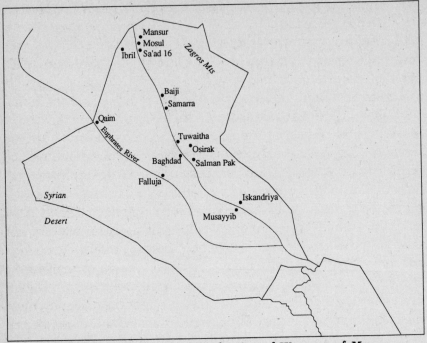

Iraqi Sites for Development and Production of Weapons of Mass Destruction

Ironically, by early 1990 some U.S. firms had also been involved in Iraqi attempts to develop nuclear devices. In March 1990, American and British customs agents arrested several Iraqis attempting to smuggle specialized electrical devices known as high-density capacitors. These are basically metal cans about the size of a toilet water tank, with special papers inside wrapped and packed with exotic fluids and gels. They hold millions of volts of electrical power, far more than any battery could ever hold, and they discharge that voltage virtually instantaneously when a special switch is thrown. They can be used for X-ray machines, but capacitors of the type the Iraqis were trying to get are normally used only to trigger nuclear weapons. They are manufactured solely by Maxwell Laboratories Company, based in San Diego, California; this firm sells its products almost exclusively to the U.S. Department of Defense and has its exports tightly controlled by the Department of Commerce. After the seizure of the 210 capacitors at Heathrow Airport in England, Saddam, concerned about a repeat of the Osirak raid, issued a blistering statement that denounced the United States, Britain, and Israel. He concluded with the apocalyptic warning "By God, we will make fire eat half of Israel if it tries to do anything against Iraq."

As late as July 1990, the Iraqis almost succeeded in legally importing from the United States a high-performance furnace from the New Jersey–based Consarc Corporation. These special furnaces can melt most modern metals, including titanium, plutonium, and uranium. Iraq claimed it intended to use the furnace, along with other high-technology furnaces from the United States and Britain, to manufacture artificial limbs for medical purposes. Iraq had also obtained from European firms the specialized components and machinery for assembling high-performance centrifuges that would allow Saddam to produce weapons-grade nuclear fuel without reliance on the type of research reactor that had been destroyed at Osirak. Normally, exports of these furnaces and components are tightly controlled because of their application in the production of weapons-grade nuclear materials, but in 1990 the United States and its European allies had decided to relax export controls on these types of devices as a result of lessening East-West tensions. Iraq was ready to buy them, and there was no automatic mechanism to block the sale or even to cause officials to question issuing a license. Fortunately, the U.S. companies themselves were worried about Iraq's intended use for the furnaces and components, and both Consarc and Maxwell reported the impending sales to the U.S. government. The capacitors were intercepted and, in June 1990, delivery of the furnaces was held up until the sale could be evaluated. The war made that evaluation irrelevant.

Iraq's biological weapons program was equally troubling. Biological weapons are the least useful weapons of mass destruction from a military point of view because their effects are so difficult to predict and because they can take a good deal of time, perhaps days, before they are militarily effective. They are banned by the Geneva Convention and by a separate 1972 treaty, both of which

Iraq signed. While nuclear and chemical weapons must be delivered by aircraft, artillery, or missile attack, biological agents can be sent to their target by more insidious methods. Insects or rodents can carry biological agents, rapidly spreading them through a target area, and covert operations can be executed to deliver biotoxins to water or food supplies. Because the agents may be difficult to detect until the medical effects begin to show, biological attack is particularly difficult to defend against. Such agents cannot distinguish between friend or foe, however, so most modern states have been reluctant to pursue their deployment.

Despite this drawback, Saddam had Iraq relentlessly pursue the development and deployment of offensive biological weapons, perhaps the only country on earth to do so. During the buildup, research facilities in Baghdad, Salman Pak, and Badush were developing and probably producing biological weapons that could have spread deadly typhoid, cholera, and tularemia as well as incapacitating diseases such as anthrax and equine encephalitis. There is no evidence that Iraq used biological agents against Iran or the Kurds during the 1980s conflict, nor did it use biological agents in the Gulf War. Had it done so in the Kuwaiti Theater of Operations, Allied forces would have been significantly slowed in their advance. The measures prescribed in military doctrine for response to a biological attack do not offer much cause for optimism. Once the attack has been detected, it is too late to do much more than treat those already infected and get everyone else out of the area.

As far as we know, Iraq was never able to deploy nuclear or biological agents in any delivery weapons. We know for a fact, however, that the Iraqi military had an extensive chemical-weapons delivery capability. Iraqi forces used chemical weapons against the Iranians in 1982 and employed them against Iranian human-wave tactics at several points in the war. Estimates of Iranian casualties caused by Iraqi use of poison gas—both mustard gas, which causes severe blistering, and nerve agents, which paralyze the central nervous system—run into the tens of thousands. Many Western sources have also confirmed Iraqi use of gas

Iraqi Chemical Agents

Type	Delivery Means	Symptoms	Effects	Rate of Action
Nerve Agent	Missile, artillery, bomb, aerial spray, landmine	Difficult breathing, drooling, nausea, vomiting, convulsions	Incapacitates or kills when delivered in high concentrations	Seconds
Blistering Agent	Missile, artillery, bomb, aerial spray, landmine	No early symptoms for mustard types; searing of eyes, stinging of skin	Blisters skin, destroys respiratory tract, causes temporary blindness	Minutes
Blood-Affecting Agent	Missile, artillery, bomb	Convulsions and coma	Incapacitates or kills when delivered in high concentrations	Minutes
Choking Agent	Missile, artillery, bomb	Coughing, choking, nausea, headache	Damages and floods lungs	Hours

against its own Kurdish population at the town of Halabjah in February 1988.

The pre–Gulf War Iraqi arsenal contained the full range of chemicals, including nerve, blistering, blood, and choking agents. Authority to use chemical weapons was held by the president of the republic, Saddam Hussein himself. Research and production facilities were known to exist at sites near Mosul, Badush, Samarra, Al Fallujah, Musayyib, Iskandriya, Baiji, and Al-Qaim. These weapons produce effects very rapidly and are almost instantaneously incapacitating to unprotected troops. Nerve agents are particularly ghastly, since they cause the body's regulatory system to shut down, resulting in cardiac arrest and cessation of respiratory function. Army training films show animals exposed to nerve agents writhing in pain and suffering severe convulsions. Those images were utmost in my memory on the second night of the war in January when I spoke so harshly to CNN's reporters in Israel who were not properly masked.

During his war with Iran, Saddam Hussein developed a procedure for the employment of chemical weapons. Once Saddam had decided to utilize the weapons, he delegated the authority to use them to the corps commanders, three-star generals. The weapons were broken out of storage and stockpiled about thirty-seven miles behind the forward line of troops. Once a chemical mission was ordered by the field commanders, the canisters of gas were loaded on aircraft and were to be sprayed from above; artillery shells were to be fired from about nineteen miles away; or rockets were to be fired from ranges of twenty-five miles (for FROG missiles) to 250 miles (for Scud missiles). This procedure was in effect during the war in the Gulf, and Saddam had already issued the order delegating such authority to his commanders in Kuwait, as evidenced at war's end when U.S. forces came across a number of caches of chemical weapons that had, fortunately, never been fired.

In addition to building these facilities for development of weapons of mass destruction, the Iraqi military machine also exploited conventional-weapons technology. Advanced systems had been purchased from Soviet, European, Chinese, and other sources. By the time the Gulf War broke out, Iraq had laser-guided bombs, radar-controlled sea-skimming antiship missiles, and high-performance jet aircraft. Iraq had also devoted great sums of money to the development of missiles of increasing range and accuracy.

Not only did Iraq attempt to extend the range and improve the lethal radius of its Soviet-supplied Scud missiles, but also the Iraqis were embarked on a long-range missile program of their own design. At a site near Baghdad, they were participating in an Argentinean missile project known as Condor. In the late 1980s this missile was by some accounts eventually capable of a range of nearly four hundred miles, but the program was reportedly canceled. The Iraqis were able to develop their own two-stage missile, however, and in 1989 test-fired launch rocket motors for their own space vehicle or for an intercontinental ballistic missile. The combination of weapons of mass destruction with delivery means of great range and accuracy gave Iraq a military capability far in excess of its legitimate defensive needs.

Missiles. The most plentiful missile in the prewar Iraqi arsenal was the Soviet-made FROG-7. FROG is the NATO standard classification for a rocket the Soviets have designated Luna. It is essentially a rocket-propelled artillery projectile, designed and first built in the mid-1960s and with a range of about forty-two miles. The Russians built it as a battlefield nuclear-delivery system. It can carry a small-yield warhead to its maximum range, although, since it is unguided once launched, it is likely to land anywhere within a mile radius of its target point. That was acceptable for Soviet purposes, since its nuclear warhead could miss its target by about that much and still have its intended effects. The FROG-7 is capable of carrying a chemical warhead.

The Iraqis used the FROG-7 against Iran, firing several dozen rockets, mostly early in the war. These were all armed with conventional munitions warheads. Although the rockets can carry over nine hundred pounds of high explosives, they had no apparent effect on the outcome of the battles in which they were used. Iraqi munitions developers added to its capabilities by developing several types of conventional warheads, including fragmentation explosives to be used primarily against people; shaped-charge submunitions to be used against vehicles and light armored systems; and improved conventional munitions that combine both fragmentation and shaped-charge submunitions for areas that include both types of targets.

The FROG is a mobile missile fired from the same truck that carries it on the battlefield. The truck, called a Transporter Erector Launcher (TEL), designated the ZIL-135, is also of Soviet design. This eight-wheeled all-terrain vehicle provides hydraulic power to elevate the missile to its upright launch position and electrical power to fire the rocket. Another model of the ZIL-135 also carries three FROG missiles for resupply. These trucks enable the FROG to move on the battlefield more rapidly than standard artillery, with preparation, erection, launch, reload, and displacement taking only about twenty minutes. The Iraqis exploited this capability during the Persian Gulf War not only for its FROG missiles but also for its infamous Scud missiles.

The Scud-B is also a missile of Soviet design, but it has much greater range and payload capacity than the FROG. The Scud-B gets its greater range from employing a liquid-propellant fuel, as opposed to the FROG's solid-fuel rocket motor. The fuel is comprised of two components, red-fuming nitric acid and hydrazine, which are carried separately along with the missile, then pumped into the missile prior to launch. The fueling process takes about an hour to complete; once loaded, the missile becomes quite volatile for the approximately twenty-four hours it can remain workable for launch.

The Scud-B as provided to the Iraqis by the Soviets has a range of 180 miles and is less accurate even than the FROG, with a fifty percent probability that the missile will land within a circle of almost two miles in diameter from the aim point. Again, from the Soviet perspective this kind of accuracy was quite acceptable, since the missile was designed to carry a nuclear warhead. It has a guidance system on board, provided by gyros linked to the fins and the vanes of the missile that are automatically turned in flight to provide corrections to keep the missile on track. The missile is carried on a TEL designated the MAZ-543, which is also an eight-wheeled cross-country truck. In addition, the system deploys a radar balloon that gathers meteorological data from high altitudes and requires a few other separate vehicles for electrical power generation, fuel transportation, and survey equipment to identify the launch site accurately.

While the Scud was designed to have nuclear warheads, the Iraqis used it only to carry simple high-explosive munitions. None of the hundreds of Scuds launched at Iran during the eight-year war delivered chemical weapons. Iraq had also modified the basic Soviet Scud design and produced its own missiles, called the al-Hussein and the al-Abbas, both of which extended the range of the basic missile to about 400 miles.

Aircraft. Iraq achieved initial surprise in its air war with Iran in 1980 but soon lost air superiority to Iran's more capable American-made aircraft. By 1985, however, Iran's inability to service its sophisticated aircraft forced it to cede control of the skies to Iraq, which steadily exploited that advantage, although never to the full extent its air arsenal could have allowed. During the war with Iran, Iraq was able to upgrade its older Soviet fleet significantly with more modern Soviet- and French-made high-performance aircraft.

Almost all analysts seriously misjudged the number of aircraft in the Iraqi arsenal. Published figures ran from about five hundred to just under seven hundred reported in the authoritative publication put out by the International Institute for Strategic Studies, *The Military Balance 1990–1991.* The Iraqi air force had actually amassed over eight hundred combat aircraft of over nineteen different types in the buildup and could pose a serious threat to any air force in the world.

The most advanced aircraft in the Iraqi air force was the French-made Mirage F-1. This single-seat, delta-winged fighter can operate in all weather conditions and has a limited night-fighting capability. Its heads-up display, navigation system, and computerized fire-control system enable it to hold its own, when well piloted, against many modern Western aircraft. A probe mounted on the fuselage allows the plane to be refueled in flight. Iraq purchased ninety-eight F-1s and later added fifteen two-seat models to its inventory.

The most advanced Soviet aircraft flown by the Iraqis was the MiG-29 Fulcrum. This airplane is roughly equivalent to the U.S. F/A-18 in size and has a look-down, shoot-down radar; laser range finder; infrared sensor; and a helmet aiming system that enables it to engage the best Western-designed fighters in air-to-air combat. Its cockpit visibility reduces the pilot's effectiveness, however, and it is further limited by the lack of Western standards of maintenance reliability. It has been a feature at air shows in recent years and has demonstrated aerial maneuverability equal to that of the latest Western aircraft. It is designed mainly as an air-to-air fighter, but it can be outfitted for ground attack as well.

The main Iraqi attack aircraft was the Soviet Su-24 Fencer fighter-bomber, which has wings that move forward for maneuverability, rearward for speed. Its special electro-optical devices and navigation systems allow it to penetrate deep into enemy territory and reach targets at great distances from its home airfield. It also has a probe for in-flight refueling. It can carry the Soviet equivalent of the U.S. tank-busting Maverick missile.

For close air support of ground troops, the Iraqis also obtained from the Soviet Union the latest Russian version of the venerable American A-10 Thunderbolt, known as the Su-25 Frogfoot. The Soviets used this aircraft extensively in Afghanistan, although they lost twenty-three of them there. It has titanium armor over parts of its body frame to give the pilot some ability to survive against ground-fired enemy antiaircraft artillery when flying low in support of ground troops. Its flight controls are hardened as well. It carries a variety of armaments including a 30mm cannon, rockets, laser-guided bombs, standard bombs, and a multibarreled machine-gun system. It mounts its own laser range finder and target designator. It can carry its own air-to-air missile, and self-defense countermeasures include a chaff dispenser to defeat radar-guided missiles, and a flare to distract heat-seeking missiles.

Iraq's bomber fleet consisted of two Soviet systems, the Tu-16 and the Tu-22. The Tu-16 Badger is a 1950s two-engine design originally intended by the Soviets as a medium-range strategic bomber. The Chinese manufacture a version that the Iraqis also had in their fleet. It carries regular bombs but can also carry air-to-surface missiles. The other bomber is the Soviet-made Tu-22 Blinder, a 1960s design; it is a supersonic jet with two engines mounted on the tail and with swept wings.

Iraq's air transport fleet was an unremarkable collection of Soviet Antonov designs, including An-12BP, An-22, and An-26 turboprop aircraft. There was one notable transport aircraft in the Iraqi inventory, a modified Soviet Ilyushin-76, which was outfitted with a rudimentary airborne early-warning radar system. This employed a French-made airborne radar system, the Tigre, manufactured by Thomson-CSF, but now made under license in Iraq. With the addition of command and control systems to complement the radar, the system had a lozenge-shaped rotating radar dome mounted above the fuselage, resembling the U.S. AWACS aircraft, and was designated by Iraq as the Adnan-1. The Il-76 Candid is the rough equivalent of the U.S. C-141 transport aircraft. Iraq had also used its Il-76s for in-flight refueling.

As well as buying jet airplanes, Iraq also pursued advanced technology in acquiring modern helicopters. It purchased eighty-one French-made SA-342 Gazelle attack helicopters in the 1980s; each can mount machine guns or Hot antitank missiles. The West German firm MBB sold a number of its BO-105 helicopters to Iraq; this aircraft can fire cannons or antitank missiles. The Soviets provided to Iraq its top-of-the-line attack helicopter, the Mi-24 Hind. This has seen extensive service in Europe with the Soviet armed forces as well as in Afghanistan, where it was used with great effectiveness in a counterinsurgency role. In the war with Iran an Iraqi Hind was credited with a kill of an Iranian F-4 fighter jet. The Mi-24 was originally designed as a transport helicopter, and its heavy lift capacity allows it to carry a large load of weapons and ammunition, including cannon, machine guns, and antitank missiles.

The Iraqi air force was formidable. It had won control of the skies over Iran during the 1980s war and had continued to expand in numbers and capability after the end of the war with Iran. There is evidence that its employment doctrine, following the Soviet model, was highly centralized and tightly controlled, thus reducing the effectiveness of the individual aircraft in its inventory. Iraqi pilots did not demonstrate any particular strength in their dogfights with Iran and did nothing to improve their flying skills between the end of the war with Iran in 1988 and the assault on Kuwait.

Tanks and infantry-fighting vehicles. Iraqi tanks were almost exclusively Soviet-made. The notable exception was the Khalid version of the British-designed Chieftain tank, which the Iraqis acquired from Jordan as retrofits to its fleet of original Chieftains. The Khalid is basically an upgraded Chieftain with a more powerful engine and a larger gun. It has a 120mm gun and a laser range finder with a passive image-intensification night sight.

Most of Iraq's tank fleet consisted of older-design Soviet T-54, T-55, and T-62 models or their Chinese equivalent, Type 59 and Type 69 tanks. But the Iraqis also had the advanced Soviet model T-72 tank, which is quite lethal. Iraq could build its own T-72s and called their own model the Babylon Lion. It uses a laser range finder, has thickened frontal armor, and has an automatic loading mechanism for the main gun ammunition. In tank-on-tank duels the T-72 can hold its own against the American M-60 series of tanks but is totally outclassed by the later-model M-1 tanks.

Iraq had a complex mix of armored personnel carriers, reconnaissance vehicles, and infantry-fighting vehicles. The most capable was the Soviet BMP-2. It was first deployed by the Soviets in Europe in the early 1980s and later saw service in combat in Afghanistan. Its two-man turret can fire a 30mm cannon or the AT-5 Spandrel antitank guided missile system, which has a range of 2.5 miles. The vehicle carries an infantry squad of six men, who can shoot out of firing ports on the sides and rear of the vehicle. It has an overpressure system for sealing the vehicle against chemical agents. The Iraqis also showed off the Soviet-made BRDM-2 scout car, which they had modified to carry a much heavier gun that could penetrate armor but with limited ability to fire at slow-moving aircraft. Other fighting vehicles were purchased by Iraq from China, Czechoslovakia, Brazil, France, and Italy.

Artillery. Iraq developed a reputation among many analysts for possessing a superior arsenal of artillery weapons. The Iraqi armed forces had an impressive array of artillery, including howitzers, heavy mortars, and multiple-launch rocket systems from a variety of providers, and most of these had greater range than Western artillery.

Iraq turned not only to its accustomed Soviet suppliers but also to several unusual Western sources for its artillery. Outcast South Africa provided its self-propelled 155mm G-5 gun, and neutral Austria sold its GH N-45 howitzer. Using extended-range ammunition, which the Austrians themselves are prohibited from using by treaty, the GH N-45 can reach out to a maximum range of nearly 25 miles, much farther than any NATO 155mm self-propelled howitzer.

Many sources were useful to Iraq in obtaining artillery, but the most prolific supplier was as usual the Soviet Union. Thus the mainstays of Iraqi artillery are those of the Soviet army, including towed and self-propelled systems of various calibers. The Iraqi artillery philosophy was the Soviets'—massed fire. They intended to saturate the battlefield with so many steel shells that no enemy could survive; hence they continually added numbers of artillery tubes to their arsenal as well as increased the range of the ammunition they could fire.

In their drive for creating their own military-industrial base, the Iraqis also designed and built their own guns with the help of Canadian ordnance designer Gerald Bull. Bull had provided the design concepts for the South African and Austrian guns and ammunition that the Iraqis procured, and they were busy turning his ideas into systems of their own when he was mysteriously assassinated in March 1990. Bull was allegedly helping the Iraqis develop a 1,000mm-bore cannon 450 feet long that could fire a shell over a thousand miles. The British government had intercepted a number of specially made steel cylinders bound for Iraq that Saddam's government claimed were intended for use as pipelines. The British claimed they could only be used for Bull's Iraqi "supercannon."

Iraq also designed and built its own artillery pieces, which it proudly displayed at an armaments bazaar in Baghdad in May 1989. Iraqi weapons designers modified a Yugoslav version of the Soviet 122mm towed howitzer and called it the Saddam. They also designed and built a 155mm self-propelled howitzer designated the Majnoon and a 210mm piece called the Al Fao. Both systems fire the Bull-designed extended-range ammunition, and the Al Fao is the most powerful self-propelled gun in the world. Iraq also manufactured its own self-propelled heavy mortar system, designated the MT-LB. This system is similar to an Austrian design, with four mortar tubes carried on a small armored carrier.

Finally, the Iraqi army had hundreds of multiple-launch rocket systems, mostly of Soviet design. A notable exception is the Brazilian-made ASTROS-II (Artillery Saturation Rocket System). This 1980s design was made by the Brazilian company Avibras specifically for the export market and is in the arsenals of several Persian Gulf states. It has a sophisticated computerized radar fire-control system, and can launch several types of rockets, including cluster types against light armor and personnel targets simultaneously. Iraq also modified this system and renamed it the Sijeel.

Antitank and air defense systems. Iraqi ground forces were equipped with an impressive array of advanced weapons for killing tanks and aircraft. Most were, of course, Soviet-supplied and included the latest in Russian tank-killing technology. But Iraq also turned to France for this kind of system and had the most advanced French antitank systems, including Hot and Milan missiles.

Iraqi antiaircraft systems included Soviet-made guns of various calibers, ranging from 23mm to 57mm, and advanced Soviet radar-controlled surface-to-air missiles covering all altitudes and ranges. These air defense systems were integrated into a national air defense system that covered all of Iraq's borders and provided close-in protection for important targets such as airfields, sensitive research and production sites, field force headquarters, and national command and control facilities in and around Baghdad. In the late 1980s Iraq also began to buy advanced French and Italian air defense systems.

Ships. Iraq had no serious maritime capability. With only limited access to the sea through its one port of Basra, and access from the Persian Gulf to that city controlled by Iranian dominance over the Shatt-al-Arab and by Kuwaiti control over the commanding islands of Bubiyat and Warba, Iraq could never hope to be a major maritime power. Iraq had ordered four frigates from Italian shipyards early in the war with Iran, and though they were completed by 1987, they were never delivered. The Italians did deliver six corvettes with sea-skimming missiles, but Iraq's ability to put these ships to sea was doubtful. Iraq did have thirty-five smaller armed craft, which were designed to conduct short raids or to drop mines.

By August 1990 Iraq had built the fourth-largest army in the world; had one of the most well-equipped air forces; had deployed a sophisticated air defense network rivaling that of any developed country in the world; and was in reach of deploying nuclear, biological, and chemical weapons of mass destruction, which could be delivered by ballistic missiles to targets within four hundred miles of its borders. Iraq's military strength was potentially overwhelming, and its strategic reach threatened the entire region from Israel, Syria, and Egypt in the west to Iran in the east, to Saudi Arabia and the Persian Gulf in the south, and to the Soviet Union and Turkey in the north.

Order of Battle

Iraq's overwhelming military power was organized into four main components, excluding the more or less inconsequential navy. The air force had grown to thirty-eight squadrons. The ground forces consisted of three separate armies, including the popular army, the regular army, and the Republican Guard forces. The armed forces were commanded personally by Saddam Hussein, who, in addition to being the president of the republic, also was general of the army, or *mushir*. The army was commanded by the chief of staff, General Fariq Awwal Rashid, who had commanded the Republican Guard after the reform of 1986. These forces were organized in a scheme that was uniquely Iraqi, combining a British military heritage with a Cold War Soviet approach integrated with Iraqi experience in its eight-year war with Iran.

The Iraqi air force. The Iraqi air force was set up in classic Soviet style with small squadrons of eight to twenty aircraft each, depending on the type of aircraft involved. These squadrons were tightly controlled by ground operations centers and, as mentioned earlier, practiced little autonomy of action.

Iraq's bombers were organized into two squadrons, one for the Tu-22 and the other for the Tu-16 and Chinese bombers. Its transport aircraft were organized into squadrons by aircraft type, with six squadrons in all, including a separate squadron for the one Il-76 airborne early-warning aircraft. Many of Iraq's MiG-25s were outfitted with special reconnaissance sensors and equipment into one reconnaissance squadron.

Iraq's fighters fell into squadrons of two groups. Those aircraft types designed for the air-superiority role were set up in sixteen squadrons of five types, including MiG-25, J-7, MiG-21, Mirage F-1, and the newest with the MiG-29. Aircraft capable of ground attack or that had a dual role were organized into seventeen squadrons, again with each consisting of just one type of aircraft, including the MiG-23, Mirage F-1, Su-7, Su-20, Su-25, and J-6.

The Iraqi air force was dispersed throughout the country on dozens of bases built specifically to protect the airplanes. There were over thirty bases within three hundred miles of Kuwait; Iraq had in the 1980s completed construction of new bases, the main ones designated "H-2" and "H-3," in its western province within two hundred miles of Israel. These bases were built with tactical considerations in mind. Support facilities such as command and control centers, ground-control radars, and fuel and ammunition storage sites were dispersed and placed within earthen revetments for protection from general-purpose, or "dumb" bomb, attack.

Many of Iraq's aircraft were housed in steel-reinforced concrete protective buildings called hardened aircraft shelters by the Allies. These were fashioned after designs created by the North

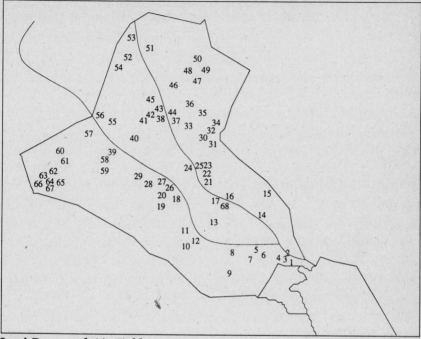

Iraqi Bases and Air Fields

1. Safwan
2. Basra/Maqal
3. Shaiba
4. Shaiba West
5. Jaliba Southeast
6. Qalib al Lukays
7. Makhfar al Busayya
8. Talil
9. Ubayyid Strip
10. Khan ar Rahba
11. Nejef
12. Diwaniya
13. Hayy
14. Amara New
15. Hawr Halfaya
16. Kut al Amara East
17. Numaniya
18. Karbala Northeast
19. Karbala
20. Iskandriya New
21. Salman Pak East
22. Salman Pak
23. Rasheed

24. Baghdad International
25. Baghdad Mutheena
26. Taqaddum
27. Habbaniya
28. Ramadi West
29. Muhammadi
30. Baquba
31. Shaykh Jasim
32. Subakhu
33. Salum
34. Sadiya
35. Jalluja
36. Injana
37. Samarra New
38. Samarra
39. Haditha
40. Mileh Tharthar
41. Jisr Ath Tharthar
42. Sahra
43. Tikrit Highway
44. Tikrit East
45. K-2
46. Fatha

47. Tall Ashath
48. Yawhi
49. Kirkuk
50. K-1
51. Qayyara South
52. Hadr
53. Qayyara West
54. Subaika
55. T-1
56. Qaim
57. H-1
58. Qasr Amij
59. Qasr Amij South
60. Shab al Hiri
61. H-2
62. Rutba
63. H-3 Northeast
64. H-3 Northwest
65. H-3
66. H-3 Highway
67. H-3 Southwest
68. Ubayda Bin Al Jarra

Atlantic Treaty Organization air forces in Europe for protection of airplanes from aerial attack and ground raids or sabotage. European firms had conducted the design and construction of these shelters, and Saddam placed great confidence in their ability to shield his air force from any attacks.

The popular army. Iraq's popular army was a militia of volunteers who could be called up in time of national emergency. They were made members of the Ba'ath Party so the regime could maintain control over the internal affairs of each region and locality in Iraq. It also served as a power balance against the regular army. Its members were mainly old men and boys with little military experience beyond basic individual military training and small-unit tactics. It was essentially an infantry force organized into platoons.

A platoon of the popular army was normally located at a base that covered the surrounding area. The members of the platoon lived close to the base so they could rapidly assemble when called. These were large platoons by Western standards and could consist of up to a hundred men organized into ten-man squads. Ten or so bases were controlled by a sector headquarters, and sectors were grouped in Iraq's eighteen national districts. The national district headquarters in turn came under the control of the popular army General Headquarters in Baghdad.

The regular army. The bulk of Iraq's combat land power was in its regular army. This was a combined arms force of considerable size and complex structure with a wide diversity of military equipment in its inventory. It was built around four kinds of combat battalions: infantry, tank, mechanized infantry, and artillery. A battalion had two hundred to seven hundred men, depending on the type, and was commanded by a lieutenant colonel, or in Iraqi parlance a *muqaddam*.

Infantry battalions in the Iraqi regular army had five hundred to seven hundred men, armed with rifles and machine guns. Each battalion had a headquarters company, an administrative company, and three maneuver companies. Each maneuver company had three infantry platoons of thirty men each and a heavy-weapons platoon with heavy machine guns and mortars.

Mechanized infantry battalions were organized around their fighting vehicle systems. Each battalion had three companies, with twelve infantry fighting vehicles or armored personnel carriers in each company. Mortars and heavy machine guns, also mounted on armored carriers, were added to the battalion in a combat support company. The standard organization for the mechanized infantry battalion called for thirty-nine armored carriers, four reconnaissance vehicles armed with antitank guided missiles, six light mortars, and various headquarters and support elements.

Tank battalions in the Iraqi regular army were likewise organized around their basic fighting vehicle. The battalion had three companies of tanks, a company consisting of three platoons of three tanks each. Including command and support systems, the battalion was equipped with thirty-five tanks, seven armored carriers, six armored reconnaissance vehicles, and up to seventy trucks for logistics support.

Battalions were grouped together to form brigades in the Iraqi regular army, and there were three types of brigade: armored, infantry, and mechanized. Armored brigades had three tank battalions and one mechanized battalion, while mechanized brigades had three mechanized battalions and one tank battalion. Infantry brigades had three infantry battalions. Armored brigades had 1,600 men, 94 tanks, and 70 AFVs (armored fighting vehicles), while mechanized brigades had 2,300 men, 40 tanks, and 160 AFVs. A brigade was commanded by a one-star brigadier general.

At the brigade level additional types of units were added to the basic combat arm to provide combat support and service support to the front-line fighting troops. These additional types of units gave Iraqi brigades an ability to fight independently. Each brigade thus had a headquarters and signal company, commandos, supply and transportation, and engineers. Smaller units—platoons—were also added to include chemical and reconnaissance capabilities for the brigade. Other support was provided by units from division level or higher, although the Iraqi infantry brigade did

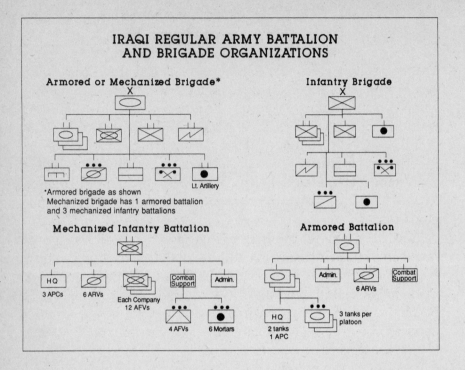

IRAQI REGULAR ARMY BATTALION
AND BRIGADE ORGANIZATIONS

have its own fire support in the form of a mortar company. Armored and mechanized brigades got all their fire support from division artillery and mortar units.

As with brigade organizations, there were three kinds of divisions in the Iraqi regular army: infantry, armored, and mechanized. Each division was commanded by a two-star major general (*liwa*) and usually had three brigades plus several supporting battalions and companies of various types. Infantry divisions had three infantry brigades plus a tank battalion. Mechanized divisions had two mechanized brigades and one armored brigade, while armored divisions had two armored brigades and one mechanized brigade. A standard mechanized division had 13,000 men, 220 tanks, and 600 armored fighting vehicles, while an armored division had 12,000 men, 330 tanks, and 460 AFVs.

Infantry divisions had three infantry brigades, but organi-

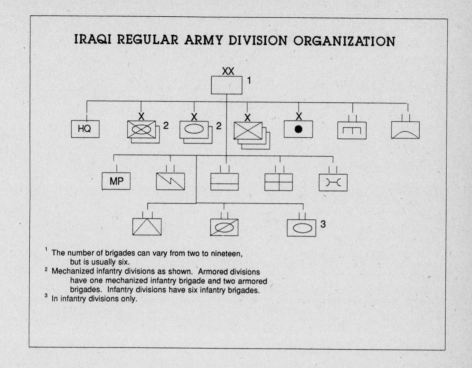

IRAQI REGULAR ARMY DIVISION ORGANIZATION

1. The number of brigades can vary from two to nineteen, but is usually six.
2. Mechanized infantry divisions as shown. Armored divisions have one mechanized infantry brigade and two armored brigades. Infantry divisions have six infantry brigades.
3. In infantry divisions only.

zations for mechanized and armored divisions were flexible; sometimes the Iraqis added more brigades, up to eight, as well as other types of units, especially artillery. Each division had a wide array of supporting troops, including artillery, commando, air defense, police, signal, supply and transportation, chemical defense, medical, maintenance, antitank, and reconnaissance forces.

The Iraqi regular army had a total of thirty-two divisions in its order of battle before the war; nine of those divisions were armored or mechanized. The Iraqi army had seven corps organizations to which these divisions were assigned. The corps was the highest operational level of command and control in the Iraqi army, with three-star generals in command. Each corps was assigned to a geographic area. Within that area the corps was responsible for all combat operations and for providing support to divisions operating in the area. The corps staff was especially

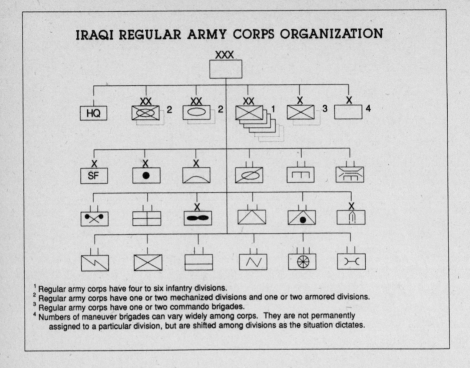

IRAQI REGULAR ARMY CORPS ORGANIZATION

[1] Regular army corps have four to six infantry divisions.
[2] Regular army corps have one or two mechanized divisions and one or two armored divisions.
[3] Regular army corps have one or two commando brigades.
[4] Numbers of maneuver brigades can vary widely among corps. They are not permanently assigned to a particular division, but are shifted among divisions as the situation dictates.

manned and equipped for planning combat operations, and there was also a political officer at the corps level who monitored adherence to Ba'ath doctrine throughout the corps.

The corps had supporting units much like the division, although they were much larger. Thus each corps had artillery and air defense brigades plus a number of battalions for support of the divisions. But at corps level there were several supporting units that did not appear at lower levels of organization. Corps was the highest level at which the Iraqi army assigned helicopter units. Corps was also the level at which the Scud missile was assigned.

The Republican Guard. Twelve of Iraq's very best divisions were not assigned to corps but were instead part of the Republican Guard Forces Command. The Republican Guard had grown from its pre–Iran War Presidential Guard days, when it was not much more than a brigade, to its corps-sized formation at the

Iraqi Division Tables of Equipment

Force	Type of Division	Number of Divisions	Personnel	Tanks	Artillery	AFVs	ADA* Guns	ADA SAMs
Regular Army	Mechanized	2	12,179	175	114	544	90	50
	Armored	7	12,129	245	114	472	90	50
	Infantry	23	14,131	35	78	6	54	0
Republican Guard	Mechanized	2	13,754	220	138	622	90	50
	Armored	2	13,734	308	144	538	90	50
	Infantry	6	14,261	44	18	6	54	0

NOTE: The figures given are the author's estimates of Iraqi forces deployed in the Kuwait Theater of Operations.

*Air Defense Artillery

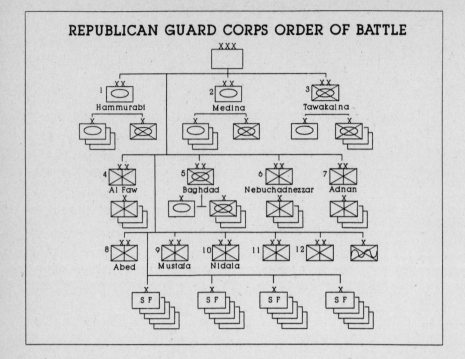

REPUBLICAN GUARD CORPS ORDER OF BATTLE

abysmal, for the Iraqis, Battle of Basra in 1986, to the oversized corps it had become for the invasion of Kuwait. It was the elite of the Iraqi army in the quality of its men and equipment. That elite status was reinforced by the assignment of names based on Iraq's martial and cultural heritage to the divisions. The Hammurabi and Medina divisions, named after the revered Babylonian ruler and the holy city, respectively, were armored. The Tawakalna and Baghdad divisions, with geographic names, were mechanized. The infantry divisions were named Al Faw, for the town at the tip of the Shatt-al-Arab; Nebuchadnezzar, after Saddam's favorite ancient Babylonian king; Adnan, named after one of Saddam's cousins; al-Mustafa and al-Abed, for two of the forefathers of Islam; and al-Nidala, which was the Iraqi name given to Kuwait City. Two other infantry divisions were assigned to the Republican Guard, as were over twenty independent commando brigades.

The Republican Guard divisions were larger and better equipped than their regular army counterparts. The infantry divisions were motorized—that is, they had sufficient numbers of trucks to move an entire division at once over rough roads. The best tanks, artillery, helicopters, and armored fighting vehicles were assigned to the Republican Guard. They received priority for supplies, and they were better paid than other Iraqi military units.

The Republican Guard not only was better trained, equipped, and led than the regular or popular army forces, but also had demonstrated its battle mettle both at the end of the Iran-Iraq War and in the invasion of Kuwait. In the war with Iran it had moved across a seven-hundred-mile front in five months, conducting five major engagements and winning every time. In each of these engagements the Republican Guard employed a different operational concept, exploiting the value of its experience in executing combined arms operations.

Tactics

Iraq had adopted its own brand of military tactics. It had a rich British heritage of pomp and ceremony from the colonial days, but the Iraqi army was not well respected in the days of the republic other than for its parades and tea service. In the late 1960s and early 1970s Iraq received Soviet advice and assistance for conducting set-piece battles, but this style of war did not work well against the more flexible maneuver style employed by the Israelis in the 1973 Arab-Israeli war. The Iraqi army and air force left the Golan Heights in 1973 with the reputation for being the least competent of all the Arab forces.

These failures and all of the foreign training and assistance were tempered by eight years of war with Iran. After enjoying initial success, Iraqi forces suffered defeat and stalemate in the war with Iran until they reformed themselves after the humiliation in the campaign of 1986. New leadership, tactics, and equipment gave the Iraqi army new life. New soldiers from the main-stream of the Iraqi middle class gave it a fighting heart and soul. With the remarkable recovery in 1988, Iraqi forces became highly proficient at both offensive and defensive tactical operations.

Offensive operations. All effective military forces in history have been successful in conducting defensive operations, yet it is not enough simply to be able to defend the homeland. The best defense is to maintain a military force capable of a good offense. The Iraqi approach to offensive operations was characterized by an attempt to achieve overwhelming superiority at a decisive place and time in a campaign.

The Iraqis adopted their offensive approach during the Iran-Iraq War when they realized they could not passively absorb Iran's human-wave attacks. While the Iraqis could beat back a few waves of the attacking Iranians, they soon realized that with its larger population, Iran's process of attrition would eventually win over the outnumbered Iraqis. Iraq therefore had to adopt the offensive or risk running out of bodies to throw into the defensive lines.

Starting in 1986, Iraq began training in offensive operations. By 1988 they had perfected a technique in which they applied over-whelming firepower against the weakest points in the lines of the Iranian defenders. During the final offensive in 1988, the attacking Iraqis sometimes outnumbered the Iranians twelve to one at the point chosen by the Iraqis for the attack.

Attacks were ordered by the political authority of the country, Saddam Hussein himself. Once ordered to plan an offensive operation, subordinate commands went through a lengthy planning process of forming their concepts of operations, preparing their orders, and obtaining headquarters approval for all aspects of the plan. The armed forces staff in Baghdad approved all attack plans, sometimes down to the lowest levels of tactical operations. Iraqi attacks were fairly straightforward applications of standard military doctrines, although the Iraqis had developed a few innovations of their own. One such creative approach was called the "silent" attack, an attempt to gain surprise by attacking at night without artillery preparation.

Attacking Iraqi forces employed four basic forms: wedge, echelon, line, and diamond. In the wedge formation, the Iraqis placed attacking tanks and armored carriers into a sort of moving arrowhead. In an echelon, the attack formation was a kind of half arrow to one side or the other. The line format was normally used to make the final assault on the objective, while the diamond was used in areas where space to move around for the attacking vehicles was constricted.

In planning for attack, Iraqi forces used a number of control measures, or markings on a map, to direct the movement of forces, coordinate the seizing of the objective, and to prevent their forces from firing on each other. First, a concentration area was selected at a place well to the rear of the front line and out of enemy artillery range. This area was where supplies and services were maintained for preparation to go on the attack. In an assembly area, also beyond enemy artillery fire, those units assigned to conduct the attack assembled and went over their plans with each other. This prevented confusion and was a final check to ensure that all the details had been covered. It also provided the opportunity for forces that had been reassigned for purposes of the attack to link up with each other. A formation line was drawn on the map about a mile away from the enemy's forward positions. At this line the Iraqi forces began to form into their assigned sectors as they moved forward into the attack. The line of departure was a recognizable terrain feature about 1,000 to 1,300 yards from the enemy, which had to be crossed at a specific time and place to begin the attack. The attack line was the place about 110 to 220 yards before the enemy's position at which the Iraqis intended to begin opening fire in close combat.

Iraqi forces could vary their approach to an attack depending on the terrain they were covering and the nature of the enemy's defense. Artillery support was planned for all phases of the attack, although Iraqi fire planning was often rigid and firmly set into precise time schedules that could not be rapidly altered to

IRAQI ATTACK FORMATIONS

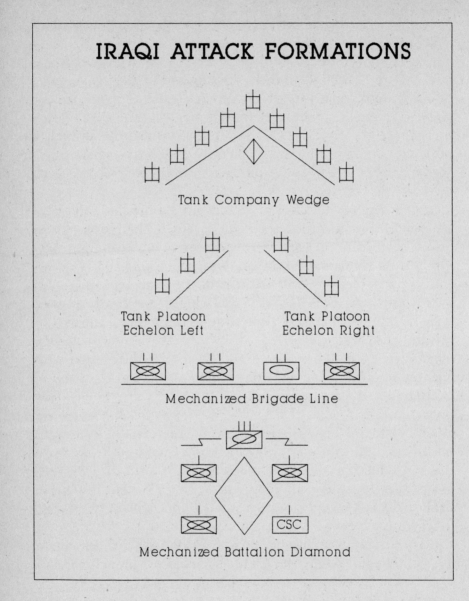

Tank Company Wedge

Tank Platoon
Echelon Left

Tank Platoon
Echelon Right

Mechanized Brigade Line

Mechanized Battalion Diamond

account for changed circumstances. When they expected resistance to be light and the ground was open, the Iraqis would place their tanks up front, especially in daytime and when they believed speed was important. They moved rapidly, employing a leapfrog technique in which one small group of tanks remained stationary to provide cover for another small group on the move. When the moving group got just to the edge of the range of the other group's tank guns, it would stop and allow the other group to move up to and beyond its position while it provided cover for them.

Sometimes infantry would be placed in front of the tanks, especially if there was a threat of enemy antitank weapons or if there were many places where enemy tanks could hide. This method was slower but more methodical and often was required where the terrain included many hills and much vegetation. The preferred method was to move infantry and tanks together along a single line, or axis, of advance. This required close coordination between tanks and infantry so that the tanks, with their limited field of vision, did not accidentally shoot at their own infantry. It also provided the best protection for both tanks and armored vehicles in the assault. Once in a while the Iraqis would move tanks and infantry at the same time but on different routes in the attack. This was normally avoided because such a tactic was difficult to control, but it could be the most effective form of the attack, since the tanks did not fire directly over the heads of their own infantry and could fire from the flanks. This gave the tanks a wider field of fire through which to provide cover for the advancing infantry.

In the attack, Iraqi commanders expected the assault force to reach its objective rapidly, get reorganized, and prepare to move on quickly. Usually, commanders at all levels would retain some part of their force, sometimes as much as a third, as a reserve to be kept out of the assault and prepared to react to unforeseen contingencies that might arise in the course of the assault. This is a time-tested principle that has proven its worth in countless instances where attacks have been surprised and spoiled by counterattacks or poor intelligence.

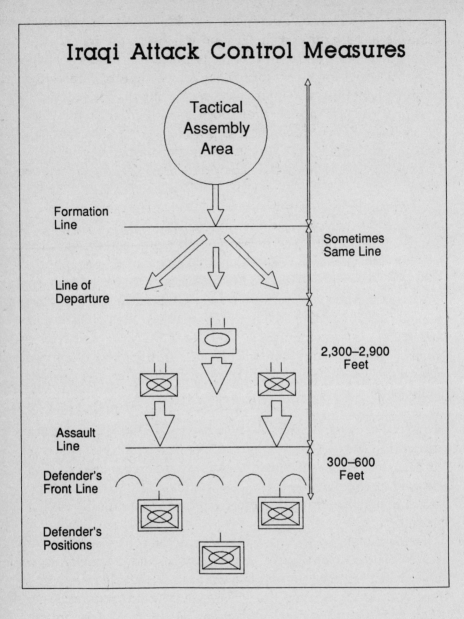

Iraqi Attack Control Measures

Tactical Assembly Area

Formation Line

Sometimes Same Line

Line of Departure

2,300–2,900 Feet

Assault Line

300–600 Feet

Defender's Front Line

Defender's Positions

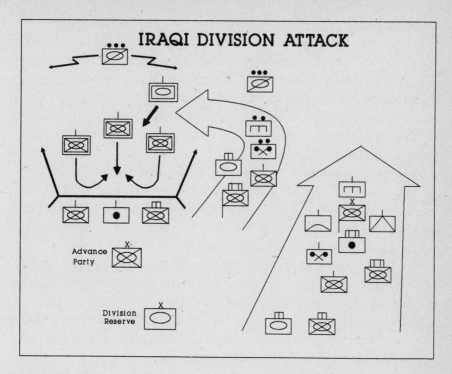

IRAQI DIVISION ATTACK

At brigade level an offensive usually began as a movement to contact—that is, the Iraqi attacker, not in contact with the defending enemy force, moved forward to find the enemy, fix it in place, and then move against it to destroy it. When the defending enemy was believed to be weak, the attacking Iraqi force would attempt to fix it with a small force, then go around it. If the defender was strong, the Iraqis would conduct a straightforward attack into its formation. Once the engagement had determined the enemy's strength and had overcome the initial defense, the Iraqi force would press on, with the main attacking force either in a frontal pursuit of the fleeing enemy or a flanking attack to move around stubborn resistance to continue the march.

Defense. Iraqi forces had four years of defensive operations in which to perfect their tactics and procedures. They were quite effective at constructing elaborate defenses and conducting defensive operations. They planned the defense in three zones. In the most forward part of the defense, they established a security zone five to six miles deep. In this area reconnaissance troops patrolled and manned outposts to provide early warning of any enemy attack. Small reserves and some heavy mortars or light artillery were placed in this zone to provide immediate response to enemy probes. In some places tanks were dug in to provide support for the infantry. Engineers constructed obstacles that would force an attacker to move to areas the defender had chosen farther back in order to concentrate his fire on the attacker. Chemical troops provided early warning of enemy chemical attacks using detection kits and alarms supplied by the Soviet Union and other Warsaw Pact countries.

At the rear of the defensive sector was the administrative zone. Here most of the defender's support operations were placed well behind the main defensive positions to provide maximum protection from artillery attack on these vital assets. The main defensive operations zone was about six miles deep between the security zone and the administrative area.

In the main defensive zone, platoons, companies, and battalions constructed elaborate defensive works throughout the depth of the area. The heart of the Iraqi defensive concept was the battalion-size "killing zone," in which the Iraqis intended to capture or kill as many enemy tanks, troops, and other weapons and equipment as possible. The base of the trap was a company dug in to a formation—for example, the "lazy W." This lazy W was simply a zigzag line of ditches with individual fighting positions linked together. In front of the trench line were mines and barbed wire. The men inside were armed with antitank rockets and machine guns. The Iraqis placed a reserve of tanks and firing batteries of artillery just behind the trench line. On the flanks of this trench line were other similarly organized lines, perhaps following different patterns for their trenchworks but essentially dug in a similar manner. With proper cover and concealment, such a U-shaped battalion formation could provide an effective trap even in the open desert. In front of the base the Iraqis placed a "bait"—a minefield with a platoon of tanks and supporting

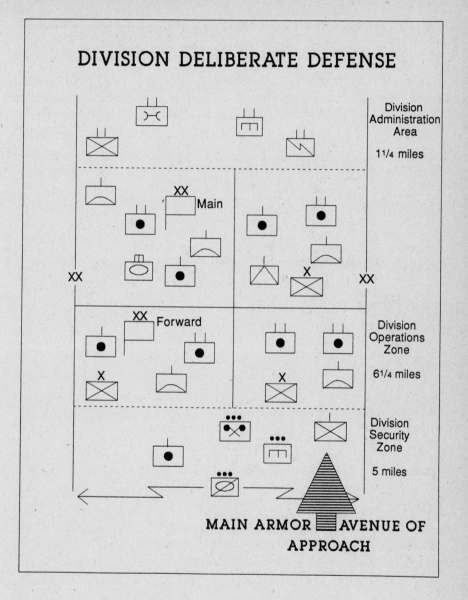

DIVISION DELIBERATE DEFENSE

Division Administration Area

1¼ miles

Main

XX   XX

X

Forward

Division Operations Zone

6¼ miles

Division Security Zone

5 miles

MAIN ARMOR AVENUE OF APPROACH

PLATOON DELIBERATE DEFENSE

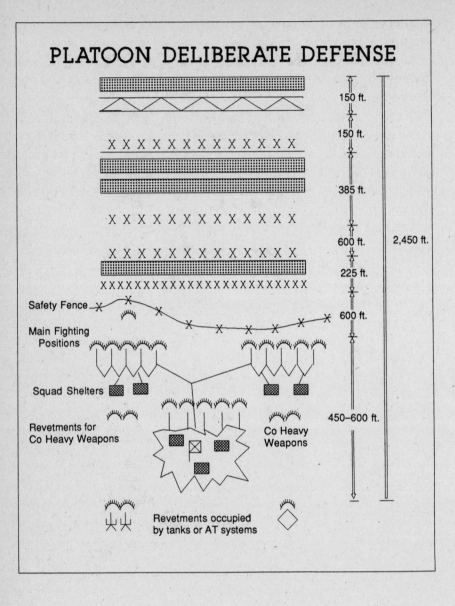

artillery tubes. This would be in the security zone and in the vicinity of the outposts and patrols in that zone.

As the attacker moved forward, the Iraqis expected him to encounter the forward positions of the "bait" and anticipated that the enemy would mount an attack to overcome those defenses. Just as the attacking enemy became decisively engaged in this forward battle, the Iraqi defenders withdrew back toward the base and flanks of the battalion, hoping to lure the attacker into pursuit. When the attacker reached the base of the defense and stopped to clear the mines and wire in front of the trenchworks, the Iraqis unleashed the full fury of their weapons from the front and flanks. They had preregistered their artillery on the obstacles so that as the attacker stopped and dismounted to clear them, the artillery would kill or wound a maximum number of unprotected soldiers.

If this defensive trap did not stop the attacker, or if the attacker

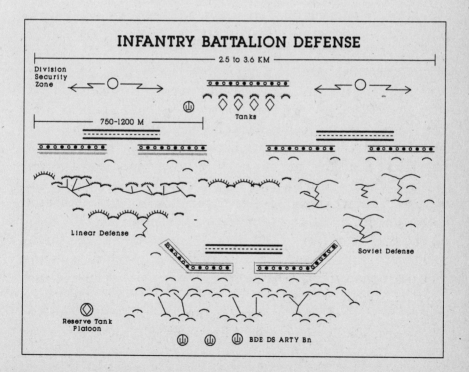

succeeded in penetrating the trench line, the Iraqi doctrine called for a counterattack into the attacking enemy by mobile armored reserves located a few miles away just for such eventualities. These "kill zones" were constructed throughout the depth of the Iraqi defenses so that even if one of them was penetrated without successful counterattack, the attacking enemy would soon run into another similar defensive position.

In both offensive and defensive operations, the Iraqi army had developed an advanced state of doctrine of its own based on much combat experience. This was an armed force that was well equipped, well trained, and well led. Its eight years of war with Iran had been a crucible of blood and battle that had given it an extraordinary ability to fight and that had provided it with a short period of military success that made strategists and analysts take note of a reborn Iraqi military threat. Iraq turned this formidable military machine against its smallest neighbor in August 1990.

The Invasion of Kuwait

The Iraqi dispute with Kuwait had three main elements. First, there was a pretense of a border dispute, which had in fact been settled long ago. Iraq claimed that the agreements from the 1960s that had settled the boundary between the two states were invalid, and Saddam demanded control over Warba and Bubiyan islands, which control access to the Shatt-al-Arab. Second, Iraq accused Kuwait of stealing oil from the Rumaila oil field that the two countries shared across their northern border. Actually, most of the field is in Iraq, with only a small portion of the southernmost tip in Kuwait. Iraq claimed that Kuwait was pumping out more than its fair share of the field's output. Finally, Iraq accused Kuwait of producing too much oil overall to undermine the price of oil offered by Organization of Petroleum Exporting Countries (OPEC). In essence, Iraq claimed that Kuwait was cheating on the price-fixing scheme established by the international oil producers' cartel.

In fact, Iraq's invasion was the result of a longer-term ambition of Saddam Hussein to control the oil resources of the Arabian Peninsula. This was part of his grand scheme to unite the Arab world under his leadership and to eject the Israelis from Palestine as a modern Saladin. With that in mind, he had started his war with Iran at a time when he perceived the Iranians to be at their weakest. And he struck at Kuwait in August 1990, when he believed he could get away with a naked theft of the entire country. He expected that the rest of the world, led by the superpowers in their post–Cold War disengagement from each other, would look the other way.

Saddam's demands on Kuwait had elevated in tone and intensity in February 1990 at various Arab and OPEC forums. In the spring, a British journalist who had violated Iraqi orders to stay away from a suspicious nuclear power project was executed by the Iraqi government, and Western intelligence sources revealed that Iraq had deployed Scud missiles to its new base in western Iraq at H-3, from which they could reach Israel. Gerald Bull was assassinated, and the British government seized the steel pipe being shipped to Iraq for the construction of the supergun.

In response to Iraqi pressure, Kuwait and the United Arab Emirates had agreed to lower their output of oil to boost prices, which had been falling at unusually fast rates. By the time of the summer's Arab League summit in Baghdad, all the oil-producing states were experiencing a decline in oil revenues, but Iraq was particularly furious with the role of the smaller producers. Saddam demanded production quotas that would result in oil at $25 per barrel. He also failed to reach agreement at the summit, as he had desired, with Syria and Turkey over water rights from the Euphrates River. By midsummer, oil prices had sunk to below $18 a barrel.

On July 17, Saddam delivered a speech to his nation threatening military action against Kuwait if it did not respond to Iraqi demands. On the eighteenth, the Kuwaitis took the threat seriously and placed their military forces on alert. U.S. Ambassador to Iraq April Glaspie reported in her Senate testimony in March 1991 that she delivered the U.S. response to the Iraqi Deputy Foreign Minister. The United States would take no side in territorial disputes among the states of the Middle East but also would insist that all disputes between Iraq and its neighbors be settled peacefully. She said that she delivered this same message every day during the crisis, starting on the eighteenth.

The CIA reported that Iraq had moved 30,000 troops to the Iraq-Kuwait border by then. On the twentieth the deployments were reported in Baghdad daily newspapers in addition to increasingly vituperative denunciations of the United States. Iraq continued to build up its force on the Kuwaiti border, and the United States on July 24 announced it was conducting joint maneuvers with Arab naval and air forces in the area. The United Arab Emirates announced that it, too, was taking part in the joint exercise with U.S. military forces, and apparently this was a sufficient surprise to get Saddam Hussein's attention.

On July 25, Glaspie was called to the Foreign Ministry to meet directly with Saddam Hussein. She was the first foreign ambassador to have an audience with him since 1984, and the summons was a surprise to the diplomatic community. Ambassador Glaspie was a career foreign service officer, one of the few who had succeeded in overcoming the politics of the State Department to rise to the rank of ambassador. She was an old hand in Arab affairs and well understood the nuances of Middle Eastern rhetoric. She had received the appointment as ambassador in 1988 but was well acquainted with the politics of the region as well as with Saddam Hussein's style, character, and ambitions.

Saddam was enraged at the United States. But, according to Ambassador Glaspie's testimony, he appeared to cave in completely at their meeting. He charged that the United States was supporting Kuwait in an economic war against Iraq, but he was conciliatory and "flummoxed" that the United States might oppose him. She said that she had responded, as before in sessions at the Foreign Ministry, that the United States would not take sides in Middle East territorial disputes but that the United States would insist on a peaceful solution. At the end of the meeting, she said, he "surrendered," and, after a call to Egyptian President Hosni Mubarak, promised not to solve his problems with Kuwait by violence.

She left the meeting assured in her own mind that Saddam would give diplomacy one more chance to resolve the dispute. An Arab conference was set to be held in Jidda, Saudi Arabia, the following week, with the Saudis to serve as mediator in the dispute. Mubarak was given similar assurances by Saddam that he would not attack Kuwait, and Saudi King Fahd was given the same promise by Saddam. In the Iraqi version of the normally secret diplomatic exchanges, Saddam did not mention the U.S. insistence on a peaceful solution and the Iraqi promise for peace. On July 30, Ambassador Glaspie left Baghdad for the United States on vacation.

On July 26, Kuwait caved in to Iraqi demands on oil production quotas and announced that it would cut back its output to the levels demanded. But the Iraqi buildup continued. On July 30 the CIA estimated that 100,000 Iraqi troops were poised on the border for an attack with 300 tanks. On July 31 Kuwaiti and Iraqi leaders met in Jidda to make one last attempt at reconciliation with Saudi mediation. The attempt failed, and the talks collapsed. On August 1 the CIA assessment was that an attack was probable. On August 2, 1990, Iraq invaded Kuwait.

It was a textbook blitzkrieg operation carried out by the Republican Guard. At 1 A.M. on the second, the Hammurabi and Medina divisions crossed the border on separate axes and moved rapidly south to Kuwait City. The assault was coordinated with attacks by a special forces commando division into Kuwait City itself. These overland ground operations were coordinated with helicopter and amphibious assaults.

The overmatched Kuwaitis were no equal to the onslaught of the Republican Guard, though a few pitched battles were fought. The Kuwaitis had even had some early warning of the attack despite the fact that the Iraqis moved mostly under cover of darkness. Kuwait had purchased a lighter-than-air ship called a heliostat from an American entrepreneur and had mounted an

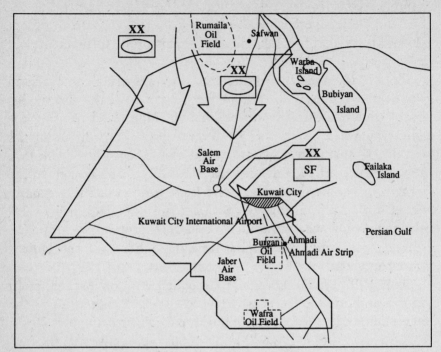

Iraq invades Kuwait, 0100 hours, August 2, 1990

early warning radar on the balloon to provide surveillance of the airspace around the tiny kingdom. The radar was operational at the time of the attack and was being monitored by a few U.S. contract people and several Kuwaitis. The Iraqi movement was so massive that the radar picked up the movements in the north and the approach of the helicopters into Kuwait City. Knowing there were no Kuwaiti operations of that size moving south from Iraq, the operators gave a few hours' warning to the government. This let them alert the armed forces and allowed the emir and the royal family to escape to set up a government-in-exile.

The Kuwaiti air force continued to operate well after Iraq fully occupied Kuwait City. Kuwait's American-made A-4 aircraft operated for a day or so out of a base in southern Kuwait, venturing out to attack Iraqi armor columns before the Iraqis finally reached the airfield on the morning of August 3 and chased the

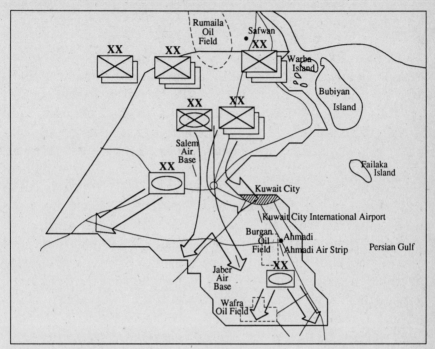

Iraq secures Kuwait, August 3, 1990

Kuwaiti pilots off into Saudi Arabia. There was a brief battle in Kuwait City near the army barracks at Shuwaik, but the Iraqis quickly overcame the small band of brave Kuwaiti defenders, led by Colonel Ahmad al-Sabah. Resistance within the city formed quickly, with its greatest strength in the Salmya district, and engaged in hit-and-run attacks on the invaders, causing some disruption of the attack. Within thirty-six hours, however, it was all over.

Kuwait had only a little more than twenty thousand troops in its armed forces, most of whom were killed or captured by the invaders. Some three thousand to seven thousand army troops escaped, along with about forty tanks. The entire Kuwaiti navy survived, a small but effective force of eight modern German-made missile patrol boats. And the Kuwaiti air force lost only thirteen of its aircraft in its heroic attempt to stall the invasion. The Kuwaiti air force thus had sixteen Mirage F-1 fighters and twenty-four A-4 Skyhawk fighter-bombers that lived to fight another day. Twenty-four armed helicopters as well as several transport aircraft made it to Saudi Arabia. In addition to captured troops and tanks, the Iraqis snatched up Kuwait's U.S.-made high-technology air-defense missile system, the improved Hawk. Not only was this a significant loss for the Kuwaitis, it also constituted a potentially dangerous capability in Iraqi hands if Saddam's technicians could figure out how to make it operational.

Iraq had obviously prepared and rehearsed the invasion well in advance. Some intelligence analysts say that the Iraqi army had been getting ready for this invasion since 1989. The divisions that made this lightning move had practiced it in full-scale mock-up in the southeastern Iraqi desert outside of Basra. After the war with Iran, that desert became the largest military training complex in Iraq and was used for maneuver and live-fire gunnery practice. The Iraqis had also strengthened their military engineer corps so that as they advanced into Kuwait they were able to build new roads along the way.

On the second day of the invasion the Iraqis pushed the elite Tawakalna Mechanized Division of the Republican Guard into Kuwait and together with the two armored divisions pushed south to the border with Saudi Arabia. Immediately behind them the remainder of the Republican Guard, six motorized infantry divisions, followed into Kuwait City to complete the occupation and to root out resistance. That same day three more divisions from the regular army moved south into Kuwait along the new roads that had been carved out of the desert the previous day. The engineers continued to make new roads in the middle of the desert running north to south.

These units were in formation not to attack Kuwait but to continue the march south into Saudi Arabia. They were accompanied by their complete logistics tail in column with them. Allied intelligence analysts concluded that the Iraqis were preparing for a subsequent move to seize the Saudi Arabian oil fields and the Persian Gulf ports. If the Iraqis executed this part of the invasion along the lines of the timetable they had used in the 1988 offensives against Iran, they could be expected to launch another attack into Saudi Arabia in about two to three weeks with objectives probably reaching another seventy to one hundred miles south of the Kuwaiti border.

This would put them in possession of the vital al-Qatif–al Qaysumah oil pipeline, the key oil fields at Khafji, Ras Safaniyah, and Manifah, as well as King Khalid Military City and Hafr al Batin guarding the western approaches to the oil fields. From there the Iraqis would be within artillery range of the port of Jubail and a scant seventy miles from Dammam and Dhahran. With the enemy that close to the main ports, Saddam figured the West would not risk sending military forces into Saudi Arabia even if they could convince the Saudis to allow them to do so. In Saddam's calculation, such a bold military move by his army would cow the Saudis into cutting a deal for the oil fields without risking the Arab backlash that he figured would be precipitated if King Fahd asked for intervention from the United States. Even if he was wrong, he would force the United States to come into Saudi Arabia from the Red Sea ports of Jidda and Yenbo, which would force them to wait for months before they could build up sufficient strength to move against him. And even then the United States would have to move through a few narrow mountain passes on easily interdicted roads then march across hundreds of miles of barren open desert before they could reach the Iraqis.

Saddam Hussein had stunned the world with his bold and rapid attack, but the world reacted. The United States mobilized its diplomatic and military forces with surprising speed to begin an international response of unprecedented size and strength.

CHAPTER FOUR

Sitzkrieg

THE IRAQI INVASION of Kuwait precipitated a crisis in the international security system—a crisis not only about the taking of a small country. More fundamentally, it was about whether the world would allow control of the most basic input to the world's economy—energy—to fall into the hands of a tyrant. Saddam Hussein and the Iraqi military machine now threatened to take over half the world's supply of oil. They had the capability to move rapidly beyond Kuwait into the northern provinces of Saudi Arabia and down along the coast of the Arabian peninsula, seizing the major Arabian oil fields and petroleum industry infrastructure along the way.

Every major country and most international organizations responded in some way to the crisis. There were diplomatic moves of unprecedented scope around the globe. The United Nations, the Arab League, and the Organization of Petroleum Exporting Countries (OPEC) moved in concert as never before. Military mobilizations in the immediately affected states of Iraq, Saudi Arabia, and the United States took place on a scale not seen since World War II.

Yet, for all the urgency of the situation as it developed in August, the crisis rapidly settled into an anxious waiting game that lasted for four and a half months. Military mobilizations and deployments proceeded on both sides as the potential battlefield was set across the Persian Gulf and the Arabian deserts.

Amidst all the saber rattling on the military side, most world leaders involved seemed anxious to avoid a war if possible, so the military moves sometimes appeared to be more bluster than brawn. Many argued for laying siege to Iraq and avoiding a direct military conflict by simply starving the Iraqi army and strangling the Iraqi economy. It became in many ways a "Sitzkrieg"—a war of sitting in place. But it was also a war that the Pentagon had been preparing for over the previous ten years.

Diplomacy

The most extraordinary response to the crisis was the Soviet Union's, by voting with the United States on the day of the invasion for the first United Nations Security Council resolution on the Iraqi action, number 660, which condemned the invasion and demanded withdrawal. For forty-five years the Soviet approach to the Middle East had been to support any groups— governments, international organizations, or terrorists—that would stir up trouble for the United States. Military hardware had been the principal instrument of Soviet policy during this time, and by the late 1980s there were more Russian-made tanks in the Middle East than there were in Eastern Europe. In the Persian Gulf crisis of 1990, though, the Soviets reversed themselves and tried to develop their own approach to getting Saddam Hussein out of Kuwait peacefully, a goal consistent with U.S. interests. Throughout the crisis the Soviets tried to cut a separate deal with Saddam Hussein involving a pullout from Kuwait. Iraq would get some kind of face-saving concessions, and the Soviets would get full credit for brokering the peace. In the end Saddam would not agree to any such deal, and the Soviet attempts failed.

The Iraqis continued to hold Soviet military advisers in Iraq along with other foreign hostages during the crisis. With so much of Iraq's military equipment coming from the Soviet Union and so much of it dependent on Soviet high technology, which the Iraqis were incapable of operating and maintaining by themselves, Saddam Hussein did not want the Soviet advisers to leave.

At one point Saddam even warned the Soviets not to pass on military secrets to the United States. The hostage situation did not help Soviet-Iraq relations either. In late November the Soviets demanded that Iraq release its 3,000 citizens being held, many of whom were indeed military technical advisers.

The crisis was not only a watershed of U.S.-Soviet relations, it was also a rebirth of the United Nations as an effective force for world action. The UN had been created at the end of World War II as a world body for the maintenance of peace, but it had failed to fulfill that role largely because of Soviet designs on empire. Non-aligned nations formed coalitions to counter the power and influence of the superpowers or the former colonial powers, and in many ways the UN became a forum for the "have-nots" to confront the "haves." Whether supported by the Soviet Union or not, hundreds of wars were fought among UN members and millions of people died in armed conflict. The most the UN was usually able to achieve was the placement of a few observers in battlefields where they could watch and report when conflict threatened. The Persian Gulf crisis challenged the world body to regain credibility and influence, which it did admirably.

It helped that the United States did not, as it had in the past out of frustration, attempt to bypass the United Nations. Instead, President Bush went through UN channels to develop international support for achieving U.S. interests in the Gulf. He worked the telephones constantly, calling world leaders to sound them out on prospective U.S. action in the crisis or to sense their degree of commitment to ejecting Iraq from Kuwait. He took three major foreign trips during the crisis, one to the Helsinki summit in September, one to the Middle East during Thanksgiving, followed by a swing through Latin America. His efforts paid off with twelve Security Council resolutions basically legitimizing the U.S. approach to the crisis.

The president was also successful in gaining Arab support for the U.S. handling of the crisis. The first and most important object of U.S.-Arabian diplomacy was King Fahd of Saudi Arabia. The king sat at the apex of a complicated pyramid of Saudi royal family politics that would make it difficult for him to accede to immediate U.S. military deployments. Some in the United States worried that the Saudis might want to buy off their powerful neighbor to the north rather than risk a rift in the Arab camp, especially after the Emir of Kuwait offered to trade some territory for an Iraqi withdrawal a few days after his country was stolen from him. In the past, the Saudis had always been helpful to the United States but insisted on keeping its military cooperation efforts quiet. The other Arab states would be likely to follow the king's lead. On August 6 the king gave his approval for deployment.

Secretary of State James Baker traveled constantly around the world to build support for the U.S. Other Arab states fell rapidly in line with the Saudis, including Egypt under President Hosni Mubarak who felt betrayed by Hussein in his earlier efforts to mediate the dispute. Even the maverick Syrian leader Hafez al Assad demonstrated a willingness to support the United States. This was a most unusual coalition, with Syria at the time still on the State Department's list of governments supporting international terrorism. On August 10 twelve of twenty-one members of the Arab League, which still included Iraq, voted to provide troops to defend Saudi Arabia.

Iran was the most critical Middle Eastern wild card in the crisis. Iran's position was a constant worry for U.S. leaders. Even after its devastating loss in the final months of the war with Iraq, Iran possessed a potent military force. Geographically, if even a small Iranian force was to side with Iraq, it would be very difficult to fight a war on the Arabian Peninsula with the entire Persian Gulf flanked by a hostile Iran. Saddam recognized this and tried a number of gambits to persuade Iran to take arms against the United States—led coalition, the most important of which was the return of all the territory he had won from Iran during the 1980s war. Iran responded by taking delivery of oil from Iraq and by promising to send food and medical supplies to Iraq in spite of the embargo. By the end of September, though, it was clear to the main Arab military powers that they, too, must stop Saddam Hussein or they would risk becoming his next targets. Iran and Syria announced their opposition to continued Iraqi occupation of Kuwait on September 25.

The president's most important allies in the crisis were the British. Prime Minister Margaret Thatcher was with George Bush at a conference on the future world strategic order in Aspen, Colorado, on August 2, the day Iraq invaded Kuwait. The president was to deliver a speech announcing his vision of the "new world order" and a new U.S. strategic approach in response to it. One can only speculate about the conversations between Bush and Thatcher as the invasion unfolded before them, but no doubt the Iron Lady shared her sentiments with the president. Her public statements were more bellicose than Bush's. Britain was the first to announce troop deployments to Saudi Arabia in support of the United States, and on November 7 Mrs. Thatcher was the first Western leader to threaten military action when she said, "Either he [Saddam Hussein] gets out of Kuwait soon, or we and our allies will remove him by force."

Other industrialized countries were not as eager to come to the U.S. side. Germany was slow to come around, eventually pledging financial support and claiming that its constitution prevented it from deploying military personnel beyond its borders. French President François Mitterand had troubles of his own with a divided cabinet. He personally seemed to want to support President Bush in a more visible way, but his defense minister M. Chevenement demurred until he resigned under pressure in early January. Japanese Prime Minister Toshiki Kaifu pledged to send noncombat military personnel and financial support for Allied efforts, plus an initial contingent of medical personnel, but he was stymied by a recalcitrant Parliament, which objected to such unconstitutional action, and the Japanese contingent was withdrawn in January before hostilities commenced.

The domestic coalition that George Bush put together in support of his war effort was in many ways even more remarkable than the international coalition. The United States was haunted by the ghost of the Vietnam War, but Bush enjoyed early support during the first few days of the crisis in August. Congress responded favorably when Bush sent official notification, "consistent with" the War Powers Resolution, that deployed American military forces were in imminent danger of armed conflict. Saddam Hussein unwittingly helped Bush's efforts when he, in a poorly concocted public diplomacy move, televised a meeting he held with foreign hostages in Baghdad. Rather than allaying international concerns regarding his intentions toward the hostages, Saddam's patronizing gestures only solidified support for the administration. The president also sent Secretary of State Baker to Capitol Hill for hearings before key congressional committees, where he outlined the administration's objectives in resolving the crisis. While from time to time the administration's rhetoric strayed from the basic line laid out in August, by and large it was consistent in seeking not the ouster of Saddam Hussein nor the dismemberment of Iraq, but four basic goals: complete and immediate withdrawal of Iraqi forces from all of Kuwait; restoration of the legitimate government of Kuwait; the safety of all westerners held against their will in Kuwait and Iraq; and the establishment of a stable structure for peace in the region. This message was articulated over and over as the administration's main message to Congress during the entire crisis period.

Ten Years of Military Planning

While the nation's leaders and the world's diplomats were maneuvering to achieve peace, the Pentagon was fully engaged in planning for war. In fact, the preparations for war in the Persian Gulf had begun ten years earlier. The military response to the crisis precipitated by Iraq's invasion of Kuwait was in many ways the culmination of a decade's worth of planning and preparation for similar scenarios.

America's post–World War II focus had been on containing the Russians. The military emphasis was on defending Europe, but there had always been concern with the Middle East and

Southwest Asia. Before the 1973 Yom Kippur War, the concern was driven solely by the potential for escalation of Arab-Israeli conflict to nuclear confrontation between the Soviet Union and the U.S. After the Yom Kippur War, the disruption of access to Middle East oil from any conflict in the region also became a factor.

The worst contingency that planners could imagine was a direct Soviet invasion of the area, which would pose both ideological and economic threats to the Western world. When the Soviets invaded Afghanistan in 1979, the same year as the fall of the Shah of Iran, that planning was renewed in earnest. The Shah had been the bulwark of U.S. containment of the Soviets in the region, and the specter of a Soviet stranglehold on the world's oil led Pentagon planners to draw up new plans to prevent a Soviet drive to the Persian Gulf through Iran.

The United States formed what it called the Rapid Deployment Joint Task Force (RDJTF) in 1981 to deal with such a contingency. Its mission was to be prepared to deploy rapidly to the Persian Gulf region, landing in Saudi Arabia or Iran, and to move quickly north to stop a Soviet push to the Gulf. The idea was to get a sizable force there before the Soviets could move through the passes in the Zagros Mountains, forming the border between Iran and the Soviet Union.

The difficulty with the plan in 1981 was getting any force to the Middle East in time to do its job. Any force required to defeat the Soviets had to be predominantly armored, as in central Europe, but armored forces are bulky and heavy, and demand massive amounts of airlift and sealift to get them anywhere. A force heavy enough to stop the Russians would be too heavy to move rapidly. A force light enough to move rapidly would not be heavy enough to win. With only a few dozen airlift aircraft in the Air Force's inventory, it was impossible to move the force by air. Sea movement was needed, but that was time-consuming. It would take over a month to get the force into the region from the United States, over 7,000 miles away, and in that time the Soviets could pour dozens of divisions down into Iran's western provinces unless interdicted. Early contingency plans thus called for a massive air campaign to hit advancing Soviet forces, delaying their arrival long enough for the American land forces to arrive by sea and mount a more credible defense. If the plan was successful, the U.S. would be able to launch a counterattack to push the Russians back into their own territory. The Pentagon's contingency planners gave the war plan a number, as they do for all war plans, and this plan was designated number 1002.

The Defense Department worked during the 1980s to improve the chances of 1002's success by adding strategic lift assets to the inventory of air and sea carriers available to move the force. The Air Force built more C-5 cargo transporters and rebuilt its C-141 airlifters, giving them greater capacity and an in-flight refuel capability. The Navy revamped its old sealift ships and bought eight new ones, which could make the transit from U.S. East Coast ports to the Persian Gulf in a little over a week.

But these additional military strategic lifters were still not

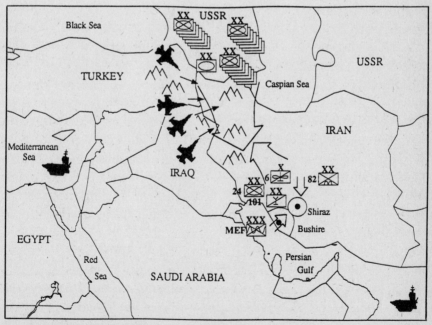

National War Plan 1002
Note: Author's estimate based on unclassified sources

enough to move the entire force in a month. The Pentagon had to create a number of additional programs to fill the gaps. For airlift, it developed a program of emergency leasing procedures in which commercial airlines agreed to allow the Air Force to commandeer commercial airliners and their crews during a crisis for use in transporting military cargos. This program was called the Civil Reserve Air Fleet (CRAF) and was designed to have three phases, each phase adding more aircraft as the progression of a crisis required. The Navy placed additional cargo ships in a semi-mothball status in a program known as the Ready Reserve Fleet. These ships could be very quickly taken out of harbor and loaded for overseas movement. Several ships even older than those were also mothballed and placed in the National Defense Reserve Fleet to be pressed into service after a longer call-up period. The Marines bought cargo ships that they used to place equipment afloat and staged them with tanks and other equipment on-board across the globe at strategic spots for rapid deployment of Marine forces.

With concern about the Middle East increasing, the Defense Department created a new command in order to fight a war that might break out in Southwest Asia or the Persian Gulf. The Central Command (CENTCOM) was carved out of territory that previously had been the responsibility of other regional commands—Pacific, Atlantic, and European—in the U.S. unified command plan. The Central Command was to be prepared to execute plan 1002 and was to be given the authority to command the assigned forces in a crisis, but it was not given control over those forces in peacetime. Because those same forces were also designated for the defense of Europe or for other contingencies, the commander of CENTCOM could plan on getting those forces if needed, but he was not permitted to supervise their training or equipment. And while the European and Pacific commands had regular exercises, REFORGER and TEAM SPIRIT respectively, through which to test the readiness of forces designated for them in their war plans, CENTCOM was not to have the same luxury. Budget constraints would not allow another such series of expensive maneuvers, and such large-scale exercises might themselves disrupt the sensitivities in the delicately balanced Middle East region. CENTCOM was allowed to conduct only a very small-scale exercise each year called BRIGHT STAR, but that never involved more than a few ground battalions and some tactical aircraft.

The Pentagon used the focus of the war plan and the small-scale exercises to develop new ideas and test new equipment in the roles they would have to play in the harsh environment of the region. The Air Force had developed its Red Flag air-to-air mock combat exercises in the desert Southwest of the United States to allow fighter pilots to work against Soviet-style fliers and aircraft in anticipation of combat in Europe. Those exercises were changed to reflect Middle Eastern combat, and the training was renamed Desert Flag. The Army built a massive exercise facility, called the National Training Center, in the California desert, where its large units could maneuver in terrain similar to that of Southwest Asia against an opposing force that also used expected enemy equipment and tactics. The Army also developed a new class of light forces designed to move more firepower using fewer numbers of aircraft. The Marines developed a training facility of their own for realistic amphibious exercises at Twenty-Nine Palms on the California coast and also experimented with various different ways of organizing their forces for combat in order to build more flexibility into their combat power.

The Navy developed its approach to the region through actual operations during the 1980s. Operation Earnest Will was the most challenging test of the U.S. military's ability to protect our national interests in the late 1980s. This was the operation initiated in 1987 to protect Kuwaiti oil tankers from attacks by either Iran or Iraq. Kuwait had reflagged its oil tankers under U.S. registry and asked for armed escorts from the U.S. Navy. In April 1988, during these escort operations, the Iranian navy came out into the Gulf and directly attacked the U.S. escorts. The Iranians were rapidly destroyed and virtually the entire Iranian navy was sunk. At about the same time, special helicopters, which had been secretly outfitted with advanced night fighting equipment, were used to destroy Iranian antiship missile launchers positioned on oil platforms on the Iranian side of the Gulf.

While the war planners were developing plans and forces for the CENTCOM mission, the Defense Department itself was undergoing profound change. In 1986 Congress had passed the most far-reaching defense reorganization law since it created the Defense Department in 1947. The Goldwater-Nichols Defense Reorganization Act strengthened the power of the Chairman of the Joint Chiefs of Staff and gave greater authority to the regional commanders-in-chief. Before Goldwater-Nichols, the chairman was not really superior to the other service chiefs of staff; he was simply the first among equals. The commanders in the field had to rely on Army, Navy, Air Force, and Marine headquarters to provide support for their deployed forces, and more often than not the support provided reflected the services' own ideas of what the priorities ought to be rather than what the commander in the field wanted. The law changed that by effectively requiring the service chiefs to respond to the needs of the field commanders.

In order to anticipate those requirements and to fully support the forces, each service created its own brain trust of officers, whose mission was to anticipate the needs of the future and to develop innovative ways of dealing with them. The Air Force created Project Checkmate, the Army called theirs the Chief's Assessment and Initiatives Group (CAIG), the Navy had the Chief of Naval Operations' Executive Panel, and the Marine Corps created an Emerging Issues Group. The officers assigned to these very small staff groups were the best and brightest from their services and worked directly for their service chiefs. To be assigned to one of these groups, officers had to be fully qualified in their combat skills and had to be well educated and intelligent. They also had to be politically astute in order to navigate the arcane bureaucratic politics of the Pentagon and the Washington environment. Their superiors began to refer to them as the Jedi Knights. Much of their work was directed toward solving the problems of developing war plan 1002 and the dilemma of rapid deployment of heavy firepower to the Persian Gulf region.

By the time General H. Norman Schwarzkopf assumed command of CENTCOM in 1987, there had been a decade of experience in anticipating and planning for a potential Soviet invasion of the Persian Gulf. But soon after he took the helm, it became clear that it was not the Soviets that he would have to worry about so much as other threats in the region.

General Schwarzkopf was by no means a unanimous choice among Defense Department officials for the four-star slot. There was in fact quite a stir about his selection. It was not so much a matter of his abrasive style and personality; both of these were well known but not really considerations in the choice. In fact the controversy had nothing to do with his character or qualifications, which had been amply proven in combat in Vietnam and Grenada and in high command and staff positions as a general. The issue was not who was to get the command; it was which service would get it.

Before the creation of CENTCOM there had been a finely tuned balance among the armed services as to which service would provide the commander for each of the prize four-star commands. The Navy had always provided the commanders for the Pacific and Atlantic commands, the Army had the European and Southern commands, and the Air Force had the Strategic Air Command. CENTCOM was the first new war fighting headquarters to be created since the formation of joint commands in 1947. The first commander had been a Marine Corps general, George Crist, the first Marine ever selected for a four-star regional command. The Marines desperately wanted one of their own to replace Crist in 1987, but lost the bureaucratic battle to the Army when Schwarzkopf was put in.

Soon after Schwarzkopf took command of CENTCOM in 1987, the Cold War began to wind down, but the end of the Iran-Iraq War brought new dangers to light. The Pentagon took a hard look at what the Iraqis had accomplished at the end of the war and became quite alarmed at the buildup they saw. In 1989 Joint Chiefs of Staff Chairman Colin Powell directed CENTCOM and the Joint Staff to begin a major revision of the old war plan 1002 to refocus it away from the old Soviet threat and toward this new potential threat from Iraq. The new plan, 1002-90, was to assume that Iraq would be the primary threat to the region and was to develop military options to deal with that threat.

A group of analysts at the Army War College in Carlisle, Pennsylvania, set about to assess precisely what the threat was from the Iraqi military. They uncovered the capabilities described in Chapter Two. Scenarios were spun out in the Joint Staff and in the services' brain trusts, and it quickly became apparent that Saddam's next likely target was either Kuwait or Saudi Arabia or both. 1002-90 was aimed at that contingency. The Air Force developed an elaborate air campaign plan based on those scenarios and even produced a mock Air Tasking Order for actual missions for the plan as a way of testing their ability to respond to a potential crisis. The new plan did not provide for any new forces—indeed, it anticipated fewer forces being available as the size of the military was programmed to shrink by about 25 percent—but it did affect the missions that would be assigned to the forces and where they would deploy.

A possible Iraqi attack scenario was developed late in 1989 and the services' brain trusts worked on it as did the various staff colleges and war colleges around the country. In June 1990 the plan had been fleshed out and was ready for its first major test, a command post exercise run by Central Command Headquarters in Tampa, Florida. All the major units called for by the plan were exercised and had an opportunity to see how prepared they were to deal with the new threat. The exercise uncovered a number of difficulties that were in the process of being resolved when the crisis erupted.

At the Center for Strategic and International Studies (CSIS), we had just completed a two-year study of the future of conventional warfare, a project entitled Conventional Combat 2002. Cochaired by Congressmen Dave McCurdy (D-OK) and John Rowland (R-CT), we had concluded that the most dangerous threat that would face the United States in the 1990s was a mid-intensity conflict somewhere in the Middle East or Southwest Asia. We expected that any number of ongoing disputes could escalate to a war which would require some kind of a military response by the United States, including conflicts between India and Pakistan, Iran and Iraq, Israel and any number of Arab states, and others. But we concluded that the most likely place for a war to erupt was between Iraq and its southern neighbors, Kuwait and Saudi Arabia. We had even simulated the outcome of such a war and published our results in the May 1990 report, "Conventional Combat Priorities." We had briefed it extensively throughout the Pentagon, the Congress, and among defense contractors in May and June 1990.

Pulling the Trigger

The first sign of crisis for the military was the July 20 CIA report of 30,000 Iraqi troops massing on the border with Kuwait. In response the National Security Council staff called an emergency interagency group meeting early on July 21 to discuss the developments and explore possible options. This meeting was held on a working level so that the staff officers from each agency could go back and brief their superiors to get recommendations from them. The session went on for hours, with the groups split over whether there should be an immediate military response or if making early military moves would foreclose any possibility of a diplomatic solution. The military options that came out of the session involved a range of possibilities including a show of force by moving ships and aircraft into the area but not engaging in hostilities, a limited deployment of aircraft into Saudi Arabia, a full deployment of all CENTCOM ground forces into Saudi Arabia, a naval blockade, and surgical air strikes in proportionate response to whatever moves the Iraqis would make.

Out of this group's work came a recommendation for the initial U.S. response. It was to be a demonstration, a show of force, that would not only display U.S. resolve but would also prepare the way for a later U.S. military deployment if ordered. It called for an aerial refueling exercise with the Air Force of the United Arab Emirates and the movement of U.S. carriers in the area. In late July the Air Force sent over seventy tankers to the Emirates, and on August 1, the carrier *Independence* was ordered to move to the northern Arabian Sea and to increase its speed of advance. The interagency group met daily to exchange information and to develop further options. When the Iraqis invaded on August 2, all agreed that the military option had to be exercised.

These initial military moves in August were aimed at deterring Iraq from attacking further south into Saudi Arabia. The Iraqis had moved into Kuwait and consolidated their hold rapidly. The day after they stormed into Kuwait, they began making menacing moves toward Saudi Arabia, deploying combat forces forward to the border and transporting thousands of tons of supplies into Kuwait and southern Iraq for a subsequent offensive south. All intelligence indicators pointed to a subsequent Iraqi move, perhaps in a few weeks, to take the Saudi oil fields.

At 0105 hours on August 2 the Pentagon issued a warning order to Strategic Air Command, Tactical Air Command, and Military Airlift Command to get aircrews into secure areas, begin wartime crew rest procedures, load and arm aircraft, and prepare to implement 1002 if the order were to be given. The other forces committed to 1002 were warned of possible deployment as well. The forces were now on a hair-trigger alert.

The initial parts of a war plan are actually quite standard no matter to what theater of war the forces are going. In any such deployment the closest carriers are directed to move to the area, the Air Force's 1st Tactical Fighter Wing at Langley Air Force Base is placed on strip alert, in-flight refueling aircraft are readied, the Army's 82nd Airborne Division begins to load up for a parachute drop, and the Marines bring in a brigade from either the west or east coast of the United States to move as their afloat equipment is launched to sea. The units that are the first to go are always the same so that they can practice loading out and getting started. A deployment order is often nothing more than a one-word execution command, soon followed with details of where the units are going and what they are to do when they get there. That is what happened in the U.S. military forces in these first few days as the political leadership conferred. If the president decided he wanted them to go, they would be ready. If he decided he did not want a military deployment, they could easily stand down and call the whole thing a good training exercise that they would have done anyway.

At 7:00 A.M. on August 2, General Schwarzkopf and General Powell met with Defense Secretary Cheney in Washington to go over the options and brief the president. When they returned to the Pentagon at 10:00 A.M., the president had decided that he could not let this aggression stand, and he made public statements to that effect. While he worked on building an international diplomatic coalition, Bush acted as if he was already resolved to use military force if he had to in order to force Saddam Hussein out of Kuwait.

On August 4 the president was briefed on the precise details of the military options under operations plan 1002. The crucial aspect of the plan was that if the military option was needed, the services required at least a month to get all the forces in place, assuming no problems arose. The president would have to order the plan initiated at that moment if he wanted military force later; he could not afford to wait. If he ordered the military to begin deploying, he could always order the military not to fight if diplomacy failed, but if he did not give the military several weeks, he would have no military option.

By then the intelligence estimates showed that eleven more divisions from the Iraqi regular army were moving into Kuwait to consolidate the hold of the Republican Guard. They were moving in thousands of truckloads of logistics supplies, and pushing it forward to the front-line troops. They had also begun to construct new roads in the middle of the Kuwaiti desert, running north to south from Iraq to the border with Saudi Arabia. With all these indicators, the military feared that Saddam Hussein intended to continue the attack into Saudi Arabia. He certainly had an overwhelming capability to do so.

The Saudis were actually the first to move against a potential Iraqi invasion of their country. On August 4 they mobilized and deployed their elite National Guard to the northern border with Kuwait and Iraq. The Saudi Arabian National Guard is not at all similar to our own National Guard. It is in fact a full-time, professional, well-trained and equipped brigade capable of rapid mobilization and quick reaction. It had been financed by the Saudis and trained by U.S. advisers for over ten years. In the

SAUDI ARABIAN NATIONAL GUARD

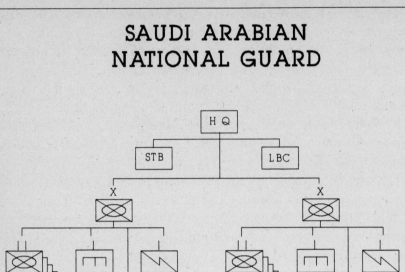

Major Combat Systems

1000 Combat Vehicles
52 BVADS
108 TOW
73 90mm

40 M102 Howitzers – 105mm
37 M198 Howitzers – 155mm
27 20mm

SAUDI ARMED FORCES

Royal Land Forces

Royal Guard

Equipment:
550 Tanks
850 Artillery Pieces
2020 AFVs
33 SAM Batteries
165(+) AA Guns

Royal Air Forces

Squadrons:

Air Defense -
3 - 57 F-15
2 - 24 Tornado

Fighter/Bomber -
4 - 98 F-5
2 - 25 Tornado

Recce -
1 - 10 RF-5E

Early Warning -
1 - 5 E-3A

Transport -
3 - 30 C-130
5 - L101
35 C-212

Royal Navy

4 Frigates
- Madina
- Hofouf
- Abha
- Taif

4 Corvettes
- Badr
- Al Yarmook
- Hitteen
- Tabuk

9 Fast Attack
- Al Siddiq
- Al Farouq
- Abdul Aziz
- Faisal
- Kahlid
- Amyr
- Tariq
- Oqbah
- Abu Obiadah
- Dammam
- Khabar
- Maccah

4 Mine Hunters
- Addriyah
- Al Quysumah
- Al Wadeeah
- Safwa

process it had grown into a coherent and capable fighting force that was well respected by its American Army and civilian technical trainers. They moved out immediately to man a screen line on their northern border, although in the event of an attack by Iraq they could do little more than provide early warning. The rest of the Saudi army soon followed suit. The high technology Royal Saudi Air Force was also involved, patrolling Saudi airspace under the watchful control of American-made Airborne Warning and Control System (AWACS) aircraft. This Boeing 707-type airplane housed a sophisticated set of radars, computers, and communications gear that could control an air battle while in flight. American technicians accompanied Saudi aircrews in constant patrol over Saudi airspace, ensuring rapid notification of American air forces of impending action as well.

But the Saudis could not hope to defend their territory alone against the assembled masses of the Iraqi army in Kuwait. The Saudi army could barely field the equivalent of a mechanized division, and it was no match for the dozens of divisions that Saddam was moving into Kuwait. Early American deployments would be key to deterring further Iraqi advances and to forming a workable defense of the northern territories. The president sent Defense Secretary Cheney and other national security officials to Riyadh on August 6 to persuade Saudi King Fahd to allow U.S. forces to deploy to the Arab kingdom. The Bush team went in with intelligence information that made it clear that Saddam was intent on continuing his march south. In fact there apparently was evidence the Iraqis had been rehearsing the military seizure of the Saudi oil fields since the end of the war with Iran. At the end of the meeting, the king surprised the U.S. delegation by agreeing to permit the United States to begin sending its rapid deployment forces to help the Saudis defend themselves.

Once Secretary Cheney secured Saudi permission, a deployment chain of events was set in motion. Bush called British Prime Minister Thatcher and French President Mitterand to solicit their participation in the military effort and found them agreeable. Cheney and Powell returned to brief the president, and on

August 6 at 9:50 P.M. the first full Desert Shield order was issued, calling for a deployment that would make feasible the execution of war plan 1002-90. The deploying units were told to move to Saudi Arabia to deter further aggression by Iraq and to get into defensive positions as they arrived.

Deterrence and Defense

Even before King Fahd agreed to the deployment of U.S. forces in Saudi Arabia, the U.S. armed forces were preparing for possible deployment. The Joint Chiefs had wargamed a potential Iraqi invasion of Kuwait and Saudi Arabia in the spring of 1990 and had developed several versions of a plan to bring U.S. forces to bear on the peninsula. The exercise, called Internal Look 1990, had revealed that if the United States could deter Iraq from attacking Saudi Arabia for about a month, the United States could get a Marine Expeditionary Force of about 45,000 men and a beefed up XVIII Airborne Corps into Saudi Arabia, which would be capable of defending the kingdom against the kind of attack Iraq could mount. The plan called for sending the entire 82nd Airborne Division, the 101st Air Assault Division, the 3rd Armored Cavalry Regiment, and the 24th Mechanized Infantry Division. It also called for deploying a Marine Expeditionary Force of about 45,000 Marines from the 1st, 4th, and 7th Marine Expeditionary Brigades and the Mediterranean Amphibious Ready Group. When the deployment order was issued, this plan was set in motion.

Air forces were the fastest to arrive. Their deployment was expedited by the fact that in the exercise conducted in late July with the United Arab Emirates, the Strategic Air Command had secretly deployed two KC-10 and seventy-two KC-135 air refueling tanker aircraft into the area. Those tankers and others from Europe and U.S. bases were conveniently located near the points needed to refuel deploying U.S. fighter aircraft en route to Saudi air bases in the Persian Gulf.

The first squadron closed in on Saudi Arabia in thirty-four hours from the time the deployment order was issued. These were forty-eight F-15C air superiority fighters from the 1st Tactical Fighter Wing in Langley Air Force Base, Virginia. Others came almost daily from across the United States. By the beginning of the war, virtually every type of aircraft in the U.S. inventory had gone to the Persian Gulf, including the venerable U-2 spy plane, the aging B-52 bomber, and the secret F-117 Stealth fighter. But in this initial phase of the crisis, key decisions had had to be made as to which types of aircraft would be sent first.

This was not easy because the limited numbers of air refueling tankers could support only a few aircraft at a time traveling across such a long distance. If the Iraqis were to continue to attack into Saudi Arabia, the Allies would need aircraft capable of hitting ground targets with great accuracy, meaning the F-15E, F-16, and A-10 aircraft. But in order to fly those aircraft to strike ground targets, the Air Force needed to control the skies over the peninsula, requiring large numbers of air-superiority aircraft. That meant even more F-15s. But if the Iraqis intended to hold what they had, then a different kind of airplane would be needed to strike deep into Iraqi territory to hit key logistics and command and control sites to force them to leave Kuwait. This kind of combat would require more bombers—F-111s and B-52s—and a host of support aircraft to suppress Iraqi air defenses and to create corridors in which the bombers could penetrate the most sophisticated air-defense network in the non-Western world outside of the Soviet Union. Alternatively, the Air Force could risk sending its most secret technology, the Stealth fighter, which would not need to suppress enemy air defenses to reach its targets. But sending the F-117 would mean risking losing one of America's most carefully guarded secrets, "low observable" technology.

The F-117 was not even acknowledged to exist until 1988. It had been used in a very limited role in the operations in Panama in 1989 but had never seen operational use outside of secret test and training flights in the Southwest U.S. desert. Its faceted body shape, shielded engines, and special skin materials keep its radar signature very low. It is so low, in fact, that most radar systems cannot detect it until it is almost on top of the radar dish. It is fitted with laser guidance systems that direct bombs to their targets with great precision.

In the August crisis, CENTCOM opted for a mixed Air Force component. They wanted the ability to control the skies but not at the expense of a capacity to disrupt Iraqi forces on the ground. For defending Saudi airspace, some air-superiority fighters were needed, but the greater risk was from an Iraqi armored thrust south into Saudi Arabia. The Air Force was tasked to send its ground attack fighters in greater proportion, and if attacks into Iraq were needed those long-range aircraft could be sent later. By the end of September, the U.S. Air Force had deployed 437 fighter aircraft to Saudi Arabia. It was not enough to destroy Iraq from the air, but it was deemed to be adequate for defending Saudi Arabia and for deterring further Iraqi moves south.

At the same time that the Air Force was moving in by air, the Navy was moving in at sea. At the time of the invasion, the Navy had deployed six combat ships to the Gulf to participate in the July exercises with the United Arab Emirates. Three French and three British warships left on August 4 for the Gulf and even one Soviet frigate was on station at the time. The U.S. Navy carrier *Independence* moved from its station in the Arabian Sea toward the mouth of the Persian Gulf. The carrier USS *Eisenhower*, stationed in the Mediterranean, moved through the Suez Canal to take up a position in the Red Sea. The U.S. also dispatched the carrier *Saratoga* along with the battleship *Wisconsin* to arrive in the Gulf by August 11. By the end of September the U.S. had fifty-four ships committed to the maritime effort.

On August 12 President Bush ordered the U.S. forces to enforce the UN embargo, and on the sixteenth the Navy established "interception zones" where all ships bound to or from Iraq would be checked for embargoed items. The carriers provided air cover for naval operations to enforce the embargo. The first naval confrontation occurred on August 16 when American warships fired warning shots at Iraqi tankers trying to get by. Iraq later attempted to invoke provisions of an agreement signed by the U.S.

U.S. Air Force Aircraft Arrivals in Theater
Through October 1990

Type Aircraft	July	Aug. 1– Aug. 15	Aug. 16– Aug. 31	Sept. 1– Sept. 15	Sept. 16– Sept. 30	Oct. 1– Oct. 30	TOTAL
AC-130	0	0	0	4	0	0	4
A-10	0	0	72	24	0	0	96
C-130	0	32	32	0	0	32	96
C-20	0	0	1	0	0	0	1
C-21	0	0	4	0	4	0	8
EC-130	0	0	7	4	0	0	11
EF-111	0	0	0	14	0	0	14
E-3A	0	0	0	0	0	0	0
F-111F	0	0	64	0	0	0	64
F-117	0	0	18	0	0	0	18
F-15C	0	48	22	2	0	0	72
F-15E	0	26	0	0	0	0	26
F-16C	0	48	48	24	0	0	120
F-4G	0	0	24	12	0	0	36
HC-130	0	0	4	0	0	0	4
KC-10	2	0	0	0	2	0	4
KC-135A	11	0	0	0	0	0	11
KC-135E	0	16	0	0	0	0	16
KC-135Q	19	0	0	0	0	0	19
KC-135R	47	10	0	10	3	0	70
MC-130	0	0	4	0	0	0	4
MH-53	0	8	0	0	0	0	8
MH-60	0	0	0	8	0	0	8
RC-135	0	4	0	0	0	0	4
TR-1	0	0	2	0	0	0	2
U-2	0	0	3	0	0	0	3
TOTAL	79	192	305	102	9	32	719

in 1987 in response to the incident surrounding the USS *Stark*. During the reflagging operations, code-named Earnest Will, the USS *Stark*, an armed frigate, had been escorting a convoy and was taken under fire by an Iraqi fighter firing antiship missiles. Not expecting an attack from the Iraqis, toward whom the U.S. had "tilted" by this time in the Iran-Iraq War, the *Stark*'s crew could not come to quarters fast enough to intercept and stop the missile. Thirty-seven crewmen had died, and the Iraqis claimed it was a mistake. An agreement had been signed by the U.S. and Kuwait to establish military-to-military contacts to avoid such mistakes in the future.

There would be no "mistakes" this time. The United States warned Iraq through diplomatic channels that U.S. forces would enforce the UN embargo and that all Iraqi military aircraft and ships were to steer clear of U.S. forces. To do otherwise would indicate hostile intent, and the Iraqis would be fired upon. On September 4 the U.S. Navy boarded and seized an Iraqi freighter filled with embargoed goods in the Persian Gulf. By the beginning of the war, over 120 combatant ships from the U.S. Navy were committed to the Persian Gulf maritime operation and coalition forces added another seventy.

The embargo was no "phony war." Starting on August 6, the day the embargo resolution passed the United Nations Security Council, the coalition naval forces ultimately conducted 8,961 interceptions and 1,185 boardings. Sixty-two ships containing embargoed cargo were diverted. The embargo gave the coalition an early military option that a great number of countries were willing and able to participate in. Dozens of states provided ships of some type, including many Arab states and ten of NATO's sixteen nations. Command and control of such a large and diverse force was complicated, but previous exercises had worked out many procedures that were used in the embargo operation. Each nation retained control over its ships, but all were coordinated through U.S. fleet commanders to Central Command Headquarters in Riyadh.

Army troops were the first ground forces to get into Saudi Arabia. There is some reason to believe that Special Operating

Forces were in the area as the crisis unfolded on August 2. The Army's Special Operations helicopter unit, Task Force 160 from Fort Campbell, Kentucky, had been deployed secretly to the Persian Gulf in 1987 to participate in the reflagging operations. They played a prominent role in attacking Iranian oil platforms in the Gulf that had been used as missile launch sites for attacks on oil tankers. The helicopters' special night fighting capability made them virtually invisible as they swooped down on the unsuspecting defenders. Not all the special helicopters had returned to Fort Campbell after Earnest Will.

While the deployment of the air forces went like clockwork, the transport of the ground forces did not go completely according to plan. The most significant glitch was in the ships that were necessary to get the heavy equipment across 7,000 miles of sea from U.S. ports, across the Atlantic through the Mediterranean to the Persian Gulf. The Navy had only eight fast sealift ships that were capable of rapidly loading tanks and armored personnel carriers, enough for just one division's worth of heavy equipment. These were designated to go to Savannah, Georgia, to load out the 24th Infantry Division and could steam to the Persian Gulf in about ten days. But some of the ships were slow to get to port, and once loaded, two of them broke down en route. The rest of the equipment, including hundreds of helicopters, had to move by slow boat and took a month to get to Saudi Arabia. One of the fast sealift ships, in fact, took so long to repair that it arrived after the slow boats.

The Navy's sealift force is assigned to the U.S. Transportation Command and had been allowed to atrophy over the years. Most of the immediately available shipping was in the Ready Reserve Fleet, which was supposed to be kept stored in a condition that would allow it to be brought back into operation very quickly. In fact only 21 percent of the ninety-eight ships in the reserve fleet were ready on time, and 60 percent showed up as much as ten days late during the first month of the deployment. Only seventy-three ships were able to be readied for service during Desert Shield, forcing the Transportation Command to rely on chartering commercial ships to make up the shortfall in shipping requirements.

For most of the years of the Cold War, the main focus of military planning was the defense of Europe, for which tanks and heavy equipment had been prepositioned in warehouses in Germany. The idea was to get the equipment there ahead of time so that in any emergency all that needed to be moved were troops. Airlift became a prime program for the U.S. Air Force. The advantage of relying on airlift was that not only was it faster than sealift but it could be done by commercial air transport if necessary. The Military Airlift Command flew 1,848 flights in just the first month of Desert Shield, including 230 civilian flights, for a total of 63,000 tons of troops and equipment. In comparison, for Operation Just Cause, the deployment to Panama in 1989, the Air Force flew 775 flights and 20,700 tons in a month to move in and then back out, and in the 1973 Arab-Israeli war the U.S. had flown 567 flights supporting Israel with 21,200 tons of equipment.

The disadvantage of airlift is that it cannot handle the capacity that can be delivered by ship. A C-5 can take about sixty to seventy tons of cargo and a C-141 can carry twenty to thirty tons, although loads can vary widely based on a number of factors. The same equipment taken on eight fast sealift ships would require over 2,500 sorties of C-141 aircraft by payload weight capacity. But the real problem with airlifting heavy forces is not weight so much as it is dimensional volume. Most of the tanks and fighting vehicles in the ground forces require an oversized aircraft to accommodate their large weight and great dimensions, and only the very largest airlifter, the C-5 Galaxy, can carry them. There are just not enough airlift aircraft to move a heavy division across great distances.

The Army's commando forces were also moved into Saudi Arabia quietly and quickly very early in the crisis. Green Berets moved into northern Saudi Arabia to help the Saudis through an intensive training and preparation period as well as to help the escaped Kuwaitis get themselves reorganized. Army Rangers and paratroopers from the 82nd Airborne Division flew in on the first flights to secure key airfields for the Air Force and for subsequent deploying ground forces.

The Marines had anticipated a potential deployment to the

Persian Gulf ever since the day the Rapid Deployment Force was created to be sent to Iran in case the Soviets attacked through the Zagros Mountains to seize a warm-water port on the Persian Gulf. To get their own supplies and heavy equipment in the region ahead of time, they had developed systems known as Afloat Prepositioning and Maritime Prepositioning Ships. Under this program the Marines bought twenty-three large cargo ships to serve as floating warehouses. They were stocked with tanks, artillery, ammunition, food, and equipment and stationed in key geographical regions of the world where the Marines might have to fight. About a brigade's worth of prepositioned equipment was at the U.S. base on the Indian Ocean island of Diego Garcia. Another was in the eastern Atlantic, and one was in the Pacific on the island of Guam. This equipment was sent to Saudi Arabia, and 16,000 Marines were sent from the United States to meet up with it.

All told, the transportation effort for Desert Shield was a military move of historic proportions. By August 21 a billion pounds equivalent of material had arrived or was on its way aboard a ship or an airplane. By the beginning of the war in January, over two and a half million tons of dry cargo had been delivered to the Persian Gulf. The effort required some unusual requests for desert supplies. By the end of 1990, the military had ordered a million and half sticks of lip balm, three million desert camouflage suits, a million atropine anti–nerve gas autoinjectors, 425,000 bottles of sunscreen, a quarter of a million pairs of sun goggles, a million desert boots, and 130,000 bullet-proof vests. American industry rose to the occasion, and in many cases made handsome profits. The defense secretary had to invoke an obscure law known as the Feed and Forage Act of 1861 to spend additional funds to feed the troops and provide other supplies. The Saudis provided food, fuel, and in-country transportation for free, and many allies sent billions of dollars rather than military forces to finance the effort.

To accomplish all of this President Bush had to call up the reserves. There were simply not enough of the right kinds of forces in the active duty components. On the first day of the

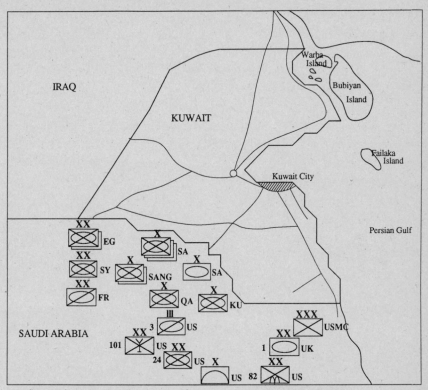

Coalition Troop Deployments for Operation Desert Shield

deployment, 595 reservists volunteered for duty, a number that peaked at over 10,000 by mid-August, but the need was far greater than volunteer numbers could satisfy and on August 22 President Bush exercised his call-up authority, activating 50,050 reserves for Operation Desert Shield.

All of these people and their equipment were sent to Saudi Arabia through two main ports of arrival. The Saudis had quietly constructed the world's most advanced and capable port facilities during the 1980s, in part to deal with future potential military contingencies. The port of Dammam is the largest military sea terminal in the world. U.S. forces departed from over a dozen ports around the world and most arrived through Dammam, yet Dammam was never stressed to its capacity during the deployment. Air fields had been constructed in the middle of the northern Saudi deserts and provided parking space for nearly two thousand aircraft; most U.S. bases house less than a hundred.

As the deployment progressed in early August, the planners at CENTCOM and in the Pentagon continued to work on assessments of what might happen if the Iraqis refused to leave Kuwait. In the early stages of the operation, the idea was to get initial deploying forces in rapidly to secure ports of debarkation, to help the Saudis secure their skies, and to demonstrate American resolve to defend the kingdom. As the force built up, the mission shifted to conducting a robust defense of Saudi Arabia.

By the end of September, the force in the theater was fully capable of defending the country. Wargames and simulations showed that the Iraqis would probably have to pay a price they were unlikely to be willing to pay in order to attack south, at least by the standards for attack they had set in the war with Iran. But the more difficult problem facing military planners in the fall of 1990 was an apparent shift in strategy by the Iraqis.

Iraq Digs In

In September, Iraqi forces began to construct massive defensive works along the border between Kuwait and Saudi Arabia, and they shifted the highly mobile Republican Guards to the north back into southern Iraq. From these dispositions, Iraq could no longer mount a surprise offensive into Saudi Arabia, although it could mount a very worrisome deliberate offensive. Simulations showed that if Saddam stayed in Kuwait he had the capability to stay for a long time.

There was much debate in the United States about the effectiveness of the embargo. At first it appeared that the embargo might strangle Iraq into submission. Indeed, the naval blockade was seemingly impenetrable and likely to stay that way for many months. It was depriving Iraq of an estimated $1.5 billion a month and industrial production in Iraq had decreased by some 40 percent. But by late fall it had become clear that the sanctions were not going to force Saddam out of Kuwait and that in fact he was strengthening his ground forces' hold on that country. Evidence began to mount that the Iraqis were stockpiling supplies for a long occupation and that the embargo, as effective as it was, would not accomplish the objective of forcing Iraq to give up Kuwait.

As broad-based as the military coalition became, it was clear that the question of defending Saudi Arabia from an Iraqi attack was not easily answered. At CSIS, a team of military analysts ran several simulations and map exercises to test the theoretical capabilities of coalition forces. Some interesting conclusions came out of those analyses. For one thing we could never figure out why Saddam stopped in Kuwait. Until the 24th Infantry and the 1st Cavalry Divisions completed their moves into Saudi Arabia in October, there were insufficient armored forces to prevent Saddam's massive army from taking the Saudi oil fields. Even the most clever defensive tactics, the most optimistic employment of American air power, and the most straightforward Iraqi attack option would result in an Iraqi breakthrough within two days. Saddam simply had so many tanks that all they had to do was move south, and they would have run rapidly through the coalition defenders by sheer weight of numbers. By the end of October, as British armored forces and the American heavy divisions arrived, the defense of Saudi Arabia became more certain.

We also tried to develop a concept of operations that would force Saddam Hussein to leave Kuwait by defeating his forces on the ground. We assumed that once attacked from the air and the ground the Iraqis would decide to leave and conduct a fighting withdrawal because they had fought that way on the defensive against Iran. With the Allied forces available at the end of October, though, such an offensive was a most uncertain option. If the Iraqis behaved logically and withdrew after losing about 50 percent of their force, we calculated they could stand and fight for about a month and that U.S. forces would suffer 30,000 casualties in the process. This was a sobering conclusion. Given the growing realization that the embargo was not likely to work, it became clear to us that if the president was intent on getting Saddam out of Kuwait, he would have to come up with a sizable additional force to do it with.

The president did amass this force by using his authority to call up the reserves and National Guard as widely as possible. In the mid-1970s, the architects of the post-Vietnam military build-down had deliberately put in place a military force structure that would require the president to call up the reserves before committing the country to a large-scale war effort similar to that which occurred in Vietnam.

Some of the methods for building this dependence on the reserves were clever. In the Air Force, whole mission areas were assigned to National Guard Air Wings and Squadrons. This allowed the active Air Force to concentrate on missions they wanted, such as the defense of Europe, strategic nuclear deterrence, and the exploration of outer space. The National Guard units were only too glad to get the remaining missions, such as the defense of the continental United States and many close air support and interdiction missions, because it meant that airplanes and fuel would be devoted to those missions—airplanes and fuel that would be flown and consumed by their own pilots and paid for out of the active Air Force's budget, not their own.

In the Army a different technique was applied. Most of the front-line combat power of the Army was in the active duty force, but a good proportion of the supporting services were in the reserve components. Even for peacetime exercises it was necessary to coordinate with the reserves and the National Guard in order to ensure that deploying ground forces had sufficient support in areas such as maintenance, field hospitals, food service, transportation, and many others. The force structure was built so that it would be impossible to fight a war of any length without a significant activation of the National Guard and the reserves.

To go along with this dependence on the reserves, the Congress gave the president the authority to call to active duty up to about 200,000 reservists, without an act of Congress, for a period of six months. The idea was that if the president wanted to get U.S. forces into a large-scale war, as Lyndon Johnson had in Vietnam in the 1960s, he could not do it gradually. In all future major conflicts, the president would have to disrupt the lives of hundreds of thousands of families by the call to active service. This was designed to generate a national debate over the value of the war itself. The call-ups early in the crisis began to shape the public debate, but when the president made his November announcement, he let Defense Secretary Cheney bring the news about additional, massive reserve call-ups and National Guard activations. By the time the war began, a fourth of all U.S. military personnel in the Gulf were reservists or Guardsmen. Even some military retirees were recalled to active duty in some critical professional skills.

Desert Shield was, of course, not just a Saudi-American operation. Dozens of other countries joined in the deployments designed to deter and defend. Britain and France sent aircraft, ships, and troops, and several other European countries sent aircraft and ships. Even Czechoslovakia and Hungary sent noncombat forces such as transportation units or medical personnel. Many Islamic countries lent their support, including substantial armored forces from Egypt and Syria. Others sent light forces, including a battalion of freedom fighters from the Afghanistan Mujahideen.

It became clear that the force that would eventually arrive in Saudi Arabia when 1002 was complete would have only the most limited offensive options. An air campaign would be devastating, but it would take a long time to get to the point where thousands of tanks could be destroyed from the air. The air planners anticipated a stiff fight for control of the skies that would take at least a couple of weeks even if the Iraqi air force performed no better than they had against Iran. Iraqi air defense had undergone a massive upgrade, and the Iraqi air force was obtaining new weapons for its advanced fighters. Many worried that the Iraqi air force would show improved performance. The way the ground forces were digging in was also troublesome. U.S. ground forces would have to attack these dug-in troops and root them out. If the Allies were to try to outflank the Iraqis with the forces available in late October, they would have to risk weakening their front lines in order to put together sufficient force to attack into the Iraqis' flanks. With the forces Iraq had in place, such an attack would invite a counteroffensive. Even if the Iraqis did not launch a counteroffensive, the simulations showed that even under the most optimistic assumptions, American casualties would be in the tens of thousands. General Schwarzkopf had resolved from his Grenada experience never to plan on those kinds of optimistic assumptions.

Schwarzkopf had been selected at the last minute to be the deputy commander of Operation Urgent Fury, second to the Navy's Admiral Joseph Metcalf. The whole Grenada operation had been planned in just a few days, and when Schwarzkopf showed up for his first staff briefing two days before Urgent Fury was to begin, he had serious doubts about the planning that had gone into it—it had been done too quickly, and not enough hard questions had been asked. What if the Cuban construction workers were armed? What if the Grenadan defenders did put up a fight, contrary to the assumptions of the intelligence assessment? His instincts had told him that the plan was flawed, but he did not speak up at the time. He regretted not having said something at that briefing, and it convinced him that he would never again execute a plan based on overly optimistic planning.

By mid-October the president had concluded that sanctions would not force Saddam out of Kuwait and that an offensive military option would have to be created in order to persuade him to leave or to force him to leave. Secretary Cheney and General Powell went to Riyadh in late October to discuss with General Schwarzkopf the creation of the offensive option. Cheney and Powell wanted to know how it might be done with the forces then available, but the CENTCOM Commander told his bosses he would need a heavy Army corps and twice the air power he then had in order to do the job. Cheney and Powell were not surprised, because the brain trusts back in Washington had told them basically the same thing.

At CSIS, we had begun to discuss our map exercises, which had revealed that under the best of circumstances the Allies could expect to suffer as many as 30,000 casualties in an offensive aimed at forcing Iraq out of Kuwait. The Pentagon was not issuing any of its own estimates of potential casualties, and we worried that we might undermine public support for the effort if we were to publish the results of our exercises. We communicated our intent to go public with the results of the exercises privately to Pentagon staffers whom we knew would pass the information on to senior officials. Their response was officially ambiguous and noncommittal, but informally they led us to believe that our estimates were very close to theirs.

Creating the Liberation Option

Throughout all these deployments the Iraqis did not sit idly by. They fortified their positions along the border between Kuwait and Saudi Arabia and added hundreds of thousands of troops to those that took Kuwait. Minefields, barbed wire, and trench lines covered all the approaches into Kuwait, even along the coastline where the Iraqis knew that U.S. Marines were capable of mounting an amphibious assault. The Republican Guard moved back into a reserve position in southern Iraq and northern Kuwait. The regular army moved in to front line and tactical reserve positions inside Kuwait. By early November there were over 430,000 Iraqi troops in the Kuwait Theater of Operations with more than 4,000 tanks. Saddam warned of "surprises" in store for the Allies if they dared to attack.

When Cheney and Powell returned to Washington in late October, the president decided to give Schwarzkopf his additional forces. On November 8 he announced that he would more than double the size of the force in the region. The plan was to move the entire U.S. VII Corps from its Cold War stations in Germany, double the number of aircraft, and send three more carrier battle groups to the Persian Gulf area to give the Allies an offensive combat option. The decision was momentous, for it meant that all of Europe was to become a line of communications for the Persian Gulf operation. The British and French made similar decisions to increase the size and capability of their forces.

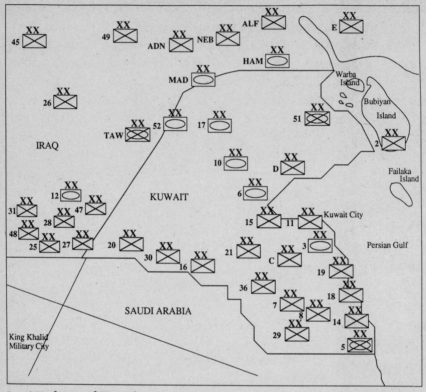

Iraqi Defense of Kuwait

The tide began to turn against the president domestically. Congressional criticism was immediate, generally holding the view that the president had not adequately consulted with the elected representatives of the people before making such a decision. Many said that he appeared to be putting in place so much force that he would have to go to war or risk losing face in world opinion if Saddam still refused to back down. Some in Congress said he should call a special session of the legislature to debate the issue before proceeding with the deployment, but the president continued to exert his constitutional prerogatives.

The forces in Europe had been given even less time than their U.S.-based counterparts to prepare for deployment. When alerted by the Joint Chiefs of Staff to deploy to the Persian Gulf, VII Corps Commander Lieutenant General Fred Franks immediately called his cavalry regiment commander, Colonel Don Holder, and told him, "Don, your regiment's motto is *Toujours Prêts*, which is French for 'Always Ready.' I hope you are because I'm giving you twenty-four hours to begin moving the 2nd Armored Cavalry Regiment to the railhead for deployment to Saudi Arabia. This is for real!" The entire corps went through an intensive period of preparation, including firing their guns and maneuvering in the field. The German government gave them top priority on their rail system for moving their equipment to port facilities near Bremerhaven. Once they arrived in Saudi Arabia they quickly assembled themselves and practiced the tactics and techniques they would soon use in Operation Desert Storm.

The Marines also doubled the size of their force. Virtually the entire Marine Corps was committed to the Persian Gulf by the end of 1990, forming two Marine divisions on the ground and a Marine amphibious force afloat. But even with their total focus on Saudi Arabia, the Marines had to divert their attention when a bloody revolt in Liberia required them to deploy a force to that African country to protect and evacuate U.S. citizens trapped by violence there. The Marines pulled it off flawlessly then went right back into preparations for the defense of Saudi Arabia and the liberation of Kuwait.

Public Debate on the Eve of War

Most major religious organizations in America, with a few notable exceptions such as the Council of Jewish Federations, criticized the administration for putting the country on a path toward war. The Senate Armed Services Committee held public hearings on the Gulf Crisis in November, and Chairman Sam Nunn invited witnesses who were largely critical of the administration's bellicose approach. House Armed Services Committee hearings later in December were more technical and offered less criticism of the policy.

On December 6 Saddam announced he would begin letting all

his foreign "guests" return home. By Christmas, the Iraqis had released all Western hostages and it was clear that if Congress took a vote on the use of military force to get Saddam Hussein out of Kuwait, the vote would be very close.

The administration marshaled its political forces in support of the war option. Secretary of State Baker and Central Intelligence Agency Director William Sessions both testified that sanctions would need a very long time to work. But the plight of the hostages and Iraq's intransigence gradually seemed to win the American people over to the president's view. By mid-December support for a war in the Gulf was around 60 percent and growing. On December 13 a federal court dismissed a congressional effort to bring the president to heel under the War Powers Act. The court ruled, as had previous courts in such cases, that the war power was a political question that the courts were not allowed by the Constitution to judge. The stage was set for a dramatic moment in American history.

When Congress returned from its Christmas recess on January 3, 1991, it was supposed to be simply for the traditional formality of swearing in a newly elected Congress and quickly adjourning to return home for the rest of the vacation. This was not to be the first act of the 102nd Congress. Its first major vote was to be whether to go to war. Resolutions of support for military action to enforce United Nations resolutions were introduced in both houses of the legislature, and debate was set to begin on January 10. The vote counters all indicated that it would be a very close call.

Every member of the 435-person body was given an opportunity to speak for the record before the vote was taken. Amendments were carefully crafted and screened by the leadership so that the vote would not be muddied. The vote in the Senate was very close, with Senator Sam Nunn leading the Democratic majority against the president in the hopes that sanctions would eventually do the job, but in the House of Representatives, where the Democratic party had an even stronger hold on the majority, dozens of Democrats voted with the president. Congressman Jack Murtha was key in swinging many votes, probably about fifty or sixty, in support of the president. On Saturday, January 12, the vote was over. Congress had authorized the use of force by a modest majority.

By the eve of war on January 15, the most powerful military force since the D-Day invasion of the Normandy beachhead in June 1944 had been assembled. In fact the analogy to D-Day was almost direct. The forces were about the same size and the Kuwait border was about the same length as the Normandy beachhead. Even the shape was strikingly similar. But once the war broke out all similarities with the past dissolved in the fury and thunder of Desert Storm. This was to be an operation the likes of which had never been seen before.

CHAPTER FIVE

Hurricane Horner

THE BATTLE BEGAN as a hurricane of bombs, bullets, and rockets swept through Iraq from the most sophisticated armada ever to take to the skies. In charge of the air campaign was U.S. Air Force Lieutenant General Chuck Horner, a master strategist and veteran combat pilot. Horner controlled just about everything that flew in Desert Storm; his official title was Joint Forces Air Component Commander (JFACC). His formulation and execution of the air component of the war, especially in the overwhelming victory in the skies won during the first two weeks of the war, vindicated the theories of air power advocates from decades past.

I watched from the CNN Washington Bureau control room as Desert Storm descended on Iraq, and the whole world watched as well. CNN reporters Bernard Shaw, Peter Arnett, and John Holliman described wave after wave of Allied attacks on Baghdad, alternately lighting up the night sky with Iraqi antiaircraft fire followed by deathly silence before the next wave of Allied bombers and cruise missiles came.

The pattern of the attack seemed obvious to me. It was the opening phase of a strategic bombing campaign aimed at the enemy's center of gravity. For years Air Force theorists had argued, mostly unsuccessfully in bureaucratic circles, that the advent of precision-guided weapons gave air power the ability to do something it had been technologically incapable of doing until then—take out the enemy's military central nervous system without damaging nonmilitary targets. The accuracy of these new weapons created the opportunity to make it impossible for a massive armed force, such as that fielded by Saddam Hussein, to be controlled and directed by its leadership. Early air power theorists had held that if a dictator's army could be disconnected from its leadership, then cut off from supplies, it would be possible to out-maneuver it with a more sophisticated, even if smaller, ground force. Such an air campaign might make it unnecessary to destroy every tank, artillery piece, and soldier in the opposing army to defeat it. The enemy would be more likely to surrender or give up without a fight.

This was the thinking of the great air power theorists like Guilio Douhet and Billy Mitchell, who had advocated strategic bombing in the past as a way to avoid the casualties inherent in ground warfare. But the airplanes of the past could not drop their bombs with certainty that the enemy's ability to fight would be utterly destroyed. As the skies themselves became a battlefield, more aircraft had to be devoted to the aerial battle and the opportunity to strike ground targets when desired diminished. Bombing runs had to go higher and faster to avoid enemy fighters, and as they did, bombing accuracy declined.

Air forces tried to compensate by dropping more and heavier bombs, but there were not enough airplanes to drop enough bombs to overcome the inevitable inaccuracies from bombing at higher altitudes and at faster speeds. With the development in the late 1970s and early 1980s of so-called "smart bombs," one bomb could finally be counted on to hit its target virtually every time. Given this capability, air power advocates concluded that strategic bombing would finally be able to force an opponent to quit without a costly ground battle. The wargames and computer simulations that analysts used to experiment with bombing techniques and technologies convinced many that air power would at last be dominant on the battlefield.

The bombing of Baghdad fit the pattern of the systems analysis that was behind the theory of the air campaign. The targets being hit in Baghdad were vital to Saddam's military machine and were distinguished very carefully from targets that had little or no military value. Taking out the main communication center meant that he could not issue orders to his field commanders.

More important, it meant that the field commanders could not send Hussein reports on what was happening elsewhere in the country as the war opened. The presidential headquarters building housed all the main offices of the ruling Ba'ath Party, the secret police, and the intelligence operation essential to Saddam's treacherous means of holding political control over his country. It was Iraq's equivalent of the White House Executive Office Building complex on Pennsylvania Avenue in Washington; it was the very nerve center of Iraq's government.

As the Baghdad dawn began to break on January 17, CNN's tired reporters described an incredible scene in the growing light of day. The attack had indeed been one of great precision. With their video transmission link reestablished, they showed remarkable pictures of the scene around the hotel. There was very little damage to anything other than the targets they had described during that long night. A solitary hole through the roof of a nearby building appeared to have been caused by an errant Iraqi antiaircraft shell. The communications tower was still standing, and the building it was standing on was intact, but a closer look at the base of the tower showed the twisted remains of the transmission station that had taken a direct hit during the attack. The destruction to civilian buildings we have become accustomed to seeing in pictures of previous bombing campaigns was very noticeably absent.

The Air Campaign

These dramatic scenes from Baghdad unveiled a new era in warfare. For a decade American military thinkers had been putting together a new form of warfare, one that integrated air, land, and sea campaigns into a synergistic whole that was designed to allow U.S. forces to fight outnumbered and win. It had been created to defeat the Soviets in a campaign across the Atlantic in Europe, and it was being applied now against Iraq in the Middle

East. On January 16 we saw the opening phase of the air campaign portion of the kind of war the theory called Air-Land Battle.

The theory of the air campaign aspect has been most fully developed by Air Force Colonel John A. Warden III in his book, *The Air Campaign: Planning for Combat,* first published in 1988 by the National Defense University. The Desert Storm air campaign plan was precisely fashioned after Colonel Warden's theories. Warden believes that every wartime enemy has a "center of gravity," the place where an attack would be decisive. He argues from history that air superiority, once won, provides the means with which to strike an opponent's center of gravity and win. Air power itself may be able to defeat the enemy without resort to the use of ground troops, or it may make it possible for ground forces to do nothing more than "mop up" after a successful air campaign. Thus, gaining and maintaining air superiority should be the first and most important goal in any war. It could be won by attacking the enemy's air force directly in the air or on the ground, or indirectly by hitting his logistics support, basing infrastructure, pilot training facilities, or command and control network. Once air superiority is won, the enemy's other centers of gravity can be attacked with impunity by the most appropriate force—air, sea, or ground. Those other centers of gravity include the national command authority, the military forces, the industry supporting the armed forces, and sometimes, the will of the people to support their forces.

The actual plan for executing the air campaign for Operation Desert Storm was worked out along the lines of Warden's theory in the Air Force's brain trust, Checkmate. Checkmate is housed in a vaulted set of rooms tucked away in a corner of the Pentagon basement. Since the early 1980s, the Air Force has used these rooms to conduct its most sensitive and secret analyses of air battle. It is equipped with the most advanced computers and simulations technologies, and only the most accomplished tacticians, strategists, pilots, and analysts can get assigned to the project. It is a place where air planners can work out campaign ideas, tacticians can try out new maneuvers, and logisticians can calculate support requirements, all using data from current Air Force capabilities and from real intelligence data on the Soviets or just about any other air force they might be interested in. The computers and simulations allow the project officers to fight realistic battles electronically and to assess the results without ever placing a single pilot or aircraft at risk. It was the birthplace of many design parameters for highly classified advanced technology projects in the 1980s and was a principal experimentation facility for the development of the Air Force's fighting doctrines for the future. It was also a place, among a few others, where the Army and the Air Force worked together on this new approach to combat operations known as Air-Land Battle.

For war plan 1002-90, the defense of Saudi Arabia and Kuwait against an Iraqi invasion, Checkmate had developed a defensive air campaign that gave U.S. forces control over the skies of the Arabian Peninsula while the ground force was being built up. Air Force fighter wings for air-to-air combat and ground attack were to provide the main defense for several months and would be complemented by aircraft from several Navy carriers. In late July, when the Iraqis began to look as if they might move into Kuwait, this defensive plan was pulled off the shelf and modified to be ready for potential U.S. involvement. When the deployment order was issued, Checkmate officers helped Central Command air staff officers to modify quickly the basic air campaign contingency plan. Those modifications in turn guided their decisions on which kinds of aircraft to send to the area, which bases to send them to, and what kinds of munitions to send for their eventual use.

The character of the plan began to shift away from the initial contingency in the first week of August. Some of the Air Force's Jedi Knights believed that the plan was oriented too much on the defensive. They convinced the Air Force staff that this war would be ideally suited to apply the theories of the air campaign as articulated by Colonel Warden. The Air Force staff allowed them to develop an offensive concept of aerial operations that would aim at hitting Iraq's centers of gravity deep inside the country, including the leadership itself and the infrastructure that supported the military forces. When General Schwarzkopf in August asked for additional help in planning his air campaign, the Air Staff was ready with a plan to defeat Saddam Hussein with an air campaign that they believed would eliminate the need for a potentially costly ground war.

The Air Staff briefed General Schwarzkopf with their plan at his MacDill Air Force Base headquarters in Tampa, Florida, in the second week of August. The commander then told them to brief the Central Command Air Commander, General Chuck Horner. Horner saw merit in the concept and asked the Air Staff to develop it in full detail and return as soon as possible. After a week of sweating out those details back in Checkmate, they came back to CENTCOM with a complete attack plan and operations order. They brought in Navy and Marine Corps air planners and coordinated it with General Powell's Joint Staff. On Friday, August 14, Schwarzkopf approved the plan and had the Air Staff take it to Riyadh to brief General Horner, who by then had moved his own staff into the theater of war. Central Command Air Force (CENTAF) then began to produce its first offensively oriented Air Tasking Order.

At this point none of the air planners knew when this order might have to be executed. For all Horner and his staff knew, they might have had to begin an offensive campaign in a week or so if Saddam showed signs of moving south. Other than the light forces of the 82nd Airborne Division, the Marines, and the few forces of the Saudis, air power was the only thing standing between the Iraqi army and Riyadh. General Schwarzkopf called an Iraqi move south his worst nightmare. CENTAF's job was to do what was necessary to prevent that nightmare from really happening.

By mid-September CENTAF had put together enough airplanes and munitions in Saudi Arabia to begin feeling confident that they could execute about a thirty-day air campaign against Iraq. They had ready an Air Tasking Order for the first two days of such a campaign. An Air Tasking Order (ATO) is a basic war fighting document that tells each pilot when he is to take off, what target he is to hit, and what weapons he will load to do it all with. Every aircraft has to appear on the ATO so that the whole effort can be coordinated. This one ran three hundred pages in length by the time every refueling tanker, electronic warfare bird, fighter, bomber, and anything else with wings was listed. It went out to everyone who played a role in getting those aircraft into the sky and back safely. This initial set of ATOs was wargamed and analyzed throughout the sitzkrieg so that by the time the execution date came around, it had been extensively adjusted and rehearsed thoroughly. Most pilots even had the opportunity to practice flying portions of it south of the Kuwait border, although they did not risk compromising the plan by flying an entire day's missions all at once.

The campaign plan called for four phases. Phase One was to concentrate on attacks on Iraq's vital centers of gravity. First and foremost, it was designed to destroy Iraq's capability to mount any kind of air campaign of its own, either offensive or defensive. This was to be done by hitting Iraqi aircraft on the ground, neutralizing the air-defense system, and knocking out of the sky any airplane that got aloft. Phase One's second goal was to destroy and disrupt Iraq's national command, communications, and control structure by destroying the central telecommunications facility in Baghdad as well as television, radio, and telephone transmission lines at critical points throughout the country. It also included the elimination of Iraq's nuclear, chemical, and biological weapons production and research infrastructure. Phase One's final goal was the disruption of Iraq's military support and armaments production infrastructure by taking out the electrical power grid, factories, transportation network, and oil industry.

In Phase Two, the air campaign was to suppress the tactical air defenses in the Kuwaiti Theater of Operations (KTO) to give the Allies uncontested access to the skies over Iraqi troops. Then, in Phase Three, the campaign was to shift to a process of cutting off the Iraqi army in the KTO from its source of supply and control in Iraq. This phase was to focus target attacks on the roads and bridges closer to Kuwait and along the Euphrates-Tigris Valley, through which Iraq transported the supplies for its army in

Kuwait. In Phase Four, air forces, working closely with ground forces, were to destroy the remaining Iraqi army units in place and force them to withdraw from Kuwait.

In late December, CENTAF began to set itself up for combat operations, dividing its growing tactical operations group into two cells, one for strategic targets in Iraq and the other for the Kuwaiti Theater of Operations. By then 300 people were managing the air campaign planning, all located in a command and control center in the Royal Saudi Air Force headquarters building in Riyadh. They had huge projection screen displays of the air situation sent down electronically from continuously orbiting AWACS aircraft so that all those involved could see the total situation at once, although the Stealth aircraft of course could not be picked up even by our own radar.

The Air Force began flying a pattern of air operations that would appear to be purely defensive but that would provide a screen behind which a powerful offensive force could be marshaled. It included two Airborne Warning and Control System (AWACS) aircraft orbiting continuously along the Saudi-Iraqi border. Inside each AWACS aircraft U.S. and Saudi officers monitored radar screens that covered all of Iraqi airspace out of which any threat might come. Satellite intelligence data was provided directly to these AWACS airplanes. Computers and radios provided control officers onboard with the capability to monitor, assess, and manage the air campaign as it progressed by watching the skies around each airplane and sending instructions to pilots as each battle unfolded.

For more close-in command and control, the Air Force deployed a version of the C-130 transport aircraft known as the Airborne Communications, Command and Control System (ABCCCS). This aircraft contains an internal module forty feet long that houses communications, command-and-control gear, and operator consoles to provide radio, teletype, and radio relay capabilities. It provided close-in control of the air campaign and direct links to air battle controllers on the ground in forward locations. The Navy also employed an airborne early warning and control aircraft, the E-2C Hawkeye, which is launched from the deck of a carrier.

A new kind of command and control aircraft had been added to the fleet late in December when the Air Force deployed its still-experimental Joint Surveillance Target Attack System (JSTARS) aircraft. JSTARS, like AWACS, was flown on a modified Boeing 707 airplane, which housed a dozen computer and communications consoles linked to an advanced radar system mounted in a canoe-shaped pod under the fuselage of the aircraft. This radar could detect, locate, identify, classify, track, and target enemy ground forces through any kind of weather. The data it collected was transmitted instantly to commanders, ground troops, and air bases. Based on the information provided by JSTARS on the ground situation, commanders could decide what kind of force to attack the enemy with. The radar was so sensitive it could even tell the difference between a truck and a tank and it could provide mapping data on ground features.

There had been some debate within the Pentagon about deploying JSTARS to Saudi Arabia in December and January. It was a highly classified program, which involved some of the military's most sensitive technology, and there was some fear that its use in this conflict might reveal its capabilities and compromise its future utility. The more sensitive issue was that it was still in development and not scheduled for operational use until the mid-1990s. Given the criticism the military had taken during the 1980s for rushing systems to the field before they had been fully tested, the Air Force was reluctant to risk revealing any program shortcomings that might become public if the aircraft were used in the Gulf.

These were valid concerns, but the Army leaders who had to worry about a potential ground campaign were more interested in exploiting the capabilities the aircraft had already displayed. In September 1990, one of the two functioning test aircraft had been sent to Europe to be demonstrated during the annual Reforger maneuver exercises. During these maneuvers, large formations of tanks would be moving around Germany amongst all the normal German road traffic. Those formations would provide JSTARS with the closest approximation to a real conflict without a real enemy to worry about during the test. U.S. VII Corps commander, Lieutenant General Fred Franks, used the system to discover where his maneuver opponent was marshaling his tanks to attack and was therefore able to anticipate where they were moving to once the exercise began. His force intercepted the mock enemy and Franks became a solid believer in the capabilities of JSTARS. His report was sent to General Schwarzkopf, who by then had deployed his headquarters to Riyadh and was very worried about an Iraqi attack. Schwarzkopf and Franks now both insisted that JSTARS be made available for Operation Desert Storm and the Air Force relented.

During the opening days of the air campaign, JSTARS was deployed along the Saudi-Kuwait border to keep watch over Iraqi armored units. If those forces were to counterattack during the air campaign, the coalition would need all the warning it could get as to when, where, and in what strength it would be coming. JSTARS would give the ground forces precious hours of warning and would also be able to direct attack aircraft and helicopters to the oncoming Iraqis to slow or stop them.

Special electronic warfare aircraft also flew a regular series of missions along the border, although the patterns were varied in order to keep the Iraqis off guard. The EC-130 electronic warfare aircraft known by its code name as "Compass Call," provided control of aircraft flying close-in and jammed and deceived enemy radars. Compass Call has a large blade antenna under each outer wing and the tail fin. There is also a smaller antenna on each side of the fuselage. Bullet-shaped canisters under the wings contain wire antennae that can be extended in flight several hundred feet behind the aircraft.

EF-111 Raven aircraft also provided electronic warfare support in the air campaign. The EF-111 is a modified F-111, which was originally designed and built as a bomber. The equipment for carrying and dropping bombs was replaced with radars, radios, jammers, and computers. The on-board AN/ALQ-99 jamming system combines ten transmitters, five exciters, and one radio frequency calibrator into a single complex, but integrated, system. It can literally "look" at enemy radar signals emissions and recognize what kind of system is sending them. The computers

analyze the threat posed by the radar, whether it is simply track-
ing or if it is linked to a missile, and provide recommendations to
the operators for courses of action. The EF-111 carries HARM
missiles to fire if needed. It not only was used to jam and strike
Iraqi radars from a distance, but it also accompanied attack aircraft into Iraq as parts of strike packages to suppress enemy radar
along the way and in the target area.

Another electronic warfare aircraft used extensively in the
Desert Storm air campaign was the EA-6B Prowler. This is a
modified version of the Navy's A-6 attack aircraft, which, like the
Air Force's EF-111, had its attack systems replaced with electronic warfare equipment. It seats four people, a pilot and three
electronic countermeasures officers, and does not have the sophisticated computers used on the EF-111. It performed much the
same functions as the EF-111, including launching HARM missiles, but the EA-6 was used primarily to penetrate enemy airspace since it does not have the fuel capacity of larger aircraft to
orbit on the perimeter for extended periods of time.

With all the analysis, planning, and rehearsal that went into
the air campaign for Desert Storm, the air staffers were confident
that the plan would achieve its objectives. They believed that the
electronic warfare aircraft, the AWACS, and the ABCCCS would
provide the kind of tight control needed to surprise the Iraqis and
manage the hundreds of attacks that would go on every night and
day. They certainly believed in the airplanes' abilities to reach
and hit their targets since they had had highly successful experiences in orchestrating such operations for the one-night raid on
Libya in 1986 and in support of U.S. forces against Iran in 1988.
But they knew they could not achieve all of their objectives right
away and they knew it would not be cost-free. They expected that
they might have to settle for hitting only 50 percent of their
targets the first day and that they might lose eighteen to twenty
aircraft in the first twenty-four hours of the war.

The campaign included large numbers of air-superiority
fighters—Air Force F-15s or F-16s and Navy F-14s or F-18s—
which flew Combat Air Patrol (CAP) to provide protection
against the expected Iraqi air force attack. The U.S. Air Force

thought it would have to fight to win control of the skies, and some believed it might take two weeks before the coalition could penetrate Iraqi airspace with impunity. Iraq's sophisticated air-to-air fighters, Soviet MiG-29s and French Mirages, certainly had the capability of putting up an impressive fight. The strikes were organized into several "packages." A typical package was sent into Iraq to hit a single installation, which might include a group of targets within the same vicinity.

These packages often included electronic warfare aircraft to go in ahead of the bombers to destroy enemy antiaircraft missiles and guns along the flight path of the bombers. They also would strike radar, communications, and command facilities where Iraqi missile launches were centrally controlled. All of the Iraqi air force ground control stations were to be hit the first night so that when the Iraqi air force tried to get into the air they would have poor information on which to base their responses to the Allies. A package also included fighter escort if it was going deep into Iraq, and command and control aircraft would go with any particularly large or complex package. The heart of a package was the set of aircraft designated to drop bombs on the various strategic targets identified by the air campaign planners as constituting Iraq's "center of gravity."

For the targets in Baghdad, the bombers were exclusively F-117 Stealth fighters. The F-117 had been developed in secret during the 1980s, and by the time the airplane's existence was finally admitted publicly in 1988, the Air Force had been operating two squadrons of over forty aircraft out of a remote base in Nevada for several years. Because of its unique arrowhead-like shape, the airplane is very difficult to pick up on radar. It is constructed out of special materials that absorb a certain amount of radar wave energy, a property that contributes to the airplane's "low observable" character. The places on an airplane that are most easily picked up by other sensors—acoustic and infrared devices—are further shielded from detection by the way the engine intakes and exhausts are located within the airframe. Although it does not fly at supersonic speeds, the F-117 was able to penetrate Iraqi airspace without ever being detected. The low observable properties of the F-117 meant that none of the supporting aircraft that had to be assigned to other strike packages were required for the Stealth fighters.

Other strikes were carried out by F-111, F-15E, F-16, A-6, and B-52 bombers. These aircraft are the mainstays of the U.S. Air Force for hitting ground targets and were all equipped with advanced computers to make sure that their bombs were released at just the right time and flight altitude for hitting their targets with the greatest accuracy. The other Allies had aircraft of similar capability, with the British Tornado and French Mirage of particularly advanced capability.

Many of these strikes were carried out using sophisticated new bombs known as precision-guided munitions (PGMs). The most accurate of these PGMs are laser guided bombs. These bombs have an electronic sensor in their nose that can "see" a laser beam and recognize a code that is transmitted on the beam. The bomb has a programmable microchip circuit that guides it in flight along the laser beam to hit whatever is at the end of the beam. A target designator aims the laser beam at the target to guide the bomb in flight.

For most bombers, this required working in teams, with one aircraft providing laser designation of the target and the other aircraft dropping a bomb into the area of the reflected laser beam "basket." Some bombers, including the F-117 Stealth, can provide their own target designation. In a few cases during Desert Storm, target designation was so sensitive, difficult, or critical that Special Forces commandos were infiltrated into Iraq in advance and used miniaturized hand-held laser pointers to designate targets for attacking Allied strike aircraft.

These same special operating forces brought their own clandestine air force into the theater of war as well as the more celebrated commando-type troops—Army Green Berets and Rangers, Navy SEALS, and Marine force recon. The air units infiltrated their commandos over long distances using MH-53 Pave Low helicopters or MH-130 Combat Talon transports. Using terrain-following radar and forward-looking infrared sights to see at great distances through darkness, fog, and smoke, the helicopters and

THE FORCES

Above, Defense Secretary Dick Cheney and Joint Chiefs Chairman Colin Powell meet in Riyadh with General Norman Schwarzkopf, Commander-in-Chief of U.S. Central Command, one week prior to commencement of hostilities. (*DoD Photo.*)

Below, Egyptian commandos in northern Saudi Arabia in training for imminent combat operations. (*DoD Photo.*)

Above, F-15C Eagle from
1st Tactical Fighter Wing,
on a combat air-patrol
mission over Iraq. (*DoD
Photo.*)

Left, Marine F/A-18C
Hornet fighters fly in
formation to take turns
refueling from Air Force
KC-10. (*DoD Photo.*)

Below, A-10 Thunderbolt
on a ground strike mission
in Kuwait Theater of
Operations. (*DoD Photo.*)

Above, B-52 bomber takes off with load of 2,000-pound bombs destined for the Kuwait Theater of Operations. (*DoD Photo.*)

Above, F-4G Wild Weasel on a mission over Iraq. (*DoD Photo.*)

Below, Marine AV-8B Harrier jump jets fly in formation to take turns refueling from Air Force KC-10 tanker. (*DoD Photo.*)

Above, Saudi Airborne Warning and Control System (AWAC) patrols the skies during Desert Storm. (*DoD Photo.*)

Above, Navy A-7K Corsair fighter takes fuel from KA-6 carrier-based refueling aircraft. (*DoD Photo.*)

Below, Portrait of an F-117 Stealth fighter. (*DoD Photo.*)

Above, F-111 bombers roll in on targets in Iraq. (*DoD Photo.*)

Right, Army M1A1 Abrams main battle tank goes through its paces during Desert Storm. (*DoD Photo.*)

Below, U.S. Marine M60 tank stops to check out damage to Iraqi vehicles on the road to Kuwait City during the ground campaign. (*DoD Photo.*)

Above, U.S. Marine amphibious assault vehicle moves across Kuwaiti desert during ground campaign. (*DoD Photo.*)

Right, Helicopter carrier USS *Iwo Jima* prepares to launch amphibious assault on Kuwait. (*DoD Photo.*)

Below, Carrier Battle Group Kennedy steams through the Red Sea. (*DoD Photo.*)

THE BATTLES

Above, F-15C from 1st Tactical Fighter Wing rolls in to engage its target over Iraq. (*DoD Photo.*)

Right, Navy F/A-18 is launched off carrier by steam catapults for attack into Iraq. (*DoD Photo.*)

Below, F-4G pilot looks up at KC-10 refueling system operator during Operation Desert Storm near Iraqi border. (*DoD Photo.*)

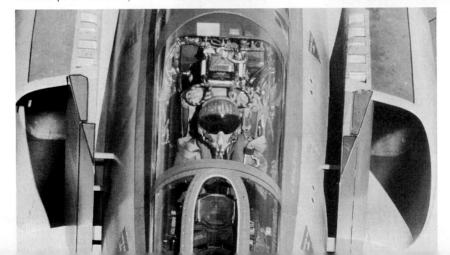

Above, Cruise missiles are blown out of Armored Box Launchers (ABLs, this one on USS *Wisconsin*) by explosive charges, then rocket motor cuts in to carry missile to higher altitude. (*DoD Photo.*)

Right, USS *Wisconsin* fires cruise missile from Armored Box Launcher. (*DoD Photo.*)

Below, Remains of Scud missile that landed in Saudi desert after intercept by U.S. Patriot air defense missile. (*DoD Photo.*)

Above, Kura Island is first piece of Kuwait liberated in raid by USS *Nicholas,* Army helicopter gunships, and Kuwaiti marines. (*DoD Photo.*)

Above, Minah Al Ahmadi Oil Terminal was blown up, then valves were opened by Iraqis to pour millions of barrels of oil into the Persian Gulf in the world's first case of environmental terrorism. (*DoD Photo.*)

Below, USS *Wisconsin* fires its sixteen-inch guns in support of ground operations off Kuwaiti coast. (*DoD Photo.*)

Above, Saudi National Guard in night operations in northern Saudi Arabia. (*Photo courtesy Vinnell Corp.*)

Above, Saudi National Guard in obstacle-clearing operations. (*Photo courtesy Vinnell Corp.*)

Below, Saudi army uses Brazilian-made Astros-II multiple-launch rocket system, shown here on a fire mission during the battle for Khafji. (*DoD Photo.*)

Above, U.S. Army M1A1 Abrams tanks move into Iraq during ground campaign. (*DoD Photo.*)

Right, Kuwaiti, Saudi, and U.S. forces are channeled into a mine field breaking point, cleared earlier by a Miclick mine-clearing charge. (*DoD Photo.*)

Below, Saudi National Guard armored vehicle hits its target in northern Saudi Arabia. (*DoD Photo.*)

Above and below, Iraqi tanks burn after the 1st British Armored Division destroys them in the Iraqi desert. *(DoD Photo.)*

Above, USS *Wisconsin* fires sixteen-inch main gun in support of ground operations. (*DoD Photo.*)

Above, Advancing Marines find Kuwait's oil fields ablaze after retreating Iraqi forces set off demolition charges. (*DoD Photo.*)

Below, An Iraqi armored vehicle that was destroyed north of Saudi Arabia. (*DoD Photo.*)

Right, Special Forces personnel along with Kuwaiti members of coalition force clear Iraqi trenches of any remaining soldiers. (*DoD Photo.*)

Below, Iraqi aircraft shelters that were bombed by the U.S. Air Force. (*DoD Photo.*)

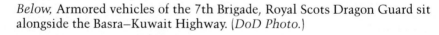

Below, Armored vehicles of the 7th Brigade, Royal Scots Dragon Guard sit alongside the Basra–Kuwait Highway. (*DoD Photo.*)

Above, Al Multa Pass north of Kuwait City, where U.S. Air Force and U.S. Army Tiger Brigade caught fleeing Iraqi troops, completely stopping their retreat. (*DoD Photo.*)

Right, Internal damage of Iraqi shelter that was bombed by the U.S. Air Force. (*DoD Photo.*)

Below, Aerial view of oil fields in Kuwait set afire by Saddam Hussein's Iraqi army. (*DoD Photo.*)

Above, Coalition troops raise national flags in celebration of the liberation of Kuwait City. (*DoD Photo.*)

Below, General Norman Schwarzkopf and Lt. Gen. Prince Khalid of Saudi forces discuss cease-fire matters with Iraqi officers Lt. Gen. Mohammad Abdez Rahman Al-Dagitistani and Lt. Gen. Sabin Abdel-Aziz Al Douri on March 3, 1991. (*DoD Photo.*)

transports were specially equipped to sneak in behind enemy lines to drop off their raiders as well as to return to pick them up undetected. Both the MH-53 and the MC-130 could also be outfitted for aerial refueling and the special air forces could thus deploy themselves over just about any distance without stopping.

For firepower the special operations air force employed the AC-130H Spectre gunship. The Spectre had two 20mm gatling-gun type cannons, a Swedish-made 40mm cannon, and a 105mm howitzer that fired out the side door of the modified transport aircraft. It was the AC-130 that destroyed Panamanian dictator General Manuel Noriega's headquarters with such precision in Operation Just Cause in December 1989.

Laser-guided bombs were not the only precision-guided munitions used in Desert Storm. There was at least one type of television-guided bomb, the Maverick, that saw use as well. Maverick is more difficult to guide to its target because it has a camera in its nose that the bombardier uses, watching a cockpit monitor, to "fly" the bomb himself in to the target. Mavericks were used against armor, air defenses, and other fixed installations in Desert Storm. Maverick first saw use in the Vietnam War, but the versions available for Desert Storm had enhanced cameras capable of seeing through some clouds and smoke. Some versions had a special infrared imaging camera, which gave it a night capability as well.

Nonprecision, or "dumb" bombs, had their uses, too. Many dumb bombs contained hundreds of smaller bomblets inside that were deposited after the larger bomb casing descended to a designated altitude. These bomblets then dispersed on and around the target and could destroy light vehicles as well as cause casualties. Some dispensers carried mines of various types. Desert Storm also saw extensive use of simple high explosive bombs similar to those dropped during World War II.

There were inventory problems with many smart bombs and with some dumb bombs as well. While they all seemed to work very well in testing and on the practice ranges, there were not very many of them in the inventory. Because precision-guided munitions are so much more expensive than conventional bombs, fewer quantities of the advanced technology systems had been purchased. In anticipation of potential conflict, Pentagon logisticians had counted the quantities on hand in the various depots around the world and worried that a prolonged air campaign might deplete their stocks before the Iraqi forces could be defeated.

The wartime plans for taking care of such problems called for mandatory surge production of the systems on order from the Pentagon, with the promise of payment to be made later, sometimes after just a phone call order. This procedure was designed to cut through the normal peacetime safeguards against waste, fraud, and abuse but the law made provision to waive all those protections in time of necessity. The problem was that the law authorizing those waivers, The Defense Production Act, had expired in October 1990 and that authority technically did not exist. Pentagon supply experts managed to get around this limitation by requesting its smart-munitions manufacturers to accelerate delivery of their current orders for the war with a promise to sort out the details later. Many smart bombs were delivered with these understandings, but it is unclear how the Pentagon and the industrial corporations have sorted out how much of a price was paid for such industrial service. In some cases, Pentagon auditors demanded the same kind of rigorous accounting and competitive pricing as in peacetime, even though the companies involved had to run up enormous labor and materials costs to add additional shifts and to get components and supplies from vendors. In retrospect, some companies actually accelerated themselves out of business because now that the war is over and the size of the armed forces is being drastically reduced, the Pentagon now has years of supply for many items.

Notable by their absence in the Desert Storm air campaign were two aircraft that just did not seem to fit. The Air Force chose not to send either its B-1B long-range bomber or its A-7 attack fighter. The B-1B could carry more conventional bombs than the older B-52 and was designed to penetrate enemy airspace, a capability the B-52 had long ago lost. Officially, the Air Force claimed that the B-1B fleet was needed for its primary role in nuclear deterrence, but the real problem with the B-1B bomber was that it had been plagued with technical problems that prevented it from being employed in the conventional role. The entire fleet had been grounded for maintenance problems in December, and design flaws had delayed installation of jamming and early-warning devices needed to give the B-1B its crucial penetration capability.

The A-7 attack aircraft was another story. The A-7 was an older attack aircraft flown by the Air National Guard and the U.S. Navy. In fact the Navy had deployed two squadrons of A-7s aboard the USS *Kennedy* for Desert Storm. The Air Force's versions of the airplane had recently been refitted with a new Low Altitude Night Attack (LANA) pod and computer that gave its pilot a night-attack capability. This capability was sorely needed during the air campaign to hit a variety of targets including mobile Scud missiles. The Air Force claimed that it did not want to send its A-7s to Saudi Arabia because it already had as many different varieties of aircraft as it could reasonably support with parts and technicians.

The Navy didn't seem to have the same problem with its A-7s, although there were some differences in the Air Force and Navy versions of the aircraft. It is unclear why the Air Force saw the logistics problems as more important than the night-attack capability the A-7s would have provided, especially since one of the Air Force A-7 wings had been assigned to the Rapid Deployment Joint Task Force in the earlier days of contingency planning for Southwest Asia. Since the National Guard was required to provide all the support for the airplane, it seems that the Air Force simply did not prepare itself to use this aircraft as it could have.

Perhaps the most unique weapon used on the first night of Desert Storm was the Navy's cruise missile, the Tomahawk. While carrier-based aircraft flew over 400 of the first night's sorties, an equally significant Navy contribution in the first night of the air campaign was the integration of the Navy's unmanned Sea-Launched Cruise Missiles into the Air Tasking Order. Over 100 cruise missiles were fired the first night of the war from nine different ships in the Persian Gulf and the Red Sea. The USS *San Jacinto* fired the first Tomahawk launched in anger, while the destroyer *Fife* fired more than any other ship during the war. Even

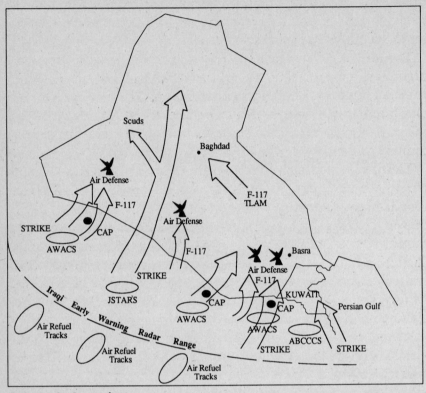

D-Day Air Campaign

a submarine, the USS *Louisville*, fired the first ever submarine-launched cruise missile used in an active conflict.

One other defining aspect of the air campaign was the integration of space-based systems. Most of the space-based assets used on Desert Storm were controlled or operated by the Air Force through U.S. Space Command. Satellites provided weather information, navigation aids, early warning of missile launch, and communications. The navigation aids proved to be the most crucial space contribution, since the open desert was extremely difficult to navigate with no recognizable terrain features for ground forces to use as references. With the Global Positioning System satellites, anyone with a special receiver could get a fix on their position with very good accuracy, enough to call in artillery fire safely if necessary. The system was so reliable that ground forces bought thousands of receivers available commercially before they deployed from the U.S.

The air campaign was thus incredibly complex. On that first night, 160 air-refueling tankers were airborne, supplying over three hundred attack aircraft and hundreds of other types as well. One hundred cruise missiles were launched. During this phase of the campaign daily sortie rates averaged nearly 2,000, the highest tempo of air operations since the Vietnam War.

The campaign included the air forces of the other Allied countries. Each nation participating had liaison officers at CENTAF to make sure that all strikes were coordinated and to check that the same target was not being struck at the same time by more than one attack. This coordination was also essential to exchange communications and recognition signals among Allies to avoid mistaking each other for enemy aircraft. In many cases, Allies were flying the same models as those flown by the Iraqi air force.

Just before H-hour (the moment the first bombs were slotted to hit) General Horner had his staff turn on CNN at CENTAF Headquarters in Riyadh in order to get real-time bomb damage assessment information for as long as the broadcast would last. Bomb damage assessment was the most difficult part of the air campaign process, and CNN became a vital part of that process. The Air Tasking Order in fact covered three battles at once. In progress at any given moment was the day's campaign, being run off of the ATO issued the night before; the generation of today's ATO, to be issued that night; and target selection for the next ATO. At around seven each morning General Horner held a staff meeting to issue his guidance for the next ATO, whereupon the planners would go over the intelligence analysis and pilot reports from the night's attacks. In many instances, intelligence reports based on satellite imagery, usually more than twenty-four hours old, were updated by network news broadcasts showing more up-to-date pictures from the target area itself. Based on that assessment they would select the targets to be hit for the next ATO. At 9 P.M. the planners would produce a notional attack plan including the targets, the time each was to be hit, and what kinds of aircraft they intended to send against each target for approval.

At that point a second shift would take over. This night shift would assign specific details for each mission, including target numbers, call signs, frequencies, and specific weapons or bombs. Target analysts would select the precise aim points for the pilots to direct their weapons against. By 4 A.M. the night shift would hand these details over to the order preparations groups, which would type out the full Air Tasking Order. The order was to be completed by 6 P.M. and distributed to each base or carrier involved. This would be the order they were to execute the following day, and the air crews and support sections needed those twenty-four hours to make all the preparations required for those missions.

The Air Tasking Order that night was so comprehensive that even the aircraft of other services were integrated into the plan. It included Marine Corps F/A-18s and AV-8B Harriers, which flew in support of the Marines in their defensive positions. Navy attack planes were assigned many strategic targets on the ATO, although because they were farther away on carriers, there were fewer targets that the Navy fighters could reach. The Navy also did not have the precision-guided munitions that the Air Force had, having opted to develop other kinds of munitions more applicable to naval air combat.

In the Vietnam War, whenever naval air forces had been committed to the theater of war, the air campaign had been divided into separate wars, one for the Navy and another for the Air Force. Targets in Southeast Asia had been divided up and each service had its own portion of airspace to wage a separate campaign. That approach was abandoned in Desert Storm and all Navy missions were included in the Central Command Air Tasking Order.

The Navy and the Marine Corps contributed hundreds of additional aircraft to the air campaign. All were integrated into the single Air Tasking Order controlled by General Horner. On the first night of the war Navy aircraft flew 415 of the over 2,000 missions flown. They flew off the decks of the carriers *Kennedy*, *Saratoga*, and *America* in the Red Sea and were directed largely at

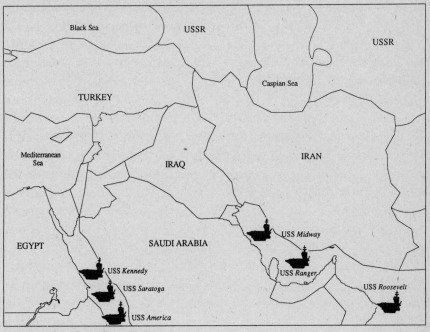

Carriers Deployed on D-Day

targets in western Iraq and outside of Baghdad. The carriers *Ranger* and *Midway* launched their airplanes that first night from the Persian Gulf toward targets in southeastern Iraq. Later the *Roosevelt* and *America* also entered the Persian Gulf and added their considerable air power to the campaign. In each area, one carrier would be designated to fly its fighters in protection of the carrier groups at sea while the others sent almost all their aircraft into the KTO. Every two or three days they would rotate responsibilities so that each carrier took its turn at covering the fleet.

Not all the penetration of Iraqi airspace was accomplished by Stealth fighters. Most targets were in fact hit by non-Stealth airplanes after Iraq's air defense had been shut down by a tactic called the Suppression of Enemy Air Defense (SEAD). Carrier-based Navy EA-6B aircraft provided vital jamming support to Air Force fighters crossing into Iraq for deep strikes. Jamming aircraft, including not only the Navy EA-6B but also the Air Force Compass Call and Army Guardrail aircraft, basically shut down

Iraqi antiaircraft radar and ground control intercept radars. Not only did these electronic warfare aircraft prevent the Iraqi signals from getting out, they also created "phantom" images on Iraqi radar screens so that the operators were often seeing aircraft appear on their screens in places where they did not actually exist. If the Iraqi air-defense system turned on a control radar to try to guide a surface-to-air missile at the attacking Allied airplanes, the F-4G Wild Weasel was close by to fire the High Speed Anti Radiation Missile (HARM) that would ride the Iraqi radar beam right down to its source. After that first night, no medium- or high-altitude missiles were ever again fired at Allied aircraft in a controlled launch because of the effectiveness of the suppression campaign.

Even some Army helicopters were from time to time included in the ATO, although normally the order only covered fixed wing aircraft. On the first night of the war, in fact, it was Army aircraft, participating in the SEAD campaign, which fired the first shots in Iraq during an operation by Task Force Normandy. Those shots were Hellfire missiles launched from Army Apache helicopters taking out two Iraqi ground-control radar sites just before a strike package of Air Force fighters came over to hit targets deep inside Iraq.

Task Force Normandy was formed from the 101st Airborne Division's 1st Battalion 101st Aviation Regiment and consisted of eight Apaches and two Air Force support helicopters. The attack force was divided into two teams of four helicopters each, and each team had a control installation to take out. They flew just above the ground for over an hour and a half to reach the target area. At about ten miles away they were able to see the installations by using special infrared scopes, and they executed their carefully rehearsed attack without ever revealing their positions to the surprised Iraqis. During the next four minutes or so, getting no closer than about two miles, they systematically destroyed radar, power generation, and communications equipment while the bewildered Iraqis scurried out of the way. At one point eight Hellfire missiles were in the air at once and several helicopters controlled more than one missile at a time.

A few days after it all happened, CNN was given a videotape of the engagement, but we decided not to show it until the Defense Department officially released it. It was a most impressive show, with one pilot firing all three of his weapons—Hellfire, rockets, and 30mm cannon—simultaneously at three separate targets and hitting every one of them. More important, the operation had successfully cleared a corridor for oncoming attack aircraft to reach deep into Iraq without being detected by air-defense radar or intercepted by Iraqi aircraft.

It all went extremely well in those first twenty-four hours or so. The Air Force lost no aircraft on that first night and they achieved total surprise. The Iraqi air force had invested billions in the construction of over five hundred hardened aircraft shelters, many of which theoretically provided protection from nuclear blast, but the Air Force's precision weaponry penetrated those shelters and demolished dozens of Iraqi planes. At Talil Air Base alone, twenty-three Iraqi fighters were destroyed while sitting inside their hangars.

At the Pentagon that first night there was no small measure of exhilaration at these early successes, but that exhilaration caused some problems. CNN's Pentagon reporter Wolf Blitzer was fairly new to his beat. He had come to the network from a successful stint at the prestigious Jerusalem *Post*, but the CNN job was his first foray into prime-time network news. He had been a frequent guest expert on Middle East affairs at CNN and was hired to replace departing veteran Carl Rochelle. Wolf and I had met several months before on a story he was doing that had brought him to CSIS to interview me. In a very short time I had come to respect his work, but on this first night of the war, some of his sources betrayed him.

Wolf had found a "highly placed source" who told him that the Iraqis had been "decimated." I pleaded with him not to use that particular term on the air in the absence of more quantifiable data, especially since the official briefers, including the president himself, were cautioning against overoptimism. He went with it anyway and the first-ever Saturday edition of the *Washington Times* screamed out in its largest banner headline type, "DECI-MATED!"

Later, someone in the Pentagon told Wolf that all the Iraqi fixed Scud launcher sites had been destroyed during the first night's air strikes and that those capable of striking Israel from the westernmost reaches of Iraq, the H-2 and H-3 airfields, were no longer capable of launching Scuds. He concluded that "the immediate threat to Israel clearly has been eased," and reported that conclusion on the late night news program. It was not the first time a source had misled a reporter, but in this instance the effect was to give viewers around the world a false sense of security against the potential for Scud missile strikes on Israel.

The Iraqi government was paralyzed. Imagine if an attack on Washington, D.C., were to take out the White House, the Capitol, the Pentagon, the CIA at Langley, the National Security Agency at Fort Meade, all electrical power was shut down, and television, telephone, and radio communications went out—all in one night. Twenty-eight power plants were hit in Iraq that first night. The bombing was so precise they were able to take out Iraqi military communications yet avoided hitting one of the government's main military communications centers in Baghdad, which was located in the basement of the Al-Rashid Hotel.

The Air Force knew that Western journalists had been centrally located by the Iraqis at the Al-Rashid, and they wanted to avoid any casualties among reporters. The Air Force sent several warnings both to network executives and to some reporters themselves that they may soon be in danger. Most of the Western journalists' leaders had decided to pull their people out, but some left the decision up to the reporters themselves. A few elected to stay put. Not wanting to place American reporters' lives in jeopardy, the targeters switched their strike away from the hotel to a bridge over the Tigris River, where the communications fiber optic cables were clumped together to cross the river. The bridge was hit by a Stealth bomber precisely on that cable during the first night.

The start of the Persian Gulf War caught the Iraqis totally by surprise. They did not appear to be able or ready to deal with the Allies' attack, but they did not simply fold up and quit. Anti-aircraft gun batteries tried to do their job. Videotape sent the next day showed streams of tracers arcing up into the night sky. Many Allied pilots reported seeing surface-to-air missiles come up into the night sky over Iraq, though none hit their mark. At the Pentagon briefing the next morning, General Powell reported that one U.S. F/A-18 had been lost during the night attack, most likely shot down by antiaircraft guns on a low-level run. A British Tornado and a Kuwaiti A-4 had been shot down, too. No word was given on the pilots until later when it was confirmed that the American had been killed.

Not all of the Iraqi air force stayed on the ground that night— 118 enemy aircraft took to the sky, although only a few more than fifty were fighters. There was some air-to-air combat as Captain Steve Tate scored the first aerial kill of the war. Eight other Iraqi fighters were shot down that night in the most intense air-to-air fight of the war. Most Iraqi fighters that took to the sky stayed about forty miles away from any Allied pilots, just beyond engagement range. The next night Saddam had a surprise of his own—Scud missiles.

Scuds and Patriots

The Scud missile was not designed to do what the Iraqis tried to do with it the second night of the war, but then neither had the U.S. intended to use its Patriot missile against the Scud in the way it was. The Scud was created by the Soviet Union in the 1960s as a nuclear warhead delivery system to be used against NATO forces in Europe. Since they had planned to place a nuclear warhead atop the missile, it was never designed to be very accurate at its maximum range of about 280 miles.

The Scud is not a particularly easy missile to launch, either. It takes about an hour to load it up with its liquid red-fuming nitric acid and hydrazine fuel, and because the mixture is highly unstable it cannot be mixed more than a day or so before launch. The missile was designed by the Russians to be launched from a rail that could be transported on a truck. The rail was fitted to the truck with a hydraulic system that raised the missile to the upright position for launch. When a firing position is located, the crew has to survey the site precisely to get a highly accurate fix on the position. Upper atmosphere meteorological readings have to be taken in order to compute how the weather will affect the missile's flight. For this purpose a balloon is released into the air, which, at preset altitudes, sends out a radar beam to scan the flight path for weather conditions. Data is then transmitted down to the launch crew, who then adjust the launch angle based on it.

The missile is not guided in flight. When launched, gyroscopes inside keep the missile aligned on its preset path by adjusting the fins on the sides, but it cannot make wide changes in flight. It basically flies up and out until it exhausts its fuel just on the fringes of the earth's atmosphere, pitches over, then falls ballistically back to earth. Iraq had used it extensively in the War of the Cities with Iran, and since then had made several modifications to extend its range out to about four hundred miles. They had not fired any Scuds during the first night of the war, although Allied intelligence had located about three dozen sites from which they knew the Iraqis had prepared Scuds for launch. The Allies also knew that Iraq had some mobile Scud launchers that could move around before setting up to launch their missiles, but they did not have precise locations on all the Iraqi launchers. While there were some false reports of Scud launches during the first night of the air campaign, the second night was different.

During the day of January 17, coalition leaders around the world had tried to assure their people that the war was necessary and going well. The military briefings given by Defense Secretary Cheney and Joint Chiefs Chairman Powell during the day provided enough information for all to conclude that the Allies were doing well. There had been some concern about Iraqi sponsored or inspired terrorism, and indeed there had been several incidents around the world during the day, but nothing serious had yet happened. There were incidents in Europe and Asia, but they appeared to be isolated and opportunistic local matters rather than a campaign orchestrated from Baghdad. General Powell made a specific point to deny reports that any Scud missiles had been launched during the first night's air attacks.

During that day I had worked on a number of stories for CNN describing the aircraft used by the Allies in the first night's attacks and assessing Iraq's preparedness. I had also gone to the Pentagon in the afternoon to learn more from sources there about what was going on. I was back at CNN studios by 6 P.M., about the time things had started the night before, to help the network decide how to carry the terrorist incidents. They had, quite responsibly in my judgment, held back on the reporting of the incidents until then but believed that it was probably time to run the stories in a low-key way. There were reports of skirmishes along the Kuwait-Saudi border as well as rumors of defections by Iraqi "line-crossers"—soldiers coming across the no-man's-land separating the two armies with hands held high or waving white flags in surrender. I was calling my Pentagon contacts to try to confirm these reports when suddenly, at 7:07 P.M., CNN's Washington anchorman David French broke in with the frightening news that air raid sirens were going off in Jerusalem; Scuds were on the way!

The next four hours were the most gut-wrenching of my life. Sirens went off at all different times in Riyadh and Dhahran, Saudi Arabia as well as Jerusalem and Tel Aviv, Israel. Scuds were landing and no one knew if Saddam Hussein had delivered the apocalyptic blow of deadly chemical weapons he had promised. The situation was very fluid, and conflicting reports had Scuds landing in several places. One network erroneously reported that chemical warheads had struck somewhere in Israel. Before dawn in the Middle East, seven missiles had hit Israel and six had landed in Saudi Arabia, all armed with conventional high explosives and none with chemical warheads.

Almost lost in the stories of the terror wreaked by the Iraqi Scud attacks and the danger of potential Israeli retaliation escalating the war, was the remarkable success of the U.S. Patriot missile system. In one report that second night from Dhahran, CNN's Charles "C.D." Jaco was visibly shaken by hearing several times in succession a "bang" followed by a "whoosh" sound off his flank near the runway while fighters were taking off. I knew that the Patriot had been deployed early in Desert Shield and that the most likely use of the system would be for point defense of an airfield such as that at Dhahran. I also knew that the Patriot had been successfully tested in a limited antitactical missile role, but I did not know if it could be specifically targeted at the Scud missiles as modified by the Iraqis. What Jaco had heard fit the launch sequence of the Patriot, and he was visibly worried about those explosions so near to him, so I tried to reassure him by speculating that perhaps Patriots were being fired at incoming Scuds. Several minutes later, Wolf Blitzer confirmed that a Patriot had successfully intercepted a Scud. I had my first journalistic coup.

The Patriot is a remarkable technological system that almost did not make it into the American arsenal. Designed in the 1970s, it was plagued with technical problems until its deployment in 1981. It was originally designed to provide protection against manned aircraft flying at medium to high altitudes and was to be a system complementary to the medium to low altitude HAWK antiaircraft missile system. In the mid-1980s the Army had begun to work on giving the Patriot a capability to intercept missiles, and in 1988 had developed a programming package to allow it to intercept missiles in a limited way. Testing was successful and the fielding of this programming change was accelerated during Desert Shield.

The system consists of between eight and sixteen launching stations. Each station has four missiles in firing boxes. Incoming enemy missiles are tracked by a phased-array radar that monitors the sky across an assigned sector. An engagement control station manages the system using sophisticated high-speed computers capable of operating the entire engagement sequence automatically. In fact, it sets up an automatic launch sequence that is verified by the human operator, who can leave the system on automatic or can intervene to stop a launch, change the sequence of engagement for multiple targets, or simply require positive launch control.

On the second night of the war, Patriots began to intercept Scuds with remarkable consistency. Not every Scud was intercepted because the Patriot was programmed to allow nonthreatening Scuds to fall harmlessly without wasting interceptors on them. The Patriot was originally designed to protect a single point on the ground, so any incoming aircraft not recognized by the computer program as threatening to the site protected would be permitted to pass through. For Desert Shield, this programming had been modified to instruct the system to protect three points at once, one on each side of the central site, so that area coverage could be approximated. It was not foolproof—there were some places between the center and the flank that were not completely protected—but it was as near to area coverage as could be achieved by the system.

By the next morning, Friday the eighteenth, President Bush was both concerned with the continued initial euphoria of the press on the success of the air campaign and outraged by the Iraqi Scud missile attacks of the night before. He took to the air again to speak reassuringly to the American people and to the world. At 7 A.M. Washington time, General Schwarzkopf gave the first of only three briefings he was to give during the war. He drilled reporters on the statistics of the day: two thousand sorties, six Allied nations taking part in air operations, three U.S. aircraft lost so far, one Kuwaiti, one British, and an Italian. He covered naval operations in the Gulf and mentioned ground forces skirmishing, repositioning, and occupying defensive positions. He emphasized that finding and destroying Iraq's mobile Scud missile launchers was going to be a very high priority for the Allies and confirmed three Scud launchers killed by A-10s. He also tried to clear up rumors that had begun to spread about Iraqi ground forces' response to the opening of the air campaign. He could not provide any information on reports that a battalion of Iraqi tanks had crossed the line and surrendered to Saudi forces along the border. The report turned out to be untrue, but it had been picked up by U.S. forces deployed just south of the Egyptians preparing to move farther west and caused them to go into a full defensive posture for several hours. It had even caused the alert of an Apache attack helicopter unit, which had been designated to be ready to react to any sudden armored thrusts the Iraqi army might launch.

Early that evening, before the next round of Scud launchings hit the news headlines, I had felt sure that the Allies were doing more than they were saying publicly about their search for Scud launchers. I knew of several systems that could be brought to bear on the problem and correctly guessed that Central Command was indeed employing them in the anti-Scud role. I convinced CNN that it would be wise to do a special report on how technology could be applied to the hunt for the Scud launchers. Not only would the network have a story none of its competitors would have, it might also reassure viewers that these missiles of terror could eventually be stopped. The producers agreed to do the piece, and it aired that afternoon.

The focus of the story was the JSTARS. I had suggested that it

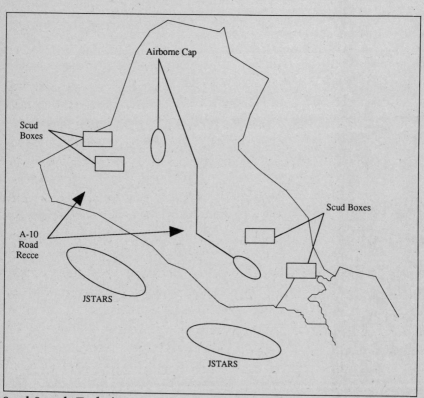

Scud Search Technique

would be an ideal system to use in the Scud hunt since any mobile launcher that moved could be detected by the aircraft's complex radar. It turned out that it *was* being used in the Scud search and when we broke the story it generated some nasty military telephone traffic to find out who had leaked it. When the Pentagon found out that it was nothing more than informed speculation on my part, the command decided that it was in fact all right for the world to know about it since that knowledge might deter the Iraqis from further launches. In any case, I had had no access to classified information for four years and was using information anyone could get from popular trade journals or newspapers.

Patriot crews came up with some innovations of their own in Saudi Arabia. The Defense Department's early warning satellite system had been turned to the problem of alerting the Patriot batteries of Scud launches. The system was giving the American missile crews about six minutes of warning time before their radar screens could pick up the incoming Scuds. When the alarm was sounded, all Patriot firing units went to a higher state of alert, but for those areas not under attack there was no way of knowing if the radar was not functioning or if the attack was going on elsewhere. To provide themselves with immediate updates, Patriot crews brought their portable radios and tuned them in to Armed Forces Radio System, which was rebroadcasting the CNN audio feed. When CNN identified where the attack was going, the Patriot crews knew, too. CNN could broadcast the news of where the Scuds were headed before the Patriot's own information systems could tell the unengaged crews where the attack had gone.

By the end of the first seventy-two hours of the war it was clear that the Allies had achieved a strategic surprise of vast proportions and that the initial successes were high by historical standards. The Iraqi air force never got more than about twenty fighters aloft during the next two days and launched only four Scuds at Israel the third night. All the Scuds were intercepted, and eight more Iraqi fighters were shot down in aerial duels. General Horner's staff was able to declare that they had achieved air superiority and set out to accelerate their bombing of the strategic targets designated for Phase One. At the same time, they could see bad weather on its way into the theater and began to adjust the Air Tasking Order to the anticipation that the sortie rate would have to drop off a little in the coming days because of it. They knew also that command of the skies would give them the ability to hit the Iraqi army in the field much earlier and with much greater effect than they had anticipated. They began to prepare to accelerate their campaign plan accordingly.

The War Under the Skies

While the Allies were wreaking havoc on Iraq from the skies, naval forces exerted their power as well. The Navy had been firing its cruise missiles as part of the air campaign and continued to enforce the embargo on goods going into and coming out from Iraq. Several Iraqi boats were destroyed in the waters of the Persian Gulf as they tried to sow mines or resupply Iraqi troops occupying Kuwaiti islands and oil platforms. Navy carrier-based fighters scored several air-to-air kills against the Iraqi air force, with a quite remarkable engagement occurring on the eighteenth when two F/A-18s from the *Saratoga*, loaded down with bombs for a strike mission, shot down two Iraqi MiG-21s. When air superiority had been won, the surface waters were clear for more aggressive operations.

The Navy began to use the battlefield as a testing ground on January 19. The submarine USS *Louisville* fired cruise missiles while submerged. Carrier-based Navy fighter jets launched developmental Stand-off Land Attack Missiles (SLAM) into Iraq. SLAM is a Navy Harpoon antiship missile modified for use against targets on land. The Harpoon's radar guidance was replaced with an imaging infrared seeker warhead combined with a television transmitter and radio command guidance receiver. With these modifications, the pilot launching a SLAM can send the missile over fifty miles away and fly it to its target on the ground with much the same precision as a laser-guided bomb. It is guided in flight by a global positioning system navigation device until it gets about a minute away from the target when the seeker switches in to provide final precise guidance.

On the night of January 18 the USS *Nicholas* slipped toward a Kuwaiti offshore oil field and launched helicopters to scout the area. Pilots had reported receiving antiaircraft fire from the area on their low-level runs into Kuwait and Iraq, and the Navy was tasked to investigate and eliminate this threat. Intelligence had reported that there were eleven platforms in the area and that nine were believed to be used by Iraqi forces for observation, communications, and antiaircraft weapons. The helicopters on board *Nicholas* were special versions of the Army's OH-58 observation and attack helicopter, equipped with advanced night observation devices and capable of firing Hellfire missiles, rockets, and cannons. They were members of the veteran Task Force 160, which had fired up Iranian oil platforms during the tanker war and had become quite expert at working jointly with the Navy.

The helicopters flew up to within range of their missiles and opened fire on two platforms, aiming for the ammunition piles. Before the Iraqi ammunition detonated, the pilots saw six Iraqis jumping out of an observation tower on the platforms onto an escape boat on the surface. Within seconds the ammunition blew up and the helicopters pulled away, their mission accomplished. At this point *Nicholas* had moved to within range of its 76mm gun and Captain Denis G. Moral gave the order to open fire. While a Kuwaiti small gunboat provided security, *Nicholas* systematically destroyed the Iraqi emplacements on seven of the platforms. When Moral realized that no fire was being returned he ordered his gun crews to cease fire and had the area scanned with their night scopes. They saw several bodies in the water and a lone figure on one platform waving in surrender.

When the skirmish was over, *Nicholas* picked up twenty-three survivors and found five Iraqis killed. The Iraqis had been ill-treated by their officers; no food had been sent out to them for days, and they had survived on fish they blew up in the water with hand grenades. Several were grateful to their captors for rescuing them. A few maroon berets of the Republican Guard were found in the area, apparently left by troops sent periodically to prevent the recent draftees from escaping from their assigned positions. Later, on the twenty-first, the *Nicholas* again saw action, this time destroying an Iraqi frigate in the only action involving a major Iraqi surface combatant during the war.

Stormy Weather

While the Navy was enjoying this small victory, storm clouds were gathering around the theater of war. The weather turned bad and slowed down the air campaign significantly. By some accounts it was the worst weather in many years, and the sortie rate dropped by about a third. The weather also hindered analysts' ability to assess the damage their attacks were causing on strategic targets.

The political weather had turned stormy as well. Israel had taken a beating on the Scud attacks, and Israeli leaders were threatening retaliation against Iraq. There were reports that the Israeli air force had been denied access to U.S. codes for identification of aircraft as friend or foe, which would be necessary for any Israeli retaliatory strikes to avoid being intercepted by coalition fighters. Israeli leaders promised to retaliate in some form although they reassured President Bush that they would delay their response in order to give the coalition a chance to halt the Scud attacks themselves. Israeli entry into the war was a serious concern for the Bush administration since it would be difficult for the Arab members of the coalition to fight alongside Israel even though they had no love for Saddam Hussein. Many analysts speculated that Saddam was firing his Scuds at Israel with precisely that in mind, and the fact that none of the Scuds seemed to be launched toward military targets seemed to support this. All fell toward populated areas, suggesting the Iraqis were using them as weapons of terror, similar to their use against Iran in the 1980s war.

To alleviate Israel's fears, President Bush decided to offer U.S.-manned Patriot missiles to Israel as a temporary deployment to help defend Israel from Iraqi Scuds. The United States, while committed to the survival of Israel, had never placed its own armed forces in direct defense of the Jewish state. For their part, the Israelis did not seek such a role for the United States. The Israelis so prized their independence that they had purchased the Patriot system and even had several launchers in their country and were in the process of setting them up and getting trained by U.S. advisers when the attacks began in January. They would not allow already trained U.S. crews to come in and operate those missiles for fear of the potential leverage the U.S. might gain over them in future relations. In the end, Israel agreed to a temporary deployment of U.S. Patriot batteries from Germany, and those forces began to arrive on the nineteenth. This seemed to reassure the Israelis about their defense from Scuds while not making them dependent upon outsiders for their defense.

On the ground, Iraq responded to the air campaign with sporadic artillery fire on close positions in northern Saudi Arabia. These were largely ineffective and caused only minor casualties. The much greater concern for the ground troops was the potential for chemical weapons being used against them. When the alarms went off in Jerusalem and Dhahran they also went off among the troops in the field. All had to suit up with their full chemical protective gear—the hot bulky suits, gloves, boots, and gas masks that provided protection from all forms of chemical agents. Suiting up took some time and made normal operations quite difficult, even for well-trained troops in good physical condition. Several false alarms went off as well and that did nothing to improve the troops' morale.

The ground forces had not been sitting idly in their positions awaiting an Iraqi attack. In fact, they had been preparing for a major assault of their own. The Marines had begun moving north closer to the border with Kuwait before the sixteenth and the Army's VII and XVIII Corps had begun their secret move to the far west near Rafha on January 13. Vast logistics bases were carved out of the desert all along the tapline road to be in place to support the planned ground offensive north. The Marines' amphibious brigade continued to adjust their position at sea to be prepared to execute a landing if needed. By the eighteenth, most of the Marine and Army units were in assembly areas and began to train and rehearse for the coming ground offensive.

On January 20, Saddam employed yet another surprise weapon in his arsenal—captured coalition pilots. Early that morning the official CENTCOM briefer would not confirm persistent rumors that coalition aviators had been taken captive. This was standard procedure in wartime; officials list pilots of aircraft known to be shot down as "missing" until evidence is found to confirm their death or capture. Saddam provided that evidence in a dramatic way when he paraded a number of Allied pilots through the streets of Baghdad and then showed a videotape of some of them on Iraqi television. The tapes showed men who had obviously been tortured making confessions under apparent duress. Many began to call for war crimes trials of Saddam Hussein and other Iraqi leaders for these violations of the Geneva Convention on the treatment of prisoners of war. This bad news was somewhat offset on the twenty-second when the Pentagon announced that at least one downed pilot had been rescued by American search and rescue teams operating inside Iraq.

The weather, already dreary, took a turn toward miserable for ground troops on the twentieth. Fog and drizzle turned to stormy downpours. Northern Saudi Arabia normally got no more than one major storm in January; in 1991 there were seven, all occurring in the two weeks after the start of the war. The temperatures plummeted to freezing. Troops that had deployed in August when the temperature was 130 degrees now shivered from the bitter, windy cold.

The artillery fire that had begun to land on the Marines near Khafji continued to land, but with no appreciable effect. The troops in the area nicknamed their unseen antagonists "eight o'clock Achmed," after the time at which the Iraqi artillery tended to be fired. Khafji had been evacuated when the air campaign began because it was within range of Iraq's artillery. In fact, the shells Iraq fired on the first night that wounded three of Task Force Ripper's troopers had been aimed not at the Marines but at the oil refinery located just outside town. Over the first three nights Iraq fired eighty-six rounds from their ASTROS rocket launchers and three FROG rockets into Khafji and finally hit the refinery. It continued to burn through the end of January.

Task Force Taro of the 1st Marine Division sent reconnaissance patrols into the town with some frequency to keep track of Iraqi movements and shelling. On the twentieth the Marines began to fire back. That night an artillery battery from Task Force Taro moved forward under cover of darkness, fired seventy rounds at the Iraqi positions, and moved back south out of range of Iraq's weapons.

Army troops, though, would have the first face-to-face encounter with Iraqi ground forces. The 3rd Armored Cavalry Regiment was screening the border between Saudi Arabia and Iraq on the night of the twenty-second when a small patrol of Iraqi infantry troops was making its way along the border just after dark. In the ensuing skirmish, two Iraqi soldiers were killed and two troopers from the cavalry regiment were wounded. The Americans took six Iraqi prisoners.

A Strategy of Annihilation

On the twenty-second, Joint Chiefs Chairman General Powell gave his second briefing of the war. It was a detailed report of how the first phase of the campaign had gone and a description of the Allied strategy for the war. He summarized the approach in few words—"We're going to cut off the Iraqi army in Kuwait; then we're going to kill it." This was an expression of historian Hans Delbrüeck's classical military strategy of annihilation.

Delbrüeck was a military historian of great talent and ability who had war experience, served as a parliamentarian, taught, and wrote regularly for military journals in Prussia in the late nineteenth and early twentieth centuries. He developed a theory of war that called on the general to choose one of two types of strategy. The first type was the strategy of annihilation. Its aim was the decisive battle, and the commander was called upon to estimate the possibility of fighting such a battle and creating the conditions for making it happen. Its aim was the destruction of the enemy's military power.

Colin Powell had been part of the U.S. military defeat in Vietnam, a defeat that was never caused by a loss on the battlefield but had come about as a result of a loss of support on the home front. He and the senior leadership of the U.S. military had resolved never again to lead the armed forces into a fight unless the political goals were clearly stated, the nation's leadership understood and would let them use necessary military means to carry the fight to a successful conclusion, and the people of the country were solidly behind the war effort. All these conditions held for the war with Iraq and so General Powell and the Allied forces pursued a strategy of annihilation.

Saddam Hussein had adopted the other form of strategy in Delbrück's paradigm, the strategy of attrition. This form of warfare is adopted by the general who knows he does not have the means to achieve a decisive defeat of his opponent's forces, but seeks to wear him out instead. It is the pursuit of the exhaustion of the enemy's means or will to fight rather than their destruction and can be aimed at the logistics support for a force in the field or even at the national willpower behind an army. Saddam had studied the Vietnam War and was convinced he could wear down the U.S. by sitting tight and inflicting thousands of casualties, even if it meant he would have to suffer tens of thousands of casualties among his own forces. He had made Iraq suffer such heavy losses during the eight-year war with Iran that he believed his political apparatus would maintain such support to cause the United States to quit, propelling him into undisputed leadership of the Arab world.

Even as General Powell spoke, Iraq began to demonstrate more clearly the lengths to which it was prepared to go to wear down support for the war among the coalition Allies. Iraq began systematically to blow up Kuwait's oil wells in the southern part of the country. Over fifty wells were ignited in the al-Wafra oil field within a few miles of the border with Saudi Arabia. It is unclear exactly what Saddam hoped to accomplish by such destructive behavior. There did not appear to be any military purpose behind it since the smoke emitted by the fires did not grow thick enough or rise high enough to disrupt coalition bombing efforts. It is most likely that Saddam was hoping to get the oil-producing Arab members of the coalition, Kuwait and Saudi Arabia, to cut a separate deal with him to stop the war and prevent him from setting on fire any more of Kuwait's oil fields. In any case the stratagem did not work. The war continued and the coalition held together.

By the twenty-third it was clear that the Allies were well on their way to achieving all their initial objectives in the air campaign. There were no Scud launches that day, and General Horner began to shift the emphasis of the targeting to the Phase Two and Three objectives, the isolation of Iraqi forces in and around Kuwait. Iraqi air activity dropped to less than forty flights a day and few if any Iraqi fighters took on coalition aircraft in aerial combat, although a Saudi pilot was awarded a double kill on the twenty-fourth. More Iraqi transports flew to Iran.

At sea the Navy took back the first piece of Kuwaiti territory to be recovered by the coalition. The guided missile frigate USS *Curts* closed in on the island of Kura on the afternoon of the twenty-fourth. Kura was about fourteen miles off the coast of Kuwait and was used by the Iraqis as an intelligence-gathering site. The crew of the *Curts*, using Army helicopters in support, took the island and a nearby mine laying ship in an engagement that ended that evening. All told, the *Curts* took fifty-one prisoners while capturing sophisticated observation equipment and weapons. On the twenty-fourth the Saudi navy scored its first kill when it launched a Harpoon antiship missile, sinking an Iraqi mine layer in the Persian Gulf.

The Marines conducted an amphibious rehearsal off the Saudi coast on the twenty-third and the twenty-fourth while a Navy A-6 fighter sank an Iraqi patrol boat and one of the Winchester hovercraft. On the twenty-fifth the Iraqis began to show signs of strain as the numbers of deserters began to increase dramatically, and Baghdad stopped showing Allied POWs on Iraqi television. Iraq opened a new chapter in the book on terrorism when it opened the valves of the Kuwaiti oil pumping station at Al Ahmadi, flooding the Persian Gulf with millions of barrels of oil over the course of the next several days. There was great risk to Saudi water desalination plants just south of the Kuwait border, but an air strike by U.S. F-111 bombers destroyed a pumping station that stopped the flow of crude oil into the sea. Before it was stopped, however, the oil streamed southward in the Gulf, creating the world's largest man-made environmental disaster in history. It seemed to serve no military purpose.

On the twenty-fifth the Marines staged their largest and most daring artillery raid to date when a battalion's-worth of 155mm howitzers drove north to the "elbow" of the Kuwait-Saudi border at about 1 A.M. and fired hundreds of shells deep into Iraqi troop positions. They encountered some Iraqi troops at the border, but the Marines quickly destroyed the truck those troops were riding in. The Iraqis fled.

Between the twenty-fifth and the twenty-eighth, dozens of Iraqi aircraft flew to Iran. This time it was mostly fighters. In his January 27 briefing, General Schwarzkopf said that the Iraqis had taken their very best fighters to Iran. There was much speculation as to why there had been such a spurt in Iraqi flights to Iran. Some wondered if perhaps Saddam was preserving his air power for some surprise desperation offensive later in the war. This would be troublesome for the coalition, particularly if Iran were to let the Iraqis use its airspace along the Persian Gulf to get deep into the rear areas of Saudi Arabia to attack coalition supply lines. General Horner did keep a contingency plan available in case it came about, but even that would only slightly upset the Allied air campaign for a brief period of time.

It seemed to me that Iraqi pilots faced an impossible set of choices. They could defy their leaders and refuse to fly, in which case they risked Saddam's brutal punishment for disobedience. If they did not fly, their aircraft were being systematically destroyed on the ground by Allied precision strikes. Yet if they did take to the skies they were sure to be shot down in air-to-air combat.

Instead, Iraqi pilots took their chances and fled to Iran. When General Schwarzkopf gave his briefing on the twenty-seventh, a total of thirty-four aircraft had flown to Iran.

On the twenty-seventh the Iraqis launched an ambush patrol into Saudi Arabia and caught Saudi border guards by surprise, but the Iraqis executed the ambush poorly, using a "V" formation, instead of the doctrinally correct line or "L" formation. Using their "V," the Iraqis caught themselves in the line of their own fire and killed one of their officers while the Saudis escaped with just light wounds to three soldiers.

On the twenty-eighth the Army tried a little field experimentation of its own in using a missile system never before tried in battle. The VII Corps fired its Army Tactical Missile System (ATACMS) at a target deep inside Iraq that night, spreading its hundreds of bomblets across an Iraqi position west of Kuwait. The successful performance of the missile in this engagement cleared the way for its more extensive use later in the war.

There was one series of naval engagements on the twenty-ninth and thirtieth, when U.S. and British aircraft and vessels finished off the Iraqi navy and destroyed a number of Silkworm missile sites. This operation became known to naval officers as the Battle of Bubiyan, after the Kuwaiti island near where the engagements took place.

On January 29 both Saddam Hussein and George Bush made public appearances to stir up support for their causes. Saddam granted an interview to CNN's Peter Arnett from his Baghdad bunker. He appeared somewhat stressed and fatigued but showed no signs of wavering. President Bush delivered the State of the Union address and was buoyant, almost exuberant. To the U.S. military personnel in the war zone, the president's speech and the Congress's positive reaction to it were the most meaningful expressions of support ever given to fighting Americans.

By the end of January the Allies had won uncontested control of the skies and seas. Iraqi Scud launches totaled fifty-two, but had tapered off to no more than one a day and on some days none at all. All strategic targets in Iraq had been hit, and Iraq's capability to manufacture nuclear, chemical, and biological weapons had been nearly destroyed. Almost two-thirds of Iraq's twenty-six command and control sites were out of action, and the entire country had only half its electrical power generation capacity. Most Iraqi airfields had been hit and seventy hardened aircraft shelters had been eliminated.

In the campaign to isolate Kuwait, more than thirty bridges had been taken out, and the flow of supplies to Iraqi forces in Kuwait had been cut to about 10 percent of the normal rate. Vast stores of Iraqi ammunition had been blown up by Allied air forces and a number of air strikes were able to destroy artillery and trucks well behind Iraqi front lines. At one point JSTARS detected a large convoy of Iraqi vehicles moving into Kuwait from Iraq, and controllers vectored strike aircraft to the site, destroying dozens of Iraqi vehicles. The Iraqi air force had lost twenty-five airplanes on the ground, including six bombers and one of their Adnan early warning aircraft. Eighty-nine Iraqi aircraft had flown to Iran by January 30. Some defecting Iraqi ground soldiers were lice infested and malnourished. Forty-six Iraqi naval vessels had been sunk or disabled. Air power had won the first phase of the war, but the war was not yet over. As General Schwarzkopf said in his January 30 briefing, "The best is yet to come."

CHAPTER SIX

The Eye of the Storm

THE FURY OF the war's first two weeks created havoc in the Iraqi government and within Saddam's army in the Kuwaiti Theater of Operations, though from Iraq's perspective it seemed as if Saddam's strategy of attrition was still working. The Iraqis had suffered much, but nothing intolerable. If they could provoke the coalition into launching a ground attack into the teeth of their extensively prepared defensive lines, the Iraqi military leadership believed that they could cause enough American casualties to turn public opinion against the war.

By mid-February Baghdad was getting distressed with progress in the war. Its late January attack into Saudi Arabia failed to provoke the kind of response they had hoped for, and the air campaign was more effective than Saddam and his generals had thought it would be, severely disrupting Iraq's ability to control and supply the army in the field. Scuds no longer caused panic in Israel or Saudi Arabia, and by late February, Allied air power was taking a growing toll on Iraqi armor. Still, Saddam thought he knew the coalition's plan of attack and believed he could ride out the storm. Amid much diplomatic maneuvering, Iraq stood its ground in Kuwait, refusing to withdraw from the "nineteenth province."

Iraqi Defensive Tactics

The Iraqi forces defending Kuwait believed they knew how the Allies were going to attack. They had studied American Air-Land

Battle doctrine and felt they understood it. They expected that there would be an air campaign that might last for a couple of weeks, then the Allies would follow that with an assault by ground forces. The Iraqi generals had analyzed the terrain in the area and had arrived at some conclusions about the character of the coming ground assault.

They were convinced that United States Marines would conduct an amphibious assault from the Persian Gulf into Kuwait. Such an assault would come at one or more of three places—Bubiyan Island, Kuwait City Harbor, and across the beaches south of the city. The Bubiyan Island approach was considered to be the least likely for a number of reasons. First, it was close to Iran and the Iraqis did not think that the Allies would risk encroaching on Iranian territory or intruding on Iranian airspace even by accident. Second, the beaches at the southern edge of the island were quite shallow and could be easily blocked with barriers. In defense, the Iraqis placed mines all across those beaches and the approaches to the Shatt-al-Arab. Furthermore, the Iraqi navy, such as it was, had its largest base just north of the island at Umm Qasr. From their small boats they could move quickly to raid approaching amphibious ships and cause significant casualties even if the Marines fought their way through. Finally, there was the question of what the Americans would do with the island once they seized it. It was a low-lying water-sogged no-man's-land most of the time. There were some oil installations, but the solid land was mostly along the coasts and across the one good road crossing the island from east to west along a man-made berm linking the two isolated outposts on the southern end of the island. This part of Bubiyan was defended by one infantry division. It was not a decisive piece of terrain and would require a great effort if the Marines wanted to use it as a jumping-off point for an attack into Iraq or Kuwait.

The Iraqis believed that the Marines would mount the most serious amphibious assault across Kuwait harbor to the westernmost reaches of the waters of the Gulf. This area just north of Kuwait City is wide open from the beaches to the north-south highway linking Kuwait City with Basra. If the Allies could take this stretch of Kuwait they would effectively cut the Iraqi army in half and could move north into Iraq, south to retake Kuwait City, or both. The Iraqi corps commander charged with defending the coastline believed that this was the most dangerous situation he could face, and he oriented his defenses against this possibility.

The coastline was defended by two infantry divisions set into extensive trenchworks covering the entire length of the coast. Throughout the harbor the Iraqis sowed hundreds of mines of various types to block the passage of both warships and amphibious craft. Antiaircraft gun emplacements were heavy since the Iraqis were acutely aware of the Marines' doctrine of sending large numbers of helicopter-borne assault troops behind the landing beaches to link up with the landing force and to defend the approaches to the landing site. The antiaircraft guns had been largely ineffective against the Allies' air campaign, but they expected that they would be much more lethal against low-flying helicopters loaded down with U.S. Marines.

Between the shoreline and the coast road the Iraqis had added extra artillery to the normal division-sized artillery force, hoping to be able to blanket the Marines with a wall of steel as they tried to come ashore. Behind these two infantry divisions, the Iraqis positioned the bulk of their regular mechanized and tank forces, including the 51st Mechanized, 10th Armored, and 6th Armored Divisions. These forces were to mount a counterattack at a decisive moment if the Marines got established on the shore. The 6th Division selected an ideal ambush site for such a battle along the road leading out of Kuwait City to the north. At a certain point the road makes a bend near a rock quarry. Excavation at the quarry over the years had created several high mounds of gravel, some reaching a hundred feet or more in height, and these hills provided perfect positions to fire at any traffic on the road below. The Iraqis fortified gun positions on these gravel mounds in the anticipation of catching the Marines' vehicles attempting to move north after the beach landings.

The Iraqis also expected the Marines to assault Kuwait City in an amphibious landing coordinated with the landings across the

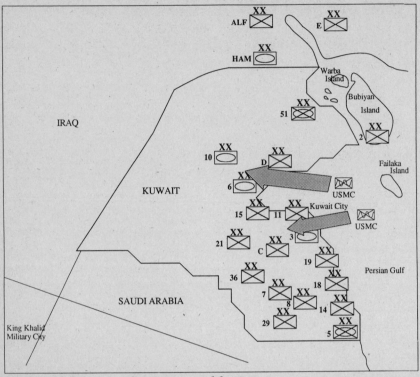

U.S. Amphibious Landings Expected by Iraq

harbor to the north. They believed that the U.S. embassy, in
particular, was so symbolically important that the Marines
would land close by in an attempt to retake it. They expected to
see an amphibious landing somewhere just south of the embassy
compound in the southern districts of the city from where the
Marines would then swing around one of the inner highway rings
to isolate the city center and await a link-up with other attacking
U.S. forces from the north and south. The 15th and 11th Infantry
Divisions were assigned the responsibility for defending the city.
All buildings facing the shore were evacuated and turned into
fighting positions. Windows were bricked up except for small
firing ports left in key places where the angles of fire were ideal
for killing Marines below. Artillery was placed in the city streets,
on building tops, and in public places. The trench line was extended throughout the city along the beach. Near the airport, the

3rd Armored Division was positioned to react by moving north or east to cut off the landing wherever it might come in the city.

While they believed the amphibious assault would come across the harbor and into the city, the Iraqis also were concerned that a landing might come south of the city, though such a landing would be less threatening to Iraq's overall defensive scheme. The 14th, 18th, and 19th Infantry Divisions were placed along the coastline to defend against this possibility. All told, Iraq dedicated four heavy divisions and seven infantry divisions to defend against the amphibious threat. Iraqi commanders were so convinced the United States would launch an amphibious assault that these divisions were ordered to face the sea throughout the entire campaign. That orientation proved fatal to the soldiers manning those positions.

Saddam expected the Allies to coordinate their amphibious assault with an overland attack. He anticipated two thrusts by the coalition ground forces, one along the coastline and another up the wadi that forms the border between Kuwait and Iraq, and he positioned his forward ground forces accordingly. One powerful mechanized division was emplaced directly on the main highway running north and south between Saudi Arabia and Kuwait. The 5th Mechanized Division occupied defensive positions between the al-Wafra oil field and the coast overlooking the approach into Kuwait from Khafji. It was to be prepared to shift on short notice if the Allies came across the desert, but Iraq's experience showed that if they themselves got off the roads they would get lost in the featureless desert, so they did not expect the Allies to attack from there. The Allies would have to use the road as a navigation guide for any attack north. Throughout this area, known as the "heel" of Kuwait, Saddam had positioned four infantry divisions, the 29th, 8th, 7th, and 36th. In reserve there was a Republican Guard infantry division due west of the Al Ahmadi oil field. If the recent conscripts manning the forward division lines did not hold the Allies, this loyal division was there to back them up. It was also there to make sure the forward troops did not flee to the rear.

From the heel west to the "elbow" of Kuwait, Iraq had placed

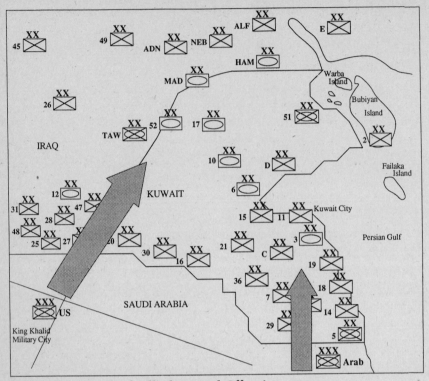

Iraq's Anticipation of Allied Ground Offensive

another three infantry divisions to maintain continuity in the
defensive line. The Wadi al-Batin cuts southwest to northeast
from Saudi Arabia to Kuwait and forms a natural avenue of approach into the Kuwait Theater of Operations. It is a wide valley
less than a hundred feet deep that contains hills and rivulets that
can mask the movement of armored formations. The Iraqis expected the Allied main attack to come up this wadi.

To block any movement west of the wadi that might outflank
the Iraqi defenses, Saddam positioned six infantry divisions
spread from the elbow to the western edge of the former neutral
zone between Saudi Arabia and Iraq. Key road junctions throughout this area were covered by entrenched infantry positions and
artillery emplacements. The 12th Armored Division was in reserve to react to any Allied penetrations of the line.

The key to the Iraqi concept for defeating the Allied ground

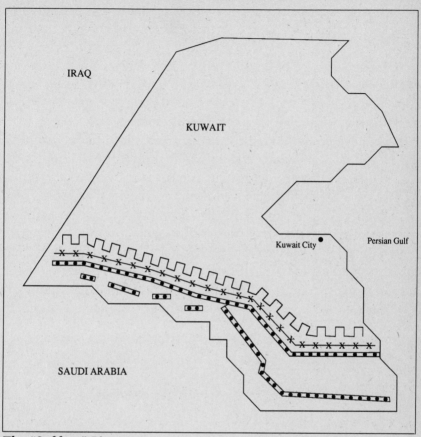

The "Saddam" Line

attack was the Republican Guard Corps. Saddam placed his elite
heavy divisions, two armored and one mechanized, just north of
the border between Iraq and Kuwait where the Wadi al-Batin
opens into an expansive flat desert. He attached to the corps the
17th and 52nd Armored Divisions out of the regular army to form
a powerful five-division armored corps. This corps was to orient
on the wadi and to mount a counterattack on the attacking Allies
at a decisive moment. Saddam hoped that his forward defensive
troops would have caused sufficient casualties among the Allies
before then so that the Republican Guard could move past the
Allied forces and into Saudi Arabia itself. The force was accordingly oriented to the south.

All along the border between Saudi Arabia and Kuwait the Iraqis constructed a defensive line. Lines and trenches closely followed their doctrinal patterns. Just north of the berm along the border was a line of barbed wire five to ten rows thick all along the border, and trenches joined lines and "lazy W's" in a continuous network of emplacements and fighting positions. Minefields were prolific. It was a textbook defense.

During the air campaign the Iraqi forces continued to improve their defensive positions even though they were frequently attacked by B-52s dropping tons and tons of dumb bombs all around them. Iraqi ammunition still moved into the area, although food arrived only intermittently. When an air strike came particularly close or even hit their positions, they moved to alternate positions nearby. They were able to construct and maintain a fully doctrinal defensive zone throughout the first two weeks of the war. To support morale among the front-line troops, Baghdad had begun broadcasting daily on "the Mother of All Battles" radio, to encourage Iraqi troops to persevere.

The Curious Battle of Khafji

Khafji was a sleepy resort and oil town of around 35,000 people on the Saudi Arabian Persian Gulf coast. It was the northernmost town in Saudi Arabia along the coast road running from Dhahran to Kuwait City and the closest piece of inhabited Saudi territory to the Iraqis occupying Kuwait. It had been evacuated by its citizens as the Allied air campaign opened on January 16. When Iraqi artillery began falling on the town on the seventeenth, the Arab forces in the coalition decided not to remain inside the city limits.

Saudi and Qatari forces dug in just south of Khafji to defend the road leading south and to provide early warning in case of an Iraqi attack toward Dhahran. The Saudi force was a battalion of the Saudi Arabian National Guard, armed with V-150 commando armored cars mounting their 90mm guns and TOW missile

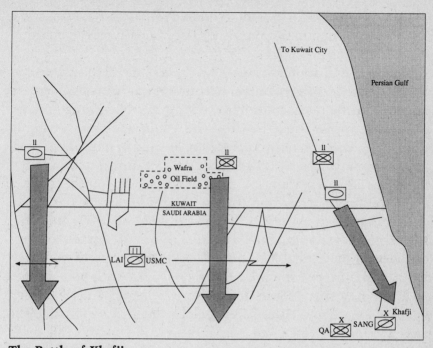

The Battle of Khafji

launchers. The Qataris had a tank battalion in place to provide a
heavy armor capability against any Iraqi advances. South of these
positions the command then known as Joint Arab Forces–East
had positioned the other of the two Saudi Arabian National
Guard battalions and the 5th Battalion of the King Abdul Azziz
Brigade of the Royal Saudi land forces. Attached to these Arab
units were liaison officers, reconnaissance troops, artillery observers, and forward air controllers from the U.S. Marines, whose
mission was to provide fire support to back up the Arabs if
needed. They also were there to provide the 1st Marine Division
with a ready link to activity on its flank.

The Marines were deployed along the border west of Joint Arab
Forces–East, stretching from a point opposite the al-Wafra oil
field to the top of the heel of Kuwait. The two Marine divisions
were in the process of passing through and around Arab forces
that, until then, had been the northernmost deployed coalition
forces. While the main Marine task forces marshaled south of

Tapline Road, the two Light Armored Infantry Battalions had moved into screening positions on the border directly confronting Iraqi troops in Kuwait.

The first indication the Allies had that something was up was on the twenty-ninth when Iraqi electronic warfare units began to disrupt Marine radio communications with a jamming barrage. This was unusual since the Iraqis had not been doing that sort of thing during the first two weeks of the war despite their capability of conducting electronic warfare operations from such forward positions. Then on the night of the twenty-ninth, at about 1900 hours, reconnaissance detected an Iraqi attack into Saudi Arabia that caught the coalition by surprise. At 2300 three Iraqi battalions moved south into Saudi territory on separate axes from just west of the heel of Kuwait to Khafji. One mechanized battalion attacked to the southwest out of the heel, a battalion of about 40 tanks moved due south from al-Wafra oil field, and a battalion of tanks mounted the third attack along the road into Khafji. The attack was unexpected, but the Allies were not unprepared. Intelligence also reported that about another 100 tanks were massing north of the Wafra oil field and beginning to move south.

On the center axis, the Iraqis ran into a U.S. Marine Light Armored Infantry Battalion commanded by Lieutenant Colonel Keith Holcomb. Keith had been a fellow at CSIS the year before and had just taken command of the battalion in the summer of 1990 after his one year of study with us. He had served for a year as a United Nations observer in Lebanon and had been shot at in anger many times before. He had positioned one company of his force astride the route used by the advancing Iraqis.

His troops were equipped with the Marines' Light Armor Vehicle armed with a 25mm "Bushmaster" automatic cannon and a TOW antitank guided missile. The Light Armor Vehicle (LAV) was not thought to be a match for any tank. Its role was to observe and report on enemy activities, although some LAVs had TOW antitank missiles for use in hasty defensive missions. The LAV was ideally suited for the desert reconnaissance role, with its 8×8 wheeled suspension system. Each Light Armored Infantry Company had fourteen LAVs with the 25mm cannon, four with the TOW, and several other types for command or support. There were a total of six companies in each battalion.

The Marines called for helicopter gunship support and opened fire with their cannons. Marine Cobra attack helicopter gunships quickly arrived, and Air Force A-10 Warthog close air-support aircraft came armed with Maverick antiarmor missiles to fire on the attacking Iraqis. The Iraqis lost twenty-four tanks and thirteen other vehicles at Wafra.

The first close combat of the war occurred when Corporal Willis, from Company A, 2nd Marine's Light Armored Infantry Battalion, opened fire at 2357 hours on the twenty-ninth of January and destroyed an advancing Iraqi T-55 tank. The battle raged through the night.

At the heel, the Iraqi attack was mounted by a mechanized battalion consisting mostly of armored personnel carriers with a few tanks attached. The Marines were only lightly screening this area but the Iraqi battalion was attacked by an Air Force AC-130H gunship from the special operations wing, firing its 105mm howitzer and miniguns at the oncoming formation. Air Force A-10 aircraft attacked the oncoming Iraqis as well. These Iraqis also quickly turned and ran back to the north, but not before four tanks and thirteen other vehicles were destroyed by the gunship.

Unfortunately, in the fog of the close battle near the heel, one of the Marines' Light Armor Vehicles was struck by a Maverick missile fired from an Air Force A-10. This was the first incident of friendly fire during the war and caused commanders to begin an urgent search for some kind of "identification, friend or foe" (IFF) device to prevent future occurrences. Seven Marines were killed in the vehicle hit by the Maverick. Four others were killed and three were wounded as a result of enemy fire.

Later prisoner of war interviews revealed that these Iraqi troops had at first balked when given the order to attack, but, when threatened with execution by their officers, went forward anyway. The AC-130 did not return to its base and its crew was listed as "Missing in Action" for the time being.

The most threatening attack came down the coast road to the town of Khafji. An Iraqi tank battalion, reinforced with infantry, moved into the town under cover of darkness. The tanks took up positions just north of the town while an infantry company occupied several buildings and the town water tower. The tower provided a commanding view of the entire area around Khafji. A Marine reconnaissance patrol happened to be in town at the time and quietly took up hiding positions in the upper floor of a building near the center of town. From here they reported back to headquarters specific intelligence on Iraqi movements and called in artillery and air strikes in response. Many times they called in strikes perilously close to their own positions while evading Iraqi detection for a day and a half.

When the Iraqis attacked, their tanks had their turrets traversed to the rear of the tank so that they advanced with their gun tubes pointed away from the defending Arab forces. Among Western armored troopers, this was understood to be a sign of surrender, signaling an advance to give themselves up. But after a short time, the Iraqis turned their turrets back to the front and opened fire with their T-55 100mm main guns in an act of treachery they had committed before in their war with Iran. This caused enough of a delay among the Saudi and Qatari defenders just south of the town to prevent them from taking quick action to stop the Iraqi advance. The Iraqis took Khafji.

On the thirty-first Iraqi forces attempted to move an additional battalion into the town but it was intercepted by airstrikes. In fact, in the early morning darkness, A-10 pilots were able to use night vision devices to target the Iraqi battalion while it was forming up for the move and swooped down to devastate the battalion before it could get to Khafji. Soon, some of those Iraqis caught in Khafji began to surrender to the Saudis south of town, simply throwing down their weapons and walking south with any piece of white material they could find, but still, rumors began to fly among the Marines that a buildup of over 60,000 Iraqis was taking place near Wafra and another attack was in the offing.

Central Command intelligence and operations analysts knew better. JSTARS had revealed that there was no follow-up attack coming; in fact, the radar showed no movement at all near Wafra. They concluded that the Iraqis were still hunkered down no matter what their intent for the attack had been. The Allies were perplexed about that intent. The attack appeared to have begun as a flawlessly planned "silent" attack. This was a tactic worked out in the war with Iran in which the Iraqis attacked at night without artillery preparation, contrary to their normal attack doctrine, to surprise the defending enemy. But the size of the offensive at Khafji and Wafra was puzzling. Iraq did not normally conduct a brigade attack with three separate battalions on separate axes without planning to follow shortly with at least two other brigades from the same division. Especially in the face of the defenses that the Allies had put in place and the capability of the coalition armored force to mount a counterattack, it seemed foolhardy even by Iraqi standards to send three battalions forward without a plan to send another brigade down the axis that provided the most success. At the very least, Iraqi doctrine required them to have a follow-on brigade in an attack position ready to move on order. Apparently the forces designated to continue the move south had either been caught by the A-10s on the thirty-first, or had become disorganized and were not capable of executing their portion of the attack. In either case, the lack of exploitation by the Iraqis gave the coalition the opportunity to take Khafji back very quickly.

The mission was given to Joint Arab Forces–East. While the U.S. Marines set up a blocking position south of Khafji along the road to Dhahran, the Qatari battalion and the two Saudi Arabian National Guard battalions attacked the city later on the thirty-first. The fighting was close-in and fierce. One Saudi guardsman single-handedly fired eight TOW missiles and destroyed eight Iraqi armored vehicles. It was over by sundown. The Arab force counterattack retook the town and killed thirty-two Iraqis in the process while wounding another thirty-five. Eleven Iraqi tanks were destroyed near the town, and fifty-one other armored vehicles were eliminated. When the last Iraqi unit surrendered, the Arab forces had taken 463 prisoners of war. Coalition Arab losses were eighteen killed, thirty-two wounded, eleven missing, and eight known taken prisoner. Only one Qatari tank was lost in the action.

The battles around Khafji and Wafra were an intelligence gold mine for the coalition. It appeared that the attack was a desperate attempt by the Iraqis to draw a response from the Allies that would bring American troops into the teeth of Iraqi defenses in Kuwait. The Iraqi command expected the U.S. to move north in response, allowing the Iraqi defenders to cause hundreds of American casualties even if such a counterattack would result in the Americans holding a piece of Kuwait. By the disorganized character of the Iraqi follow-up to the initial night attack, it was clear that Iraq no longer had a viable offensive option of sufficient strength to threaten Allied defenses, and the lack of any support for the initial attack was an indication that command and control in the Iraqi forces was worse than estimated in Central Command bomb damage assessments.

The physical condition of Iraqi soldiers at the battle of Khafji was also most revealing. The poor condition of the few dozens of line crossers from the first two weeks of the air campaign did not constitute a sufficiently large sample size from which to draw any conclusions about the status of all the frontline divisions, but here was an entire division in an attack gone awry whose soldiers had been initially unwilling to fight. Those that had attacked the Marines were well-fed and fought fiercely, at least initially. But those that had briefly held Khafji and had been captured by the Saudis were, in some cases, undernourished and had been mistreated. Most were glad to be in Allied hands safe from their own officers. Central Command concluded that the air campaign was taking a devastating toll on the morale and will to fight of the Iraqi army.

The Coalition Prepares for the Ground Campaign

At the same time as the Iraqis were moving into Khafji, the coalition navy was finishing off the Iraqi navy. At the Battle of Bubiyan, naval gunboats and strike aircraft hit three amphibious landing craft in the Shatt-al-Arab, four small boats north of the island, and three more at the naval base at Umm Qasr. At the island of Maradin, a Navy pilot had noticed a message spelled out in rocks, signaling "S.O.S. We Surrender." When other aircraft were sent to check it out, Iraqi gunboats opened fire but were quickly destroyed.

On February 1 the Navy hit Iraqi facilities at al-Kalia naval base, destroying two patrol boats, which had mounted Exocet missile launchers, and helicopters from the USS *Nicholas* hit other boats. A-6s struck an Iraqi patrol boat moored in Kuwait harbor. British naval forces participated in these attacks, which effectively eliminated the Iraqi navy. Allied naval forces continued to watch for Iraqi mines in the Persian Gulf however, as a total of thirty-seven had been discovered and destroyed during the first two weeks of the war.

On February 3, Marines retook Failaka Island although by then it had been abandoned by its Iraqi antiaircraft artillery gunners. With the northern Persian Gulf thus cleared of any threat to the Allies' big ships, the U.S. Navy moved north in force. The *Missouri* moved to within range of Iraqi positions in Kuwait and began firing its sixteen-inch shells into a command and control bunker complex. The next day it took out an Iraqi artillery emplacement and an antiaircraft radar and a surface-to-air missile launcher.

The air campaign continued at a record pace with the weather having cleared considerably by the fourth. Targets shifted to the Kuwait Theater of Operations with about seven hundred sorties going in against Iraqi positions in Kuwait and an additional one hundred or more specifically against the Republican Guard. Allied air losses continued to be minimal, although any pilot flying below 20,000 feet still risked getting hit from the extensive array of Iraqi antiaircraft gun systems. The Allies enjoyed particular success against Iraqi supply columns backed up at bridges that had been knocked out by precision-guided munitions. Strategic bombing continued to strike targets deep into Iraq where Saddam's command and control system was attempting to work around the destruction of the fixed facilities.

All of this also wore down the Iraqi air force. In a burst of

activity from the third to the sixth of February, another forty-five
Iraqi jets fled to Iran, although by this time the Allies, having
established a combat air patrol to intercept them, shot down a
total of seven others. Scud launches tapered off; only three were
fired during the first week of February and for four days straight
there were none.

In a significant skirmish on the ground on February 5, the
Syrian army drew its first blood. The Syrians had been cause for
much concern among the Allies. Their motivations were suspect
and more important, Syrian willingness to fight against Iraq was
still in question. All suspicions disappeared on February 5, however, when Syrian artillery fired on an Iraqi patrol that had penetrated Egyptian positions along the border.

That same day, President Bush announced he was sending Defense Secretary Cheney and Joint Chiefs Chairman Powell to
Riyadh to confer with General Schwarzkopf. He said he was
skeptical that air power could eject Iraq from Kuwait, but wanted
his highest military advisers to go for a first-hand look. In fact,
during this time the land forces had been preparing in earnest for
the ground attack, which for them was much more than just a
distant option.

The basic concept of operations for the attack had been developed back in November and December when the president had
directed Central Command to develop an offensive option. To the
Air Staff's air campaign plan, Schwarzkopf's own Jedi Knights at
CENTCOM had developed a sweeping idea to envelop and turn
the flank of the Iraqi defenders while punching through the front-
line defenses at several places simultaneously. It bore a striking
resemblance to the concept we had developed in 1990 at CSIS.

The plan was that while the Marines afloat kept the Iraqis'
attention glued to the threat from the Persian Gulf, the Marines
and the Arab forces on land would reduce the Iraqi barrier line and
penetrate the defenses in three broad thrusts along the Saudi-
Kuwaiti border. The combined Saudi-Qatari-Kuwaiti troops of
Joint Arab Forces—East would move up the coast road from Khafji,
while the 1st and 2nd Marine Divisions would move northeast
from the desert opposite Wafra. The Egyptian and Syrian troops

in Joint Arab Force—West would attack just east of the Wadi al-Batin and swing east toward Kuwait City. Meanwhile the U.S. VII Corps would penetrate the line west of the wadi, bypass the front-line divisions and move swiftly north to turn the flank of the Republican Guard. To bottle up the Iraqis and prevent them from escaping, XVIII Corps would make a bold move deep into Iraq as far as the Euphrates River, then push east to Basra and close off the routes to the north. If successfully executed, the Iraqis would have nowhere to go and would have to surrender or be annihilated. It was an ambitious plan, but time had allowed the coalition to put the force in place to execute it. It had been wargamed and simulated hundreds of times and was deemed workable if the air campaign was successful. Given that the air campaign had surpassed their expectations, the plan was ready to go.

By this time all of the U.S. Army VII Corps had arrived in Saudi Arabia and was in its assembly area. Their orders were to prepare for offensive operations, so while brigades rotated duty, screening the border against any possibility of an attack, the rest of the corps rehearsed its plan for an attack into Iraq. The corps had issued its operations order back in January, but at that time, the plan was not much more than a concept of operations. As the brigades and divisions of the corps trained and practiced their procedures, the corps staff under Lieutenant General Fred Franks worked out the plan in finer detail.

Franks is a career armor officer who had commanded a company in Vietnam. His leg had been blown off by a mine, and while he sports a wooden leg, his career has never missed a step from the disability. He was an English professor at West Point, has commanded at every level, and has served in the most prestigious Pentagon jobs. He is also a master of the new doctrine of Air-Land Battle and he prepared VII Corps, the largest armored corps in history, to execute it with a vengeance against the Iraqis. He had his commanders go over the plan in command post exercises several times and made each of them take their troops out into the desert to rehearse it. They adjusted their use of tanks, Bradleys, and Apaches from the techniques used in the rolling hills and forests of Germany to the wide open deserts of the

Arabian Peninsula. One of his concerns was that Allied artillery, outranged by that of the Iraqis, would pose an added burden on the movement of the corps, given that the U.S. artillery had inferior mobility in comparison to the fast-moving Abrams and Bradleys. They planned to overcome this deficiency by moving more artillery forward with the leading elements of the attack. The VII Corps was given twice its customary complement of artillery for Desert Storm, and the British 1st Armor Division was placed under VII Corps control for offensive operations.

The other U.S. Army corps, XVIII Corps, was equally over-stocked with artillery. In the grand strategic concept for the offensive, General Gary Luck's XVIII Corps was to strike deep for the Euphrates River from its secret jump-off point near Rafha in northern Saudi Arabia. Luck is an officer of rare experience, having served in tank, infantry, aviation, and Special Forces units throughout his career and having been wounded in Vietnam while commanding his cavalry helicopter troop.

Luck's corps, normally assigned light infantry missions, was much more heavily armed than it had been while at its Ft. Bragg, North Carolina, duty station. During Desert Shield the 3rd Armored Cavalry Regiment, the 24th Mechanized Division, and the 1st Cavalry Division had been assigned to the corps in addition to its customary control over the 101st and 82nd Airborne Divisions. Additional Apache attack helicopters had been assigned to XVIII Corps for its special offensive mission. The French Light Armor Division had been attached as well. The corps rehearsed its offensive operations while preparing for combat in the far west.

These U.S. corps had been equipped with the latest American armored fighting vehicle systems. Their M1A1 Abrams Main Battle Tanks, some of which had been received as late as January 23, were the best in the world. Its 120mm gun fired a secret new round made of depleted uranium that reportedly could penetrate any known armor plate in the world. Its mobility was unsurpassed, capable of firing on the move at over forty miles per hour and still score first-round hits at 1,200 meters. Its crews had trained in hitting Soviet tanks at 1,500 meters and its forward-

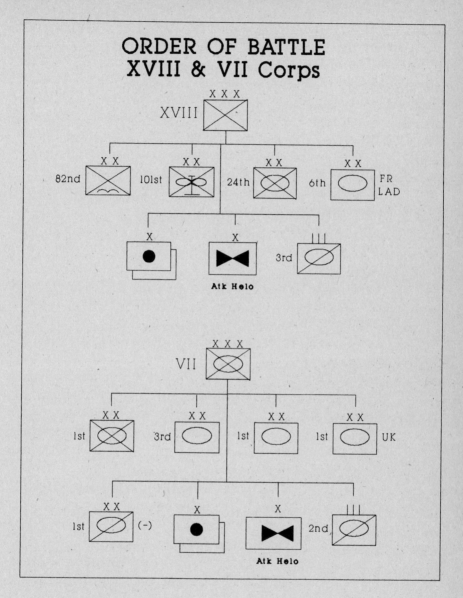

looking infrared sights gave it a capacity to engage the enemy through fog, smoke, and darkness.

The Armored Cavalry and Mechanized Infantry units in VII and XVIII Corps were equipped with the Bradley Fighting Vehicle System. The Bradley carried three to eleven crewmen depending on the configuration and was used in reconnaissance, antitank, and infantry roles. Its aluminum armor could defeat most Soviet infantry fighting vehicle weapons, but it would not stop a tank main gun round. More important, it carried both the TOW antitank missile and the 25mm chain gun automatic cannon, which could pierce most Soviet armored fighting vehicles smaller than a tank.

BRITISH armored forces brought their latest technology to the Persian Gulf war as well. The British Warrior Mechanized Combat Vehicle was the rough equivalent to the U.S. Bradley. Its main armament is a 30mm cannon. Some variants mount an antitank guided missile. British tank forces were equipped with the formidable Challenger. Like the American M-1, the Challenger has a 120mm gun and uses thermal imagery for superior fire control.

French armored forces were later in arriving in the Persian Gulf than the American and British heavy units, and the French armored equipment modernization program was several years behind that of the U.S. and Britain. As a result, French armored forces went into the Persian Gulf war with older tanks and infantry carriers that were barely equal to those of the Iraqis.

Egyptian and Syrian divisions prepared as well. These forces were powerful additions to the coalition. Organized as heavy divisions, they formed another armored corps to anchor the center of the Allies' line. The Egyptians came equipped with American-made M-60 tanks and M-113 armored personnel carriers. They had participated in exercises with Central Command during the 1980s and were experienced in U.S. operational procedures. Egyptian commander General Ali Nabil was also a veteran of the 1967 and 1973 campaigns against Israel. Syrian forces were less comfortable operating with the U.S. and came with Soviet-made T-72 tanks and BMP armored fighting vehicles. They were kept farther away from U.S. forces than from other Allies.

The Marines under General Walt Boomer executed a complex maneuver to shift from their orientation along the coast to attack positions in the interior. They constructed an elaborate deception scheme to mask their movements and even created the impression of a huge tank force that in fact did not exist. In addition, Schwarzkopf had attached to the Marines an armor brigade from the Army's 2nd Armored Division to shore up the Marines' capability in tanks.

The shift from a defensive posture to an attack posture was completed between January 23 and February 23. Thousands of tons of logistical supplies had to be moved and hundreds of thousands of troops had to be shifted around to be in place for the attack, if it was to be launched. Central Command carefully orchestrated the movement of units to keep the Iraqis confused as to what was where along the border. While VII and XVIII Corps moved west, the Marines along the coast shifted toward the interior. The Egyptian and Syrian forces moved north closer to the border, and the other Arab forces moved north of Khafji later in February.

The command relationships among the Allies were lashed up in an ad hoc fashion, compared to the well-integrated network employed in NATO forces, but they seemed to work well enough. General Schwarzkopf commanded U.S., British, and French forces while Saudi General Prince Khalid commanded all Arab forces. In Riyadh it was all brought together in the command center housed in the Royal Saudi Ministry of Defense building. Inside, all operations were continuously updated by officers from each country so that all could see what was happening across the battlefield. To ensure there were no surprises, American forces also assigned liaison teams of U.S. soldiers with the requisite language skills to all other Allied ground forces and set up separate communication links directly to American forces close by.

On February 8, CENTCOM issued its first quantitative report on damage to Iraqi forces in Kuwait. Up to this point, military officials, General Schwarzkopf in particular, had avoided citing any numbers of enemy troops or equipment destroyed in battle. Their hesitation reflected not only the uncertain art of bomb damage assessment, but especially the U.S. generals' reluctance to issue anything that might remotely resemble the "body counts" of the Vietnam era when ground operations began to grow in intensity. They did not want to mislead the public about progress made, and they wanted to avoid putting pressure on subordinate commanders to come up with statistics that meant little on the battlefield. But on this day, Central Command reported that over 600 tanks had been destroyed and on the next day, February 9, the number was updated to over 750. CENTCOM also reported that 650 artillery pieces had been destroyed along with 600 armored personnel carriers. These numbers were issued as Cheney and Powell met with General Schwarzkopf for eight hours in Riyadh on the ninth.

The President Decides

The president's military men went over the situation in great detail. They assessed the Iraqi situation by examining a mosaic of indicators, from numbers of tanks destroyed to estimates of the rate of resupply into the KTO. Every Iraqi division was assessed individually across a range of dozens of evaluation factors. Their conclusion was that the Iraqis showed no intention of withdrawing and could still mount an effective defense, but that it would crack if attacked deep and fast on the ground. There was not much hope that continued bombing would dislodge the Iraqis. Soon air power would reach the point of diminishing returns, where too much risk and effort would have to be exerted to achieve any more destruction. The readiness of coalition forces was assessed to be good, and after some discussion, they decided to recommend to the president that G-Day, the day to launch the ground attack, be established on February 24 if Iraq had not withdrawn. After examining reconnaissance reports on coastal defenses and seeing how extensively the Iraqis had mined the Persian Gulf approaches to Kuwait, they decided not to launch an amphibious landing unless it was needed later to support the land attack. The amphibious force would remain at sea—it had been afloat continuously since August—as a feint to continue to draw Iraqi defenses away from the attacks in the west.

After Cheney and Powell returned to Washington, President Bush announced that he saw no reason not to continue the air campaign for some time. The Air Force began to report some success in hitting Iraqi mobile Scud launchers, and the bomb damage assessment from the air campaign continued to show progress. On February 12, Allied ground forces reported about fifty fires burning in Kuwait in the Wafra oil fields.

On the twelfth, the 1st Marine Division initiated one of its largest raids ever when it coordinated a three-hour strike on Iraqi positions in Kuwait employing a 155mm artillery battalion, three battalions of Saudi artillery, and eighteen rounds from the battleship *Missouri*'s 16-inch guns. Baghdad was subjected to the most intensive bombing of the campaign since the first few days, and the Iraqis responded by moving aircraft to civilian areas to avoid Allied attacks. The next day Kuwaiti Gazelle attack helicopters knocked out two Iraqi tanks in a bold move across the border along the coast. From my perspective in the CNN control room it seemed as if the pace and intensity of the conflict were beginning to pick up.

A bunker or a bomb shelter? Then on the thirteenth, the Allies were stunned by video news reports of the results of an Allied air strike on a command and control bunker in Baghdad. For two days this incident dominated the news as Iraq brought Western journalists to the site to show the death and destruction wrought by the Allied bomb that had penetrated the bunker's eight-foot-thick concrete roof.

The Iraqis insisted that the target was a community air raid shelter; the United States claimed that it was a strictly military command and control center, one of many throughout the city of Baghdad. The circumstantial evidence certainly seemed to support the Allies' claim; it looked nothing at all like a community shelter, with a barbed wire-topped chain link fence surrounding it and a camouflage-painted roof. But the deaths were undeniable. Whether the people inside had been families of government or party officials or innocent citizens who had been cruelly told they would be safe inside, we may never know. In briefing after briefing for the next several days, the Pentagon claimed it had incontrovertible intelligence evidence that the facility was a command and control center that had been actively engaged in military activities only a short while before and was therefore a legitimate target.

Meanwhile, back in the Gulf, the carrier *America* entered the Persian Gulf, bringing the total number of carriers in that restricted sea to four. It was incredible that even one carrier was there; Admiral Tom Moorer had told me that it was risky bringing a carrier into the Persian Gulf even in peacetime because the Strait of Hormuz was so narrow and the navigable channel was strictly confined. Here the United States was in a shooting war and mines were everywhere, yet not just one but four carriers were there. Something was up.

That afternoon, the ruling Revolutionary Command Council of Iraq announced that it would withdraw from the territory it had seized in Kuwait and that the move would begin very soon. There were celebrations in the streets of Baghdad when Iraqi radio passed on the announcement and CNN's cameras were there along with a hasty translation of the statement. Although the early translations were rough, it soon became apparent that the withdrawal offer was not unconditional. In fact the offer contained all the old conditions stipulated by Iraq and added some new ones. It was soon rejected by the Allies. President Bush called it a cruel hoax; he called on the Iraqi people and the Iraqi military to take matters into their own hands and force their dictator aside. This invitation seemed to some to signal a willingness to provide help, perhaps clandestinely, if only some group would take up the call. Meanwhile Iraq launched five more Scuds that day, a peak since the tapering off that had begun in late January. So much for the peace initiative.

About this time I had noticed that we were no longer getting pool reports from correspondents located with the VII and XVIII Corps. We had seen plenty of video from them before, especially during the move out from their original defensive positions, and the press reporting had been quite regular. In fact, when I thought about it, the last we had seen of these very large formations was about a week earlier, when it had been reported that they were moving north. The 82nd Airborne Division's Sheridan light tanks were shown being transported on large trucks north along the coast road. And the attachment of the 2nd Armored Division Tiger Brigade to the 1st Marine Division had been featured in a story by a pool correspondent with the Marines. These moves of elements of the XVIII Corps seemed consistent with my previous speculation that the XVIII Corps would be close to the Marines and the Arab forces along the Dhahran–Kuwait City road for an attack across the Saddam Line near the coast. But the absence of reports from VII Corps was another matter.

Someone wanted to obscure the location of VII Corps and that could mean only one thing—the corps had been moved west to prepare for an imminent ground attack and CENTCOM did not want the Iraqi high command watching CNN to know where the corps had been moved to. That seemed fine by me—I had no desire to speculate on that issue, but it meant that we had better soon be ready for the start of a ground offensive. I alerted the network's executives of my thinking, and they agreed to prepare some ground warfare segments for later use. We spent a day at the CSIS situation room taping in front of the large map boards we had assembled, exploring various options the Allies might use and explaining tactics and techniques for ground operations such as obstacle breaching, tank attacks, and the like. It was a prudent move.

Actually my guesses were only partially correct. The 7th Corps had moved west, but something had happened to the corps in the process. It became the largest armored corps ever assembled. Its complement of artillery was doubled and it was assigned one of the ATACMS batteries available to the Americans. It also received additional engineer battalions to assist with crossing the obstacles and to help clear pathways for trucks and supply convoys following the advance. The British armored division had been attached (the technical term for the relationship is "operational control" or "OPCON") so that at the dawn of the ground campaign Fred Franks had under his command over a thousand tanks, a hundred Apache attack helicopters, and a hundred thousand soldiers. And it was farther west than I or my colleagues had imagined it would go.

The most carefully guarded secret was the composition and location of XVIII Corps. The 82nd had not been moving north in that video, it was moving west along Tapline Road. It moved nearly three hundred miles west to an assembly area near Rafha. And the 101st Airborne Division (air assault), with its over three hundred helicopters moved itself likewise. The attached French Light Armor Division was deployed even farther west to Rafha, and the 24th Infantry Division took up its attack position outside of Nisab. The 24th's commanding general, Barry McCaffrey, issued his general order to attack on the fifteenth. His words were inspiring: "Soldiers of the Victory Division—we now begin a great battle to destroy an aggressor Army and free two million Kuwaiti people. We will fight under the American flag and with the authority of the United Nations. By force-of-arms we will make the Iraqi war machine surrender the country they hold prisoner. . . . There will be no turning back when we attack into battle. . . . We shall do our duty."

On that same day a battalion task force from the 1st Infantry Division ("The Big Red One") moved forward and reduced the border berm in twenty locations. The force moved into Iraq and set up a hasty screen about three miles inside Iraq. From this location the division moved artillery across the border for quick raids into Iraqi positions. Corps headquarters was nervous with the battalion so far in front and ordered it withdrawn back into Kuwait the next day.

All across the front on the fifteenth, the Allies were getting ready to commence the ground assault on a moment's notice. The rest of VII Corps moved into its attack position, called Forward Assembly Area Garcia, along the tapline road. The 1st Cavalry Division, down to two brigades with the detachment of the Tiger Brigade to the Marines, was assembled in the Wadi al-Batin under the direct control of the Army component commander for Central Command and was to be the theater reserve. It was also to move up the wadi in a feint to convince the Iraqis that they had guessed right about where the Allies would attack.

The Marines had completed a massive shift to the west of their own. They left the positions they had occupied south of Wafra for a month and concentrated their power along the edge of the heel and the elbow of Kuwait. In their place they left a small group of Marines called Task Force Troy whose mission was to make the Iraqis believe the entire 1st Marine Division was still there. Task Force Troy had been creatively equipped for the mission. It had dozens of wooden tanks and artillery mock-ups, one battery of real artillery with six tubes, five real tanks, and some TOW missile launchers mounted on HMMWVs. A few Light Armor Vehicles were assigned as well to make it look as if Keith Holcomb's battalion from the 2nd Marine Division was also still there, when in fact it had been withdrawn along with the entire 2nd Marine Division to attack positions west of the heel. Many of the Marines' green camouflage nets had been left in place during the night moves in order to make it look as if a much larger force was still there.

The Marines' deception techniques were not just optical. A psychological warfare unit was added to Task Force Troy to provide amplifiers and speakers similar to the types used in Panama in 1989 to surround Manuel Noriega with rock music. The Marines played sounds of tanks moving. Electronic warfare specialists jammed Iraqi radio nets, and a truck flailing a chain stirred up the dust signature of armored columns on the move. The plan called for the six tubes to fire an artillery prep on the Iraqi positions, and just to make it more believable, the Marines rigged a remote control truck with TNT and dummies to be sent forward into Iraqi lines to blow up on command.

The 1st Marine Division engineers crossed the border on the night of the seventeenth to conduct reconnaissance of the obstacle belt they would face. At one time during this period, division Commanding General Mike Myatt issued his advice to his troops: "Don't take counsel of your fears; that son-of-a-bitch is as scared of us as we are of them."

The sporadic fighting along the border continued. On the seventeenth, another friendly fire incident took its toll when an Apache helicopter mistakenly hit a Bradley fighting vehicle and a ground surveillance radar on an armored personnel carrier. Two American soldiers were killed and six wounded in the incident and it raised new calls for a more effective method of identifying U.S. vehicles to Allied aircraft firing from long range. The Defense Advanced Research Projects Agency issued an urgent order for thousands of hastily designed devices that emitted an infrared flashing light, but the war ended before very many of them made it into the hands of the forward troops. The commander of the Apache battalion responsible for the incident was later relieved of command.

New evidence began to emerge in mid February that the Iraqi occupiers of Kuwait were committing new atrocities. While Iraqi Foreign Minister Tariq Aziz was negotiating in Moscow, reports began to flow out of Kuwait that its citizens were being tortured and deported. And in the Gulf waters more mines were discovered when the amphibious ship *Tripoli* and the Aegis cruiser *Princeton* struck mines within three hours of each other in the early morning darkness. *Tripoli* was not seriously damaged, but *Princeton* had to return to port for the rest of the war for repairs.

By February 19 the Moscow-Baghdad negotiations had produced a plan that was carefully considered but rejected by President Bush. With that rejection the pace of the skirmishing stepped up noticeably. General Schwarzkopf reported that the air campaign was now destroying over a hundred tanks per day. Pentagon intelligence officials showed sketches demonstrating Iraqi duplicity in staging the destruction of mosques in Iraq and blaming it on Allied bombing. The border incidents grew in scope too. In some cases entire battalions were fully engaged.

Ultimatum

On February 20, President Bush told the Russians he had had enough of Saddam's endless attempts to work out a deal for withdrawal under favorable conditions. He told Soviet President Gorbachev that he would give Iraq four days to begin to withdraw, release all prisoners, and show the Allies the locations of all minefields in Kuwait. That same day in a helicopter raid nearly five hundred Iraqis surrendered to U.S. forces. Iraqi forces continued to be subjected to withering air attacks as they tried to shift positions in the KTO and moved among logistics sites for resupply. The Pentagon briefers that day spoke of the resiliency of the Iraqi military infrastructure and how intelligence had detected some Iraqi success in working around the effects of Allied destruction.

In the air, Iraqi sorties had dropped to zero. No more aircraft tried to escape to Iran. Allied pilots had shot down thirty-five Iraqi jets in aerial combat and could confirm another fifty-five destroyed by bombing. The Allied air planners knew they had hit 375 of Iraq's 594 hardened aircraft shelters and estimated that they had destroyed another 141 aircraft in those shelters. Of fifty-four targeted key bridges on the rail and road routes into the Kuwaiti Theater of Operations, forty had been rendered unusable and another ten had been damaged. Through all of this, over a hundred thousand air sorties had been flown, but only twenty-nine American aircraft had been lost in combat and just nine Allied planes had been lost.

On the twenty-first, Saddam Hussein made his most defiant statement yet, refusing to accept President Bush's demands of the previous day. On the twenty-second, President Bush gave Saddam twenty-four hours to withdraw, and he accused Iraq of starting a scorched earth policy in Kuwait. Iraqi troops in Kuwait began lighting more oil wells on fire, and Allied forces on the border began dropping napalm on Iraqi trenchlines that had been filled with oil. The night sky was ablaze with fires on the eve of battle and on the twenty-third President Bush authorized the commencement of the land attack. The time had come to finish the war.

CHAPTER SEVEN

Schwarzkrieg

ON SUNDAY, FEBRUARY 24, the weather in the Kuwait Theater of Operations was terrible. A chilly rain fell, and fog rolled in at dusk. Smog from the oil fires clogged the air around Kuwait, while dust was the demon in the Iraqi desert. The coalition ground troops of Operation Desert Storm never thought that treading the burning sands of the Arabian desert would be like this. But the ground war was on, and the conditions were bearable for the troops, knowing that the way home lay ahead through the gritty darkness into the remnants of Saddam's occupying forces. They also knew that they would have to fight more than just the weather to get home. The artillery raids and reconnaissance patrols revealed that while some of the Iraqi forces were demoralized and devastated, most of them intended to stay put and fight.

The Iraqi troops had suffered incredible conditions and treatment from both the Allied air campaign and their own leadership. The air campaign had taken a tremendous toll. The divisions along the Kuwait-Saudi border were low on food and water although they were not starving. They had been subjected to tremendous psychological stress from the constant Allied bombing. Although the bombs did not usually land directly on the Iraqis' bunkers, they did land close enough to terrorize anyone within range of the concussion wave. But the Iraqis did have ammunition and they did have their orders. They were to stay there and fight to the end. They had been told that the Americans were all light infantry and that the Iraqi artillery would so break up the attack-ing coalition forces that the Iraqi infantry would only have to meet scattered opposition from a few formations that might man-age to break through. Having issued their orders that week, some of the Iraqi officers then left their posts. One division commander went home to Basra and telephoned his staff every few days or so. A battalion commander had taken his officers back into Iraq and told his men they were called back for a meeting. Many who were closer to Iraq stole away in automobiles carrying with them all the consumer goods they could carry, including televisions, ste-reos, refrigerators, and much, much more. Those who did stay took care of themselves while their soldiers lived in squalor. The officers' bunkers in some instances had refrigerators well stocked with fresh fruit, cold drinks, and bread, while the troops barely got one meal a day. It was the worst imaginable form of leadership. It certainly was no way to motivate an army that was about to be attacked.

And attacked they were. The date for the commencement of the final ground offensive, "G-Day," had been set for February 24. H-hour was 0400. All the raids, patrols, and deceptions had been carefully designed and meticulously executed to mask this crucial moment to give the Allies precious time to reduce the obstacles that formed the "Saddam Line." Once the offensive was set in motion it could not be recalled; it was like a huge coiled spring that had been pulled back, set and ready to be launched. If the precise locations of the points along the line were known by the defending Iraqi forces, they could concen-trate their artillery fires and position their mobile reserves to repulse the attackers before the breaching of the obstacles could be completed. A successful linear defense required maintaining the continuity of the line, and if the attacker could get entangled in the obstacles or even delayed for a few hours, then the de-fender could shift fires and forces to strike where the attacker was most threatening. The Allies knew this and had gone to elaborate lengths to deceive the Iraqis as to the breach sites because the coalition ground forces, as strong as they were, still were outnumbered along the front line and outgunned in tanks and artillery. The Iraqis knew that a ground attack was coming, so the Allies could not hope to surprise them strategically. They would have to rely on achieving tactical surprise to give them an advantage they lacked in numbers.

How to Conduct a Land Offensive

There are three ways to mount an attack on the ground. The simplest method is the head-on charge. If it is to be directed against a defensive line, such an attack would become a penetration. If it is undesirable to conduct a penetration, the attack can be made against the sides of a defender's position, in which case the offensive is called a turning movement. A third method is called an envelopment, where the attacker tries to slip all the way around the defensive line and attack from the rear. Of course, no real attack is a pure version of one of these three classical types, but instead it is made up of some modification or combination of one or more of the types.

The terrain leading from Saudi Arabia into the Iraqi forces in the KTO lent itself to any of the three classic kinds of offensives. Along the Persian Gulf coast the ground is composed of very loose, powdery sand that tends to move with the prevailing winds in dunes. Improved roads form the main routes of movement for military formations because heavy vehicles have difficulty dealing with the blowing sand. Not only is it a strain on tanks to push through the sand, but the machined parts of internal combustion engines are easily damaged by the hard silicon particles. Inland from the coast the sand is gritty while the ground is harder and more rocky. The Wadi al-Batin is just about the only terrain feature in the area; it is a wide valley cut into the desert floor forming the border between Kuwait and Iraq. It can serve as an avenue of approach from Saudi Arabia through Kuwait and into Iraq for about a division-sized armored formation. Farther west the terrain is wide open desert stretching north to the Mesopotamian basin when it reaches the Euphrates River valley.

The coastal road and the desert interior form suitable avenues of approach for penetration operations, and the wadi and deserts to the west would afford ideal space for a turning movement or envelopment. In their operational planning, Central Command's Jedi Knights had modeled and simulated dozens of differing options before they had settled in December on Schwarzkopf's "Hail Mary" concept.

The idea was to create so many different penetrations into Iraq's formations that the Iraqis could not anticipate where the main attack was coming from before it was too late for them to do anything about it. The Saudi, Kuwaiti, Omani, Qatari, and Bahraini brigades were clustered together under the organizational grouping of Joint Arab Forces—East (JAF-E) and assigned an attack sector along the coastal road. West of JAF-E were the U.S. Marines (MARFOR) organized as 1st and 2nd Marine Divisions. Just east of the wadi the Egyptian and Syrian divisions were formed together into Joint Arab Forces—West (JAF-W).

JAF-E was to attack straight up the road and take Kuwait City. The Marines were to attack from the southwest to the northeast to secure the airport and the approaches to the city while JAF-W was to support the Marines protecting their left flank. To keep the eleven Iraqi divisions along the coast preoccupied, the Marines left a brigade afloat to conduct amphibious demonstrations. They would not actually conduct a landing unless the attack got bogged down. The Marines' reconnaissance of the beaches showed that there were too many mines in the waters near the shore, and they would be likely to suffer heavy casualties in any amphibious landing.

Centered on the wadi was the U.S. 1st Cavalry Division, less the Tiger Brigade, which had been attached to the Marines. The 1st Cavalry's task was to attack up the wadi as a feint, in an attempt to make the Iraqis believe that they were the leading element of VII Corps at the head of the main attack. But in fact the cavalry was all alone; it was to fake an attack then pull back and serve as Central Command's theater reserve.

In reality VII Corps was to conduct a turning movement with the 1st Infantry Division forging a breach in Iraq's line just west

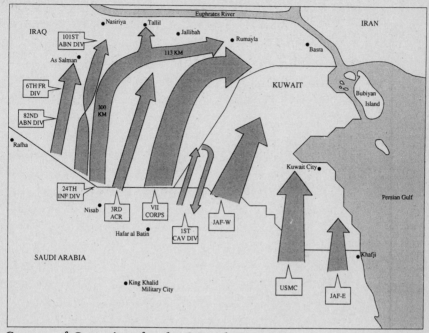

Concept of Operations for the Ground Campaign

of the wadi then passing the British 1st Armored Division through. Once the British were in Iraq, they were to turn immediately east and begin to roll up the flank of the Iraqis front lines while the 2nd Armored Cavalry Regiment, 1st and 3rd Armored Divisions, having gone around the end of Iraqi lines to the west, were to push farther north then turn east into the Republican Guard to complete the turning movement.

Central Command estimated that the Iraqis would still be able to maneuver their mechanized forces even after the air campaign, and that once the ground campaign began they would have the capability to conduct a fighting withdrawal. They had successfully conducted this most difficult kind of operation many times against Iran, and CENTCOM planners wanted to make sure they could catch and destroy enough of Iraq's armored forces in the ground campaign to eliminate the Iraqi army as an offensive threat in the region for many years to come. It would not be out of character for Saddam to order his best divisions to withdraw while forcing his forward infantry conscripts to stay in place and sacrifice themselves as they tried to inflict maximum casualties among the advancing Allies.

To guard against this possibility, General Schwarzkopf ordered the U.S. XVIII Corps, which was organized to include the French light armored division, to conduct a deep envelopment designed to close off any escape routes the Iraqis might attempt to use to head north away from the forces during the penetration and turning movement maneuvers. The French, with a brigade of the 82nd Airborne Division and a group of U.S. engineers attached, would secure the far western flank, while the 101st Airborne Division, with its hundreds of helicopters, would fly to the Euphrates and cut off the routes leading into the KTO. As the western flank and the northern approaches became secure, the 24th Infantry Division and the 3rd Armored Cavalry Regiment would race over land to Highway Eight, which runs parallel to the Euphrates River from Nasiriya to Basra, then swing along the highway to the southeast toward Basra. Just before reaching the city, they were to set up a blocking position at the Rumaila oil fields to catch any retreating Iraqi mechanized forces that would be moving north out of the KTO. It was to be an envelopment of epic proportions.

In fact the entire operation was to be one for the history books. Not only was it to be the largest tank attack since World War II, but the operational concept combining all three classic offensive maneuvers at once had never before been attempted. Schwarzkopf was modest when he said that he intended it to work like the football "Hail Mary" play, where you just send everyone out to receive and throw the ball to one who can get open. Actually, he left nothing to chance in one of the most complex operational plans ever conceived. Every unit had a precise objective and mission, all coordinated and sequenced to complete the destruction of Iraq's army before the Iraqi leadership could comprehend what was happening and do something about it.

Into the Breach

At 0100 on the twenty-fourth, naval gunfire initiated the amphibious demonstrations. Both U.S. battleships, *Wisconsin* and *Missouri*, opened fire with their mammoth 16-inch guns along the Kuwaiti shoreline, confirming in the minds of the Iraqi commanders their idea that the Marines were about to launch an assault over the beach. At the same time, intelligence sources indicated that the Iraqis were committing new atrocities in Kuwait among local citizens. Later, Central Command briefers told of "unspeakable" acts on the part of the Iraqi occupiers, which began as the Allies opened the ground campaign.

At 0400 the Marines crossed the border to begin their breaching operation and at 0500 the 1st Infantry Division pushed forward in its sector. These were to be the two main penetration points. The others would come later in the day.

The Marines 1st Division crossed at a point defended by the Iraqi 29th Division. The Iraqi division had been reduced to less than half its strength as a result of the air campaign, and in the black of the night, engulfed in the smog of the oil fires, they could hardly see Task Forces Taro and Grizzly on the left and right plowing up their minefields. Task Force Ripper followed in the center by blowing up the minefield, although several times Ripper's explosive line charge automatic detonator malfunctioned, causing a certain consternation among the infantrymen whose duty was to crawl out and detonate it manually. By 0700, Task Force Ripper had secured the center breach and Task Force Papa Bear moved in to breach the line on their right. By 1200 the entire 1st Marine Division was through the first line of minefields, and the Iraqis had hardly fired a shot in response. Many Iraqis surrendered to the Marines. When the Iraqis finally did open up, firing a massive artillery barrage into the Marines' formations just before noon, their guns were quickly silenced with airstrikes from the Marines' F/A-18 and AV-8B fighters.

The Marines pressed on, reaching the second minefield obstacle belt just after noon when the leading companies of Task Force

Ripper crossed into an area called the "Emir's Farm," just south of the Burgan oil field. Here the Marines received a warning of a chemical attack and had to stop briefly to don their protective clothing and gas masks. When the "all clear" was given, after a check of the atmosphere showed it had been a false alarm, they encountered small arms, machine gun, and tank fires from an Iraqi battalion in a defensive position. Task Force Ripper deployed, still garbed in their chemical protective outer garments, and swept through the position, silencing the enemy with their own tanks, TOW missiles, and heavy machine guns.

The 2nd Marine Division had a tough fight on its hands. Three days before G-Day, the division's light armored infantry battalion had infiltrated the Iraqi lines along the heel of Kuwait. They had suffered a withering artillery barrage unlike any other in the war. While the air campaign had been particularly successful in hitting artillery emplacements elsewhere among Iraqi forces, the 2nd Marine Division was again hit with an artillery barrage as it attempted to breach the Saddam Line in its assigned sector. Keith Holcomb's battalion, again selected for a difficult task, took its most significant casualties as Iraqi artillery impacted on his men and, uncharacteristically in comparison to other places along the front, shifted as they moved. By the end of the day, Iraq's guns were silenced and the Army's Tiger Brigade, attached to the Second Marines, were through and on their way to the town of Jalibah, astride the highway interchange controlling the western and northern approaches to Kuwait City. Later assessments determined that only 10 percent of Iraqi artillery facing the 2nd Marine Division had been silenced by air power.

As dusk began to settle in, the 1st Division had reached its first day's objective south of the Burgan oil field and readied itself for the next day's mission—to take the airfield at al-Jaber and continue the attack toward Kuwait City. Commanding General Mike Myatt moved his headquarters far forward to a position just south of the oil field, which by then was ablaze and covered in smoke. They were farther forward than they normally liked the headquarters to be, but felt safe enough since it seemed as if no one would be able to come at them out of the hellish fires burning in the oil field. Just to be sure, they took a platoon out of Task Force Ripper to provide local security for the command post. All day the stream of surrendering Iraqis grew, and the Marines had to toss them some food and water, then send them south on foot to be picked up later by others following so as not to delay their advance.

The Army's 1st Infantry Division had conducted its "stand-to," the traditional military get up and get ready drill, at 0300 on the twenty-fourth. Their scouts reached the border at 0538, and soon after the advancing troops began to receive mortar fire from the defending Iraqis. Counterbattery fire quickly silenced the Iraqi mortars, and the division never missed a step in its advance through the Saddam Line. By dawn, Iraqis were beginning to come up out of their holes to surrender to the "Big Red One," and while there were numerous sightings of Iraqi vehicles, there was very little initial contact. By 1000 hours the leading combat elements of the division were through the defensive line, destroying dug-in tanks and APCs along the way, and the artillery was brought forward. In the process, 1st Infantry destroyed the Iraqi 25th Infantry Division defending the sector, and by 1800 the division was guarding the breach with two brigades forward, ready to continue the attack on order. They had taken over 5,500 enemy prisoners of war and were busy through the night cutting and marking a total of twenty-four lanes for the Corps to use the next day.

The night was not uneventful for the 1st Marine Division outside of the Burgan oil field. General Myatt's Kuwaiti liaison officer had warned that the Iraqis might be able to push some tanks through the burning oil field after all. While the Americans were skeptical, they did have the security platoon from Task Force Ripper orient their defenses toward Burgan. It turned out to be a prudent move, as during the night the Iraqis attacked into the division's command post with a sizable tank force. The platoon was able to defeat the attack, killing three Iraqi tanks in the process. It was to be a harbinger of a larger, more threatening counterattack the next morning.

The combined forces of JAF-E met little resistance in their

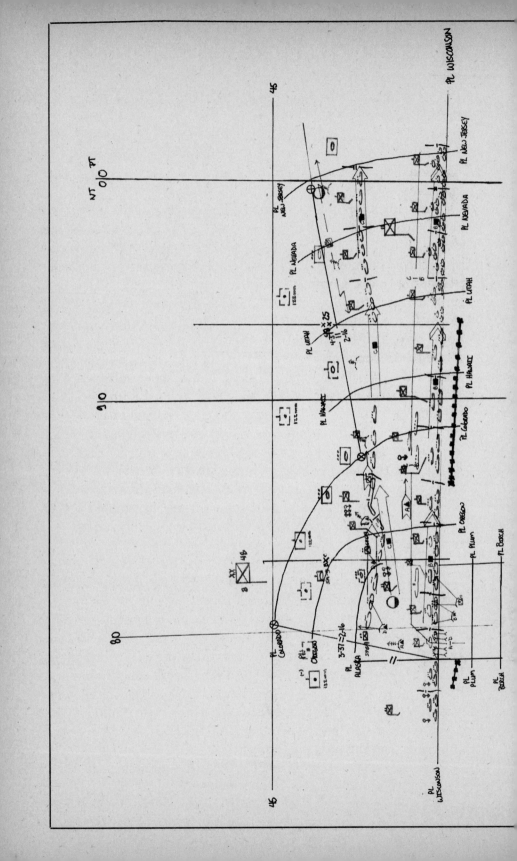

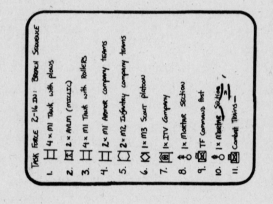

TASK FORCE 2-16 IN: BREACH SEQUENCE

1. ⊟ 4× M1 Tank with plows
2. ⊠ 2× AVLM (MICLIC)
3. ⊟ 4× M1 Tank with Rollers
4. ⊟ 2× M1 Armor company teams
5. ⬚ 2× M2 Infantry company teams
6. ◁ 1× M3 Scout platoon
7. ▣ 1× ITV Company
8. ⚲ 1× Mortar Section
9. ⊡ TF Command Post
10. ⚲ 1× Machine Section
11. ⬛ Combat Trains

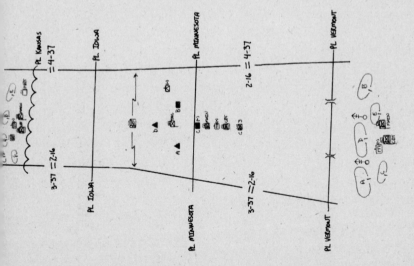

The 1st Infantry Division (Big Red One), 2nd Battalion, 16th Infantry map overlay showing their battle plan for breaching the "Saddam Line" along the Iraq-Saudi Arabia border.

attack north along the coast road, slamming into the remnants of the Iraqi 5th Mechanized Division which had been largely destroyed in the botched battle of Khafji. JAF-W, with the Egyptians in the lead, made slight progress but did succeed in crossing the burning trenches before the end of the day. The 2nd Marine Division, farther north along the heel of Kuwait, was given an objective closer to their line of departure for the first day's attack in order to keep the Allies' line from forming a potentially dangerous salient in the center. They, too, successfully reached their first day's objective against light resistance and took many Iraqis prisoner.

While the main fighting force of VII Corps waited for the 1st Infantry Division to secure their breach for the next day, the 2nd Armored Cavalry Regiment had moved nineteen miles into Iraq and the XVIII Corps was moving north, pouring across the Iraqi border and racing to the Euphrates. The first to fight were the French, who were assigned to take a critical road junction in the middle of the desert—an objective they named "Rochambeau." After crossing their line of departure at 0530 hours, the French, with Gazelle helicopters in the lead providing forward reconnaissance, neutralized a brigade defending an Iraqi communications outpost located at Rochambeau and quickly occupied the objective with their ground forces. They then set up a hasty defensive perimeter during the evening to prepare to take their objective for the next day, the town of As Salman, defended by the very effective and near-full-strength 45th Iraqi Infantry Division. The 101st Infantry Division moved by helicopter fifty miles into Iraq. Four battalions of infantry carved out a huge piece of desert twenty miles in diameter, each occupying a corner blocking position to defend. A huge logistics base was established inside the perimeter formed by these battalions and the division brought in thousands of tons of fuel, ammunition, and supplies to support the coming days' attacks north. The place was known as Log Base Cobra. Late in the afternoon a brigade of infantry was pushed northward toward Nasiriya, the next day's objective.

Once the 101st and the French were successfully in place, the 3rd Cavalry and the 24th Division crossed the line of departure in a blinding sandstorm at 1500 hours on the twenty-fourth. They had taken advantage of their long-range scouts who had signaled back that there weren't any significant Iraqi defenses to stop them. By 1900 they had driven hundreds of tanks and armored vehicles undetected twenty-five miles into Iraq.

In Washington, the start of the ground campaign brought about a drop-off in official information about the war. In a brief and terse statement to the press, Defense Secretary Cheney said that there would be much less information forthcoming from the Pentagon in order to preserve the operational security of the offensive phase of the war. The president announced that the liberation of Kuwait had entered its final phase.

The Battle of As Salman

Just before dawn on the twenty-fifth, leading elements of the French Division reached out beyond Objective Rochambeau to the north. The morning's mission was to seize Objective White, which was a large defensive position near the crossroads town of As Salman. The position had been occupied by the Iraqi 45th Infantry Division, which was, despite the air campaign, still at nearly 75 percent strength. But the Iraqis were oriented with their combat power—five infantry battalions, two tank battalions, and an antitank company—to stop an Allied drive to the northwest out of Kuwait. It was as if the Iraqis were expecting the coalition ground forces to drive on Baghdad; they never anticipated an attack from the south.

But that was precisely where the French and the 82nd Airborne were coming from. In the early morning hours the French swept through the 45th Division. With their Gazelle helicopters in the lead, the French picked off Iraqi tanks from two to three thousand yards away. The Iraqis never knew what hit them. As tank turrets flew into the air from the impact of the French HOT antitank missiles, AMX-30 tanks swept through, firing up artillery pieces and FROG missiles.

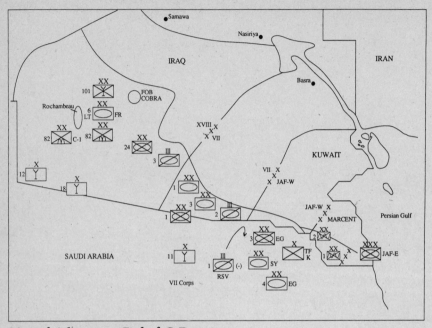

Line of Advance at End of G-Day

The airborne troopers and mechanized infantry platoons cleared out bunkers throughout the area, and a French camera crew picked up the action, sending back brilliant videotape of the combined arms action. It was a textbook example of the coordination of helicopters, artillery, tanks, and infantry. The most impressive sight was the surrender of hundreds of Iraqi soldiers. As the French infantry squads methodically checked each hole in the ground, dazed Iraqi soldiers emerged, gratefully surrendering to the conquerors.

It was pitiful, and the commander of the U.S. airborne brigade remarked, "Every soldier I saw surrendered." The French commander quickly brought the American engineers forward to clear the roads for the forward movement of the rest of the XVIII Corps' support forces. By mid-afternoon it was all over; Objective White was secure. They had taken over 2,900 prisoners while suffering three killed and fifty wounded.

By 0150 hours on the twenty-fifth, the 101st Airborne had reached its objectives along the Euphrates River, sealing off High-

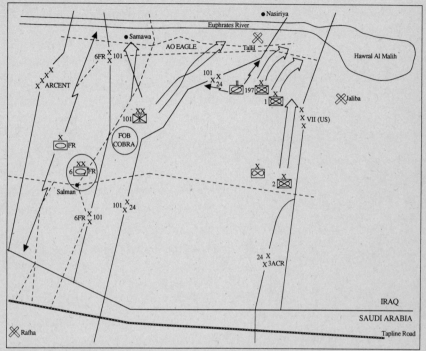

XVIII Corps Operations, February 25, 1991

way Eight at key points in a wide open space designated as "Area of Operations Eagle." AO Eagle stretched from Samawa to Nasiriya, giving the Air Assault Division a front of over fifty miles to cover. Infantry battalions placed at key places provided direct blocking positions while attack helicopters served as mobile reserves.

The 3rd Cavalry served as a screen on the far right of the XVIII Corps sector while the powerful 24th Mechanized Infantry Division began its drive to the Euphrates on the ground. The division's 2nd Brigade and 197th Infantry Brigade seized blocking positions on the As Salman–Bussayah Road and the 1st Brigade pushed north of the road taking up a blocking position just south of Tallil and Jalibah airfields. From these positions the division prepared to attack Iraqi forces defending near those airfields the next day. The Iraqis still had no idea of the kind of combat power that was lurking in their rear areas.

The Battle of Burgan Oil Field

The Marines of the 1st Division had been preparing all night for their attack on al Jaber airfield and the Burgan oil field. The air was dripping with oil from the spurting wells, and although they were aflame, the crude still fell from the sky in an oozy drizzle mixed in with the chilly fog. Many Marines had begun to develop respiratory ailments; before it was over several would come down with pneumonia. They fought on anyway.

The airfield was defended by an Iraqi brigade, the oil field was protected by the better part of a division. Task Forces Grizzly and Taro provided flank security while Task Force Ripper swept across the airfield neutralizing the one Iraqi brigade defending. Task Force Papa Bear followed, moving around the oil field since it was too hot to go close to the wells themselves, while Task Force Shepherd moved around to the north of the field itself where it was feasible to proceed. After an intense artillery preparation, Papa Bear found itself in the midst of two tank brigades trying to conduct a counterattack into the advancing Marines. In the murk of the oil fires and the artillery, the Iraqis could not get their attack together to stop the advancing Marines. Parts of four divisions, the 15th, 5th, 50th, and 20th, had been brought together by an Iraqi general desperately trying to comply with his impossible orders from Saddam Hussein. The Marines had bypassed one brigade from the 20th Division, which tried to counterattack to the north once they realized they were in the Marines' rear. But it was to no avail—the Marines countered every move of the Iraqis with tanks, antitank missile firing armored vehicles, or Cobra attack helicopters. By the end of the twenty-fifth, the Marines were solidly in control of the objectives that had been assigned to them for the next day and were taking thousands of Iraqi prisoners.

There had been several surprises for the Marines in the battle of Burgan oil field. One was that a few T-72 tanks had been spotted participating in the battle. It had been thought that only the Republican Guard had T-72s and that these regular army divisions did not have them. Yet here they were, though they proved to be no problem for the attack helicopters or TOW missiles the Marines used against them.

The other surprise was the condition of the Iraqi soldiers. Those who were surrendering were obviously shell-shocked, hungry, and glad to be taken prisoner by Americans who they knew would treat them better than their own army had. The Marines had seen this as they moved forward the day before, but on the twenty-fifth the numbers of surrendering Iraqis began to swell enormously. The surprise, though, was in the conditions under which their officers had been living. They had clearly not been suffering the same hardships as their men in the trenches. Task Force Ripper uncovered one officer's bunker that had an operational air-conditioner and a fully stocked refrigerator. Sleeping mats and overstuffed chairs provided them with a luxuriously appointed staff meeting room and U.S. Meals-Ready-to-Eat (MRE) were available as well.

By 1930 hours on the twenty-fifth the 1st Marines had secured their objectives and turned their attention to the east, toward Kuwait City, which would be their next objective area. In the battle of Burgan oil field they had defeated about the equivalent of a division, destroying eighty Iraqi tanks in the process and taking 2,200 prisoners of war. One Iraqi brigade commander had valiantly remained with his troops, but saw the futility of his efforts and decided to surrender.

The 2nd Marine Division had run through its objective area as well and was by now occupying a blocking position just south of the main road intersection west of Kuwait City. During the day the 4th Marine Amphibious Brigade had conducted an amphibious demonstration at As Shuaybah to reinforce in the Iraqis' minds that the main attack was yet to come in the form of a major landing. Meanwhile the 5th Marine Amphibious Brigade came ashore farther south in Saudi Arabia to serve as the Marines' reserve force.

The advance of JAF-E and JAF-W had been slower than anticipated. By the twenty-fifth they had moved only a couple of miles north into Kuwait and were now lagging behind the Marines immediately on their west and east. At 1530 on the twenty-fourth the Kuwaiti "Shaheed," or "martyr," brigade had been the first of JAF-E to cross, followed by the Qataris, then the Saudi Royal Land Forces brigades and the brigade from Bahrain. The Saudi Army National Guard had been left to screen the border and to serve as a mobile reserve if needed. By 0400 on the twenty-fifth the Saudis had reached Al Zour but their advance had been slowed by the thousands of surrendering Iraqis. The Egyptian Armored Division had been first across for JAF-W, followed by the Syrian Division, then the Egyptian Mechanized Division. If the Iraqi mechanized forces positioned just ahead of the Arab forces could reorganize themselves with the time given to them by the delay of JAF-E and JAF-W, the Iraqis might be able to mount a counterattack on the now dangerously exposed Marines who were in effect in a salient.

The Marines were in an operational dilemma. They had advanced more rapidly than they had planned and were now on a line that they had not expected to get to until the next day. They could use a halt to regroup, but they also had the Iraqis on the run and disorganized. The 1st Marine Division commander, General Mike Myatt, faced a crucial decision point. He could order a halt in place to allow the Arabs to catch up, but that would risk allowing the Iraqis in their sector to flee and prepare to fight again on another day. Or he could order his leathernecks to continue to advance, taking that risk in order to catch the greater part of several Iraqi divisions on the run or by surprise. In the end, he reasoned that if they were going to die it would be better to do it at one hundred miles per hour than standing in place. He told his operations officer that he had no intention of dying anyway, and he ordered the division to prepare to continue the attack early the next morning.

The Battle of Busayya

In the VII Corps sector, the 1st Infantry Division had worked through the night to clear open twenty-four lanes through the

Saddam Line. At 1200 hours on the twenty-fifth, the British 1st
Armored Division began passing through, an operation that took
until 0200 hours to complete. West of the British, the U.S. 2nd
Armored Cavalry reconnoitered the way into Iraq. On the Corps'
left flank, the 1st and 3rd Armored Divisions had cut their own
breaching lanes through the border berm beyond the Iraqis' defensive positions, where there was little opposition.

The British Division turned east after passing through the
breach and immediately attacked into the Iraqi 12th Armor Division, which was at about half strength. By the end of the day the
British had silenced all opposition in their objective area and prepared to continue to move east. They had destroyed 200 tanks, 100
APCs, 100 artillery pieces and had taken 5,000 Iraqi prisoners.
They had lost twelve of their own killed in action, including the
tragic loss of nine to friendly fire from an American A-10 that had
mistakenly fired on a British Warrior Infantry Fighting Vehicle.

Northeast of the British fight, the American units in VII Corps
ran into the Iraqi 26th Infantry Division. The 26th was still in
fighting condition at about 75 percent strength, but they were
completely surprised and totally overwhelmed by the size and
speed of the attack on the twenty-fifth. The 3rd Armored Division attacked into one brigade of the Iraqi 26th; 1st Armor attacked another; and the XVIII Corps' 24th Mechanized Infantry
Division hit the other brigade and the division command post.
There was a stiff fight, but the battle was over by 1200 on the
twenty-sixth. The VII Corps then turned east from Busayya, using
the British as the pivot point to take on the Republican Guard.

The Battle of 73 Easting

On military mapsheets, grid lines are superimposed over the
terrain features to give everyone a common reference system.
These grid lines are numbered and it was along the 73 north-
south grid line that the climax of the war to liberate Kuwait
occurred. The engagements that took place there from the

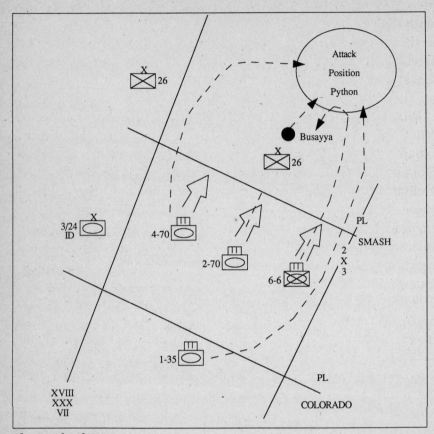

The Battle of Busayya

twenty-sixth through the early hours of the twenty-eighth of
February have been called the "Battle of 73 Easting" because there
is not much urban construction in the area, just wide open desert
crossed by ridges and wadis that form natural routes of movement and defensive lines for armored forces. Along this grid line
the VII Corps decimated the Iraqi Republican Guard.

The Republican Guard had been subjected to the most intensive aerial bombardment in history. Thousands of sorties had
been directed their way during the first three phases of the air
campaign, and when the ground offensive began the strikes grew
in magnitude. As the VII Corps neared the positions of these six
divisions, which were still at 75 percent to near full strength, the

air attack shifted to allow General Franks's tanks close contact with their enemy. General McCaffrey's 24th Division lay in wait at the northern escape route out of Kuwait while the 1st Infantry Division, now backed up by the remaining two brigades of the 1st Cavalry Division, sealed the southern edge of the line. It was to be an all-American battle.

With the 2nd Armored Cavalry Regiment in the lead, the entire VII Corps turned east and began to move on the Republican Guard. The Iraqis were still expecting the Americans to attack from the south up the wadi and were facing the wrong way when Colonel Don Holder's cavalry troopers made first contact with them. Behind the cavalry, 1st and 3rd Armored advanced, tightening their frontages as they moved to concentrate their firepower. By mid-afternoon on the twenty-sixth, the regiment had fixed the locations of elements of the Tawakalna and Adnan Republican Guard divisions and had run into positions held by the regular army 52nd Armored Division. Some were holding their position and returning fire; others seemed to be moving north toward Basra.

While the cavalry was in contact, General Franks ordered his two armor divisions to pass through to the north and take on the Iraqis with the full fury of their armored firepower. Both divisions preceded their tank attacks with a massive barrage of artillery and Multiple Launch Rocket System fires followed by attacks on Iraqi T-72 tanks by Apache attack helicopters. As the Apaches broke off to rearm and refuel, the artillery fired another barrage into the Republican Guard, pinning them down and destroying trucks and APCs. The sequence was repeated before the tanks and Bradley fighting vehicles of the 1st and 3rd Armored Division slammed into the Iraqi positions. The 1st Infantry Division was called up from the south. It passed through the 2nd Cavalry and was thrown into the attack against the Tawakalna Division's southern flank brigade and a brigade of the adjoining Iraqi 12th Tank Division.

Apache helicopters were also sent deep into the Republican Guard positions, striking the Medina Division in its defensive area. By late afternoon the entire VII Corps was in contact with the Iraqi Republican Guard, the Tawakalna Division had been overrun, and the Iraqis' main logistics area had been captured. Thousands of tons of supplies had been stockpiled by the Republican Guard. One division commander told me that in his estimate they had enough ammunition and food to defend for two years, and that he had never seen so much ammunition in his entire Army career. It was to take weeks for the American forces in Iraq after the war to destroy all the ammunition stockpiled by the Iraqis.

The Mother of All Retreats

But the Iraqis were not finished. On the twenty-sixth Saddam Hussein realized that he had been outmaneuvered and was about to be annihilated. The 2nd Marine Division, with the Tiger Brigade, had taken Jahra, west of Kuwait City, and sealed off any escape routes for his divisions along the coast. The forces that had been so prepared to defend against an amphibious assault were overrun, had surrendered, or were putting up a final stand at the Kuwait City International Airport. The 1st Marines finished off that fight. Saddam had lost over half of his army in less than two days of fighting, but he still had his best forces in some semblance of order. He gave the order to withdraw, starting what became, in U.S. Defense Secretary Dick Cheney's words, "The Mother of All Retreats."

The movement to the north was immediately picked up by the JSTARS aircraft. The two roads leading out of Kuwait City were jammed with traffic from Iraqis who had given up their military pretensions and tried to leave with at least some loot to show for their months of occupation and weeks of suffering under the Allied air campaign. With the Marines blocking the road south, Central Command turned loose the air forces to strike the fleeing Iraqis along the highway leading north to Basra.

The Air Force knew well how to stop a convoy, even though the Iraqi movement was not at all organized into anything resembling a tactical road march. Strike fighters hit the vehicles at the head of the column blocking the road and causing a massive six-lane-wide traffic jam with thousands of cars, trucks, and military vehicles lined up behind. Ironically, the line of vehicles was backed up to the very place where the Iraqis had planned to spring an ambush on the Allied forces pushing in from the sea. For hours, Allied pilots struck the vehicles on the road with impunity, destroying them with devastating precision. Most Iraqis abandoned their vehicles but many did not escape. It came to be called the "Highway to Hell," and later photographs verified the apocalyptic nature of the destruction along this route. Flying over the scene a few days after the war, I thought it seemed to be a scene straight from Dante's *Inferno*.

The Iraqi forces north of Kuwait City tried to withdraw along the desert ridges and wadis that run generally south to north into the Euphrates River valley. The VII Corps arrayed all along the 73 grid line were waiting for them. For nearly two days the Corps fought and continued to advance to the east. The 2nd Armored Cavalry was counterattacked by a brigade from the Iraqi 52nd Tank Division. Later interrogation of Iraqi officers revealed that Saddam's forces still had not realized what was happening. This counterattack was a contingency plan designed to cut off a main road supporting an attack up the wadi. The Iraqi commander exclaimed to Colonel Holder, "Everywhere I looked there were tanks and more tanks; the whole earth shook!"

The attack was repelled in fierce tank-on-tank fighting. Some Iraqi tanks got so close that some of the regiment's Bradley fighting vehicles fired their 25mm cannon at the advancing tanks in desperation. To their surprise the cavalrymen found that the cannon's depleted uranium bullets, which had been designed to be used only against armored personnel carriers and other lightly armored vehicles, penetrated Soviet-made T-62 and T-55 tanks' frontal armor.

The Battle of Medina Ridge

While the 3rd Armored Division completed the destruction of the Tawakalna and 52nd Armored Divisions, the U.S. 1st Armored

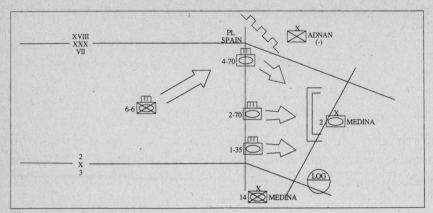

The Battle of Medina Ridge

Division pushed a brigade through to engage the Medina Division. At about 1200 on the twenty-seventh of February, the 2nd Brigade of the 1st Armored Division spotted dozens of Iraqi tanks dug in to the reverse slope of a ridge line over a mile or so away. The Iraqis were the 2nd Brigade of the Medina Division reinforced with about a battalion from the 14th Mechanized Division, arrayed in a solid line about six miles long. They had moved up to a defensive line in the path of the advancing American forces to stop the attack and cover the withdrawal of the remainder of the Iraqi forces in the KTO.

Using their thermal sights to see through a sandstorm, the M-1 tank crews took precise aim at the Iraqi T-72s and rapidly destroyed them all. The Iraqis fired back at the muzzle flashes of the American tanks, but because they had dug themselves in with the crest of the ridge between them and the oncoming Americans, they could not elevate their guns to get off an effective shot. It would not have mattered anyway since the Abramses were firing from beyond the range of the Iraqis' Soviet-made T-72 tanks.

Artillery, attack helicopters, and close airstrikes added their firepower to the battle, and it was all over in less than forty minutes in the early afternoon of the twenty-seventh of February. The 1st Armored division had totally destroyed the defending Iraqis, killing sixty of Iraq's most advanced T-72 tanks equipped with laser range finders and nine older T-55s. Only fifty-five prisoners were taken. One cavalryman in the 2nd Armored Cavalry Regiment called it a corner of hell.

The Battle of Bloody Heels

North of VII Corps, the 24th Infantry Division, now with operational control of the 3rd Armored Cavalry Regiment, attacked to seize the Iraqi airfields at Tallil and Jalibah. Jalibah was defended by about a battalion-sized force from the Adnan Republican Guard division. There were still a number of Iraqi fighter jets on the runway apparently not hit by the Allied air campaign, although they obviously were not being flown from the base either.

The division's first and second brigades attacked the field beginning early on the morning of the twenty-seventh. They caught the Iraqis by surprise, but a company of T-55 tanks opened fire on the advancing lead Bradleys. Abrams tanks were brought up and artillery quickly silenced the defenders. As the men of the Victory Division swept across the airfield there was yet another case of friendly fire, this time from tanks of one brigade mistaking Bradleys of the other for enemy vehicles.

As the 24th moved in, the Iraqis came out. A hundred or more eventually emerged to surrender to the division. One lieutenant noticed that many of the Iraqi soldiers' feet were bare and bloody. He figured that they had run out of supplies and could not get replacements for worn-out boots, but after interrogating several Iraqi prisoners it turned out not to be so. In fact, the bloody heels had come as a result of wounds inflicted on the men by their officers. Fearing that their soldiers would attempt to flee into the hands of the advancing Americans, the Iraqi officers had deliberately sliced their soldiers' Achilles tendons, rendering them incapable of moving very far in any direction. Having thus protected their own reputations from the ignominy of desertion, those officers then fled to the north themselves.

After consolidating their hold on the airfields, the 24th continued its attack to the east, moving at 1300 hours toward the Rumaila oil field, which had been the ostensible object of the whole crisis between Kuwait and Iraq in the summer of 1990. The Adnan Republican Guard Division occupied positions around Ar Rumaila Airport Southwest, and at 0800 on the twenty-seventh a battalion of the 1st Armored Division, which was operating slightly out of its own assigned sector, ran into a reinforced infantry battalion just south of the airfield. The 1st Armored fixed the position and hit it with artillery. The 24th Division marched into it, crushing the remainder of the Adnan Division and forcing the Nebuchadnezzar Republican Guard Division to withdraw to the north.

The Nebuchadnezzar Division raced across a major water obstacle, the Hawr al Hammar, a lake fed by the Euphrates River, by speeding over a recently built causeway just west of Basra. In the process, the 24th overran another huge Iraqi logistics site containing over 1,300 bunkers filled with artillery and air force ammunition. It had been left largely intact by the Allied air campaign.

At 1700 hours on the twenty-seventh, VII Corps forces had been notified that a cease-fire was imminent. All elements of the Corps were to push as far as they could as fast as they could go in order to complete the sealing off of Kuwait from Iraq before the cease-fire was implemented. The 1st Infantry pushed its helicopters beyond its front lines to the Basra road and the coastline. The 1st Armor conducted an attack east beginning at 0530 on the twenty-eighth, catching the remnants of the Medina Division fleeing toward Basra.

General Schwarzkopf had informed General Powell and the president that he was close to completing his mission of ejecting Iraqi forces from Kuwait and eliminating the offensive threat from the Iraqi military machine. While the exact sequence of the discussion among the president and his military advisers was a matter of some public debate a few weeks later when Schwarzkopf seemed to state in an interview that he had desired to continue the attack for a while longer, the president issued a cease-fire order to become effective on the twenty-eighth at 0800 hours Kuwait time. It would be exactly one hundred hours since the beginning of the ground war.

The Marines had encircled Kuwait City and watched as soldiers from JAF-E were passed through to conduct the liberation of the city. A number of reporters, including CNN's Charles Jaco, had raced ahead to send back live pictures from inside the city as the Arab forces entered. By 0800 the cease-fire order was in effect. The Allies halted offensive operations and consolidated their positions. On the twenty-ninth the 1st Infantry was ordered to move north to Safwan, Iraq, to secure the airfield there, which was to be the site for military-to-military cease-fire negotiations. The airfield was still occupied by Iraqi defenders, who nonetheless vacated their positions when informed of the cease-fire and issued an ultimatum by the Big Red One's interpreters.

Inside Kuwait City, Allied forces began the tedious process of rooting out the last pockets of resistance. Several Iraqis remained in the city as snipers but they were all cleared out over the next few hours. Many fled to safety in the hands of the U.S. Marines after they were pursued by members of the Kuwaiti Resistance bent on revenge. U.S. Special Forces troops moved into the embassy compound with military versions of dune buggies for transportation. The embassy compound was carefully checked and cleared of the many booby traps the Iraqis had left. But surprisingly, they had neglected to take down the American flag, which still waved proudly overhead. In a dramatic outdoor ceremony, U.S. Ambassador Edward "Skip" Gnehm resumed his post and began superintending the daunting task of helping to rebuild Kuwait.

One Last Shot

But it was not quite over yet. Not all Iraqi forces had gotten the word that they would not be fired on if they held their positions, and some did not believe that they would be allowed to pass if they just laid down their arms. At about 0630 hours on March 2,

Barry McCaffrey's 24th Infantry Division scouts detected the movement of a large armored column northward on the road to the causeway across the Hawr al Hammar. By the time they could get closer to investigate, about two hundred Iraqi vehicles had slipped across the causeway and hundreds more were arrayed to follow. Many tanks were on heavy equipment transporter trucks; some were moving tactically along the road obviously providing cover for the movement.

McCaffrey had his 1st Brigade move forward to challenge the move, ordering the Iraqis to stop or be fired on. The Iraqi response was an artillery barrage that landed among his troops. He ordered the brigade to attack the column, careful not to engage those Iraqi vehicles that had already escaped across the causeway though they were within range of the 24th's artillery and attack helicopters, and to stop firing when the Iraqis showed sign of surrender. The Iraqis did not stop; they continued to move north into an engagement area executed by the division's armor, mechanized helicopter, and artillery forces. When it was over, the division had destroyed another 187 armored vehicles, thirty-four artillery pieces, over four hundred wheeled vehicles, and nine multiple rocket launchers. About a battalion of the Iraqis got the message and halted, saving approximately forty armored vehicles and two hundred trucks from a similar fate. By 1500 hours on March 2, the last shots of the war had been fired.

The Talks at Safwan

Safwan, Iraq, is a rather isolated place. It springs out of the middle of the desert between Kuwait City and Basra around wells that provide water for about 25,000 people. There had been an airfield there with a single asphalt strip tucked up against a rocky hill that jutted up from the desert floor. The U.S. 1st Infantry Division had secured the site and set up a meeting tent and special communications sites for U.S. and Allied leaders to use for consultations. It was to be used for talks between the Allies and the Iraqis in setting forth the terms for the formal ending of the war.

Through an unusual set of circumstances, I had become CNN's Washington anchorman for the live coverage of the talks. I sat in the studio from 2 A.M. until 8 A.M. engaged in discussion and commentary with the Atlanta anchor, Jonathan Mann, and reporters around the world as we witnessed the historic moment live via satellite.

The Iraqi delegation was first to arrive. They had been picked up in an American Bradley fighting vehicle at a secret location and escorted to a sequestered area away from the meeting tent. General Schwarzkopf and Prince Khalid arrived later in heavy security and walked briskly to the tent. As they walked, Schwarzkopf issued instructions to the 1st Infantry Division officers who would bring the Iraqis in front of the cameras to the tent—the Iraqis were not to be disarmed or humiliated.

The Iraqi delegation arrived shortly afterward, appearing rested and clean though somewhat bewildered by it all. The talks apparently went well for the Allies. A few hours after they began, Schwarzkopf and Khalid emerged to announce that the Iraqis had agreed to all the Allies' demands and would soon be allowed to disengage near Basra, while a demilitarized zone around the Kuwaiti border was created. Eventually United Nations forces would replace Allied forces in the zone and take over responsibility for the growing refugee problem in the area.

At the cessation of hostilities, Allied forces began immediately to serve the needs of local citizens for food, water, medical care, and sanitary conditions. Soon thousands came to the Allies not only for basic needs but increasingly for political asylum. Within days, Iraqis around Basra, Nasiriyah, and Najif took up arms against their government in an attempt to eject the Iraqi army from their towns and cities, but it was to no avail. The Allies had not annihilated the Republican Guard; they had only defeated them. There was enough fight left in them to put down the insurrections in several weeks of ruthless fighting, some even in holy places. A similar fate awaited the Kurds in the north who took up arms, although the Allies later created safe havens to protect Kurdish citizens from further attacks.

But the war with Iraq was over. In the Kuwaiti Theater of Operations, Iraq had deployed 4,550 tanks, 2,880 other armored fighting vehicles, and 3,257 artillery pieces. The war had caused the destruction of 3,847 tanks, 1,450 fighting vehicles, and 2,917 artillery pieces. The remaining 1,600-plus tanks in the Iraqi army will not be likely to invade a neighbor soon, but they do form the core around which Saddam Hussein may be able to rebuild an offensive force in the near future. More important, Iraq maintains over five hundred combat aircraft throughout the country, although the best fighters were destroyed by the Allied air campaign. The most telling destruction was to the Iraqi air-defense network, which had been one of the most effective in the world. It was utterly devastated and will not be soon rebuilt. Most important, Iraq's capability to design, build, produce, and deploy weapons of mass destruction has been set back at least ten years, if not more. The Persian Gulf War had achieved its objectives of ejecting Iraq from Kuwait and eliminating the offensive military power of Iraq.

CHAPTER EIGHT

How This War Was Won

THE IRAQI ARMY was well trained, battle-tested, and highly skilled at conducting combat operations after eight years of war with Iran and two years of continued building and expansion after the end of that war. It was basically a medium-technology, Third-World armed force, the kind anticipated by many of us as the frequency of mid-intensity conflicts increases in the post–Cold War era. Its strength was its mass that, once in motion, developed a powerful momentum.

In the concluding months of the Iran-Iraq War, Iraqi forces outnumbered Iranian defenders sometimes by as much as twelve to one. In the Kuwait Theater of Operations, Allied officials contend that Iraqi forces had a numerical advantage in tanks and fighting troops—as opposed to support troops—of as much as three to one. In the end, the Iraqi leaders betrayed their soldiers, and their experiences against Iran were no preparation for what the Allies did to them. The constant aerial, artillery, and naval gunfire pounding broke the will to fight for more than half of the defending Iraqis. Those who had some fight left in them were swiftly and violently outmaneuvered and destroyed by the most effective armor lightning thrust in history.

Superior People

The Allies fought with largely volunteer forces. America's all-volunteer force did not happen by default. It was carefully built and preserved out of the hollow force that had been allowed to develop in the 1970s. It capitalized on the natural American talents for self-motivation and self-improvement, which were disciplined and allowed to flourish in a force that encouraged people to excel.

These good people had good leaders. To be sure, there were a few exceptions, but the overwhelming majority of the military leaders of the campaign were men and women of character, integrity, skill, and experience. Professionalism permeates the entire officer and noncommissioned officer corps; that did not happen by accident. Single-mindedness of purpose, vision for the ultimate outcome of the fight, and perseverance in adversity characterized the national leadership behind the force. President Bush appointed the right people to lead the effort, gave them the resources to conduct the fight, and provided the national and international leadership to see it through to a successful conclusion. He was helped in this effort by a Secretary of State, Secretary of Defense, and Chairman of the Joint Chiefs of Staff who supported these efforts well. Special recognition should be made of the fact that the theater commander-in-chief, General H. Norman Schwarzkopf, was uniquely suited to the role called for in the Allied commander.

The U.S. Congress was also important in providing the democratic leadership support of the force in the field. Several leaders in the Congress provided key support on a number of votes leading up to the deployment and initiation of hostilities. And during the deployment and fighting, a number of congressional delegations traveled to the theater to visit the troops and find out from commanders what other support the Congress could provide.

U.S. military force structures underwent a fundamental transformation during the 1980s. All the services had shed their post-Vietnam organizations by the mid-1970s, but the conversion to an all-volunteer force had devastated the armed forces. In the 1970s, too many holdover draftees, who should have been released, hung on far too long. Discontent permeated the ranks, while drug and alcohol abuse were rampant. Pay was miserably low, and motivation to work suffered from the lack of a sense of mission. The problems had caused Army Chief of Staff General Edward C. "Shy" Meyer to testify at one point before Congress that the United States had a "hollow" force.

The buildup and modernization of the 1980s changed all that. New equipment was purchased, pay and allowances were raised substantially, and training conditions improved. More important, U.S. forces were given a new strategic focus. After the Arab-Israeli War of 1973, the concept of combined arms warfare was felt to be the best means to meet the most important threat—the Soviet conventional military machine—that U.S. forces would have to be prepared to meet, especially in what was then the most threatened theater of potential war, the central plains of Europe.

Army divisions, Air Force, and Navy fighter wings and ships were reorganized from top to bottom. Battleships were brought out of mothballs and refitted with new high-technology radar and missiles. New frigates were designed, and new classes of cruisers, capable of managing complex battle campaigns, were created. Aircraft organization became more diverse, integrating ever more advanced technologies into ever more sophisticated and complex squadrons and wings for air superiority, defense suppression, close air support, interdiction, and strategic bombing. Ground forces became highly specialized, with the Marines concentrating on amphibious operations while the Army developed eight kinds of infantry, among other kinds of forces.

All of this required investments of time and money in developing the right organizational schemes to exploit both new technology and the steadily increasing quality of people coming into the force. Many experiments were conducted and some organizational ideas were discarded. Innovation was encouraged; the only bad idea was the one not raised for consideration.

One idea that was widely hailed at the time of its inception was that of the "total force." This was the idea that some part of the armed forces could be in the reserves or the National Guard, where costs were lower because the organizations did not train on a full-time basis. For World War II, the reserves had been mobilized as a huge new force with each division being formed up from scratch, trained as basic fighters, put through the paces of larger unit maneuvers, and then shipped off to the war as a whole.

The problem with this approach was that it took so long to get entire divisions, and even larger corps, ready to go to the war that, had the Germans and Japanese been only a little more powerful or more fortunate on the battlefield, there might not have been sufficient time to wait. After the war, military leaders wanted forces that were ready to fight on short notice.

Increasingly, in the 1980s, the Defense Department could not afford to man all the complete divisions, ships, and wings that it felt were necessary to deter the Soviet threat, so greater reliance was placed on the reserves. The total-force policy was designed to incorporate greater reliance on the reserves without creating new vulnerabilities from long training times after call-up. The design was to have much of the logistics infrastructure of the active forces in the reserves and most of the combat power on active duty most of the time. A somewhat delicate balancing act was maintained between being ready to fight on a moment's notice and building in some reaction time to a developing crisis, for if all potential crises had to be met with forces in being, the country would likely go bankrupt in the attempt to finance such a large standing force.

Eventually, by the mid-1980s, much of the combat power of the force was also in the reserve or National Guard structure. Many air wings required for early deployment contingencies were in the Air National Guard, and much of the military airlift capability and all of the air interceptor squadrons for defense of the continental United States went to the Guard or the reserves. In Desert Storm these air units performed their tasks well, while some ground units did have difficulties.

The Army and Marine Corps chose different paths to integrating reservists and National Guardsmen into their forces. The

Army took a two-tiered approach. Individuals and small units were given support roles such as supply, transportation, civil affairs, and administration, among others. Combat functions were largely reserved for the active force, with the exception of a few brigades. These "round-out" brigades were formed and trained within particular geographic regions and were designed to become part of active duty divisions when a national emergency or war was declared.

Those active duty divisions assigned Guard brigades were reduced in strength proportionately, so that to get an entire full-strength division to the field, its affiliated National Guard brigade was needed. It was assumed by force planners that a certain short amount of train-up time was needed and would be available to get these Guard brigades ready to go with their active duty counterparts.

In Desert Storm it did not work out that way. The 24th Infantry Division had only two brigades in peacetime; it was to rely on its round-out brigade, the 48th Georgia National Guard, if it were to be called into action. When Operation Desert Shield was ordered in August 1990, the 48th was not called to active duty, and the 24th Infantry went to Saudi Arabia with another, separate brigade from the active force. When the 48th was later called to active service, it was not declared ready for deployment before the war ended. Other National Guard round-out units had serious disciplinary problems.

The Marines had a different approach to the integration of reservists. The Marine Corps kept its force structure almost entirely in its active components and pursued a "round-up" approach. With this idea, a fully combat-ready Marine division consisted of three brigades, all in the active forces. Additional combat and support units were in the reserves and were designated to be added to the Marine divisions if they ever were deployed in combat. Most Marine operations in peacetime are at brigade level or below, and rarely do the Marines expect to operate a full division in the field as a complete force. This is a function of the role the Marines are called on to perform as the nation's primary contingency force around the globe.

Thus, when the Marines were called on to deploy two divisions in Desert Storm, reserve battalions were integrated into division task forces already formed from among the active battalions in the divisions. Virtually all the combat power of the Marines was in Saudi Arabia by December, including substantial portions of the Marine Corps Reserve.

This experience must cause Pentagon force planners to re-evaluate the total-force concept. While the integration of reservists and Guardsmen on an individual or small unit basis worked for supporting forces, the reliance on larger units for combat arms must be reassessed in the light of Desert Storm. If the practice is to be continued, either more time must be planned for before deployment or more resources will be needed to keep Guard combat brigades ready to deploy on short notice.

The greatest payoff from the attention given in the 1980s was in training. Huge investments were made in modern training facilities such as at Nellis Air Force Base, where pilots routinely practice their skills in mock aerial combat with a specially trained and equipped "aggressor" squadron that employs enemy tactics. The Navy's version of this concept was popularized in the motion picture *Top Gun*. The Army and Marine Corps have built huge training complexes in the U.S. desert Southwest, where entire brigades operate in a near-combat environment against a foe that practices enemy tactics. It is the most realistic training in the world. The soldiers I spoke to in Iraq just after the war's end credited their National Training Center experience with giving them the confidence they needed on the eve of battle. Many said that the Iraqis were not anywhere near as proficient in combat as were the NTC Opposing Forces soldiers.

Much of this training was made possible by the development of sophisticated training devices and simulators. Pilots can push the performance of their aircraft to their limits and suffer a "crash" without danger to valuable jets or risk to human life. Low-power laser beams replace bullets and missiles while sensors can detect target "hits" to let people know when they have been careless or caught off guard. Extensive computer networks keep track of every engagement and movement to evaluate the performance of individuals and weapons afterward from every possible vantage point.

Another element of the way the people of Desert Storm worked together so well was the set of command relationships put in place for the war effort. Whenever large armies are fielded, the sheer size of the force requires the appointment of several generals to command the force. A 700,000-man army is too much for one general to command by himself. Problems can arise when subordinate generals are forced to work together under one of their own, especially at the highest levels. The basic problem is that the self-confidence, aggressiveness, and accomplishment that are the prerequisites for successful command make it hard for such a person also to be a team player. Personal rivalries can become institutional rivalries as well. Thus, over the years, the American military establishment had developed particular service approaches to warfare in the Army, Navy, Air Force, and Marines that often reduce the effectiveness of U.S. forces operating together or "jointly."

As we saw in the sitzkrieg stage of the war, the Goldwater-Nichols Act was the key element toward remedying that situation. Among other things it attempted to tear down the walls of rivalry that had been built up over the years among the military services that increasingly had come to hinder combat operations. Congress pointed to operations such as the ill-fated Iranian hostage rescue mission during the Carter administration, and the bombing of the Marine barracks in Beirut, Lebanon, as examples of the worst effects of interservice rivalry. Even successful campaigns such as the 1983 liberation of Grenada were seen as less than satisfying by the proponents of the measure because so many casualties might have been avoided if command arrangements had been more clear-cut.

The Goldwater-Nichols Act aimed to overcome those difficulties by legislating two measures. First, the law elevated the position of the Chairman of the Joint Chiefs of Staff and placed him in the chain of command. In the past, the chairman, while the highest-ranking military officer in the U.S. armed forces, was an adviser to the Secretary of Defense and the president, but he could not often express his own views because the old laws required him to represent the views of the other service chiefs as well, a requirement that resulted more often than not in his bringing to the nation's political leaders the least controversial positions that the five flag officers could agree on. When an individual service chief did not like the direction being taken, he could obstruct progress by holding out for his own view before the chairman could take a joint position to the Secretary of Defense.

The other part of the wall of service separation was the control the service chiefs exerted over the forces in the field. Each component of a force in the field was tied by logistics support, personnel policies, and doctrinal practice to its service headquarters rather than to the overall commander in the geographic region to which the force was assigned. This usually resulted in theater commanders having little actual control over military operations in their own areas of operations.

The Goldwater-Nichols Act cut through the wall of service separation by elevating the position of the chairman of the Joint Chiefs of Staff and by placing full command of all forces in the field squarely under the command of the commander-in-chief in the theater. In Desert Shield and Desert Storm, both General Colin Powell, Chairman of the Joint Chiefs of Staff, and the theater commander, General H. Norman Schwarzkopf, exercised this new authority with tremendous effect. General Powell made the basic decisions on what the objectives of the war were to be, the strategy to achieve them, and the forces that would be sent to the field to accomplish them. General Schwarzkopf was given wide leeway to develop the operational plan, to decide on its execution, and to resolve disagreements among air, sea, and ground components as to which would have priority at differing phases of the campaign.

Better Ideas

America's superior people were empowered by better ideas. This was not just a clash of wills, nor was it only a conflict of national interests. The Persian Gulf War brought into battle a fundamental conflict of values, strategies, and operational concepts. In the end the Allies prevailed as much because they were fighting with the right ideas as because they had great people. This was one of the few clear-cut ideological struggles of the post–World War II era. Saddam Hussein's idea was that if he wanted it he could take it. He was a dictator of the worst kind. Not only did he deny his people their basic rights as human beings, he also treacherously sacrificed their lives for his own selfish satisfaction. He was willing to sacrifice hundreds of thousands of Iraqi people for his own glory. He did so not only in this fight but in his eight-year war with Iraq as well.

The Allies held a clearly superior moral ground. Virtually the entire world agreed that what Saddam had done in taking Kuwait by force was wrong. Even those few countries that did not support the war did not deny that Saddam was wrong to take matters into his own hands by force of arms. The world recognized that Saddam's brand of aggression, like Adolf Hitler's in 1939, had to be stopped or it would spread rapidly to affect the entire world. More than any other recent conflict, the Persian Gulf War was one of right versus wrong.

The second idea that prevailed was one of strategy. Saddam Hussein was pursuing a strategy of attrition while the Allies adopted a strategy of annihilation. Saddam believed that he did not necessarily have to win on the battlefield; he merely had to outlast the Allied coalition. He was convinced that he could break up the coalition perhaps by offering separate deals to some of its less committed members. He believed that America's commitment would evaporate once casualties started to come back to the States.

He was wrong on all counts. President Bush put together an amazing international coalition in a few months' time, and he held it together even when at times it appeared that the Soviets might break the whole thing apart with their diplomatic maneuvering. Saddam also completely missed the lesson of Vietnam. He was willing to suffer a hundred thousand casualties in order to inflict a few thousand on the United States in the belief that, as with Vietnam, the American people would support a war halfway until it got rough, then cut and run. This time, indeed, Americans were not going to support a president halfway through a war; they were prepared to support him all the way. The coalition set forth its goals clearly at the outset of the operation and never wavered until it won.

Iraq stubbornly stuck to a losing strategy long after it became clear that it would not succeed. The amazing thing about Saddam's stubbornness is that with so many of us military analysts and commentators predicting his defeat well before he had been cut off by the 100-hour ground campaign, Saddam never began to pull back or even offer to do so until it was too late.

In the final analysis, a campaign is won by the side that has the better operational concept for defeating the enemy. In this case the Iraqi concept was to hunker down and stick it out. The Allies, in contrast, fought a combined arms campaign of maneuver. There is nothing inherently wrong with an attrition strategy if the enemy's force can be forced to attrit itself. This happened to the United States in Vietnam, with disastrous results for the country. It did not happen in the Kuwaiti Theater of Operations because America had learned its operational lessons from Vietnam.

There is a bogus debate going on in the aftermath of the war that one of the services might have won all by itself if only it had been allowed to prosecute the war its way. Many argued that the Navy could have forced Iraq out of Kuwait simply by continuing the maritime embargo initiated in the summer of 1990. Air power advocates claim that if the air campaign had been allowed to continue just another couple of weeks, so many of Saddam's tanks would have been destroyed that he would have been forced out anyway. These adherents argue for a single-service approach to future wars, with one arm dominating and the others playing minor roles supporting the primary air or naval force.

The fact is that no single service won this war; all of them did. None was singularly sufficient and each was absolutely necessary. It may be that naval blockades can bring a country to its knees, but in the case of the Persian Gulf War the prospects for maintaining an effective embargo around Iraq for the twelve to eighteen months that would have been necessary to do so were daunting. Even if the air campaign could have been sustained another two weeks, there is no way of knowing when an enemy will quit or how long he will stay when hunkered down. In any case, neither the politics nor the weather gave the coalition another two weeks at the end of February, when the ground campaign was launched. In the end someone had to go in on the ground and take Kuwait back, and the fight was no mopping-up operation.

The fundamental quality of war is that it is infinitely unpredictable. The force that best preserves its options against the unpredictable is the force that will prevail. It was the inherent flexibility of the Allied force that gave it the ability to respond to Saddam's every trick and stratagem. Indeed, most of the changes imposed on the Allied plans were caused not by Saddam but by natural forces that no one could anticipate. In the end, the ability to bring multiple arms to bear on Saddam's land force meant that even if Iraq had enjoyed some measure of success early on, Saddam's forces were going to lose. The only questions were when and at what cost.

Things

The basic dilemma presented by the great success of Desert Storm has to do with how we deal with weapons systems in the future. The good news is that everything worked. The bad news is that we still cannot afford it all. The United States will face incredibly difficult choices in the 1990s over how to preserve the keys to this great victory even while we reduce our defense spending to account for the reduced threats we face in the foreseeable future. If we look in isolation at each system used in the war we will want to buy them all. If instead we look beyond the performance of individual weapons systems to how force packages can work together in the future, I believe we can exploit our natural advantage in technology at an affordable cost and remain the world's only superpower well into the twenty-first century.

We must begin by taking a new look at how we plan to deter war through strategic systems. For decades we have relied on the threat of nuclear retaliation to deter any adversary from ever striking us with nuclear weapons in the first place. For a long time we even told everyone that we reserved the right to use nuclear weapons first if our interests in Europe were threatened by a massive Warsaw Pact attack. Now those doctrines are being challenged by the irrelevance of the Soviet threat and by the emergence of conventional warfare threats from strong Third World states such as Iraq. We must find ways to deter future Saddam Husseins from taking other Kuwaits.

One thing the war showed us in this regard is the value of ballistic missile defenses. The Patriot was never conceived to be an antimissile missile, but it filled that role nicely against a crude threat from Iraq's modified Scuds. Other ballistic missile threats are more sophisticated and we will have to have systems much more capable than Patriot. They must be able to provide wide-area defense, and they must be rapidly deployable to any part of the world.

The war also revealed our increasing dependence on space-based systems for deterrence. The United States received early warning of Scud launches by means of our spy satellites, which detected Scud launches instantly. Launch data were relayed quickly to both the Allied command in the theater and to the Israelis. This early warning made it possible to get Patriot crews ready for intercepts and to prepare populations for proper protective measures. It almost became routine after the first couple of launches.

But no one was shooting at our satellites. Those "eyes in the sky" were so valuable that, had they been shut down, there would have been much more panic when the missiles struck and more resources would have been diverted to hunting down and killing those mobile Scud launchers. The Soviets already have a functioning antisatellite capability, and many other countries are developing such systems. The United States' dependence on space-based systems is so critical that I believe we need to concentrate on developing counters to emerging antisatellite systems, we need to deploy our own ASAT capabilities, and we must develop redundancy in our satellite coverage and launch capability to be prepared to fight the next war in the high ground of outer space.

In land warfare, Desert Storm demonstrated a continuing need to deploy highly lethal and agile systems capable of moving very fast across the battlefield. Given the ineffectiveness of Iraq's artillery against Allied armor, it should be possible to lighten the armor protection of our heavier systems—tanks and fighting vehicles—in order to get even more speed and agility out of combat vehicles. The next tank must be considerably lighter, faster, and perhaps stealthier than the M-1 Abrams.

The effectiveness of Multiple Launch Rocket System (MLRS) should be exploited. More applications of the concept of using fewer people to deliver more firepower can be found just as a single MLRS launcher manned by four men can deliver more firepower than an entire battalion of five hundred World War II artillerymen. Precision-guided munitions, for example, can give MLRS the ability to hit and destroy tanks.

Ground forces in Desert Storm did not have adequate surveillance and reconnaissance capabilities. No commander ever has enough information to fight his battle with complete certainty, but future wars are going to be so fast-paced that a premium will be placed on the ability to see farther and sooner. U.S. ground forces should expand the exploitation of Unmanned Aerial Vehicles for this role and should experiment with light satellites that could be launched on short notice to provide coverage more responsive to battlefield commanders.

In the air much can be done to exploit our technological lead over any foreseeable foe. American planes fly faster and higher, are more survivable, and can deliver more effective ordnance than any others in the world. The key to winning the air war in Desert Storm was the ability to win command of the skies so quickly. Even if the Iraqi air force had put up a stiffer fight early on in the campaign, they would have lost, though Allied aircraft losses would have been higher. We must continue to maintain our lead in the design and production of high-performance aircraft.

Once air superiority is won, the effectiveness of precision bombing can have a salutary effect on the outcome of the campaign. Smart bombs killed more tanks than any other aerial weapon. The United States leads in these technologies as well, but Allied air forces possess weapons of equal effectiveness in many respects. The Iraqis also had a number of precision-guided munitions they had purchased from the French and the Soviets, so this is an area that deserves continuing efforts to maintain our lead. It will also be important to keep up with technological developments in other countries in these weapons in order to develop counters to their potential use against U.S. forces.

The success of the first few days of the air campaign was in many ways a result of defense suppression measures taken in secret in the opening hours of the war. Active measures designed to shut down enemy air defenses included electronic warfare, Apache helicopter raids, and HARM missile strikes. The most effective passive measure was, of course, the use of the Stealth fighter, but it is unclear how much of the success was due to the passive versus the active measures. Before we invest billions on fielding a new generation of Stealth aircraft, we should carefully analyze the trade-offs between the two approaches. Perhaps some mix of the two would be most appropriate for the future.

Naval combat was, of course, not a significant factor in the campaign of Desert Storm, but maritime supremacy was vital to the success of the effort since most Allied forces deployed by sea. Carriers, submarines, and surface combatants will still be needed in the future, since there are several blue-water navies around the world capable of posing a significant threat to America's sea lines of communication.

One glaring weakness again revealed by operations in the Persian Gulf is in mine warfare at sea. The United States still does not possess adequate minesweeping capability, even though deficiencies in this area were revealed throughout the 1980s in the very same Persian Gulf during the Iran-Iraq War. We have been content to rely on our Allies to perform needed countermine operations for us, and so far we have had Allied support when needed. But in the future we cannot be certain that those same Allies will support us against a different foe in different circumstances. The United States must develop a more robust countermine capability of its own for the 1990s.

Strategic mobility was sorely stressed in Operation Desert Shield. The story of the airlift and sealift to deploy the force was truly remarkable. The United States is the unquestioned leader in this regard, but the demands of the future will be at least as tough as those for Desert Shield and are likely to be even more stressful. We cannot assume that our transport planes and ships will have unquestioned access to the skies and ports needed to deploy our forces on such a scale again. We must anticipate that there will be some interdiction of our deploying forces, and we must have sufficient backup transport available to replace some losses.

Moreover, this war has severely stressed the existing fleet of ships and planes. We need many more fast sealift ships in order to get more heavy ground forces to a distant theater. Greater use can be made of Maritime Prepositioning Ships afloat to have supplies nearby because we are not likely to enjoy an extensive support infrastructure of modern bases built into the region as we have had in Saudi Arabia. The fleet of ships bearing the bulk of the load, the slower Ready Reserve Fleet, needs a comprehensive overhaul and must be maintained in a better state of readiness for future contingencies.

The military airlift fleet was flown to the limits of its performance capabilities in Desert Shield. Our C-141s and C-5s will need to be overhauled sooner than previously planned because so much of their design lifetime was used up in airlift operations for Desert Shield. A replacement aircraft is not likely to be available for some time, so we will probably have to invest in a service life extension program to essentially rebuild much of our current fleet. Finally, we must reevaluate whether we need a costly new transporter, the C-17, or if we could get more lift for the money by reopening the assembly lines for the older craft and buying newer versions of the older models in greater quantities.

Our ground transportation assets were inadequate to the task set before them for Desert Storm. Early in the planning phase of the war, when General Schwarzkopf contemplated ordering the great deceptive shift in tank forces to the west, he quickly discovered that there were not enough Heavy Equipment Transporter (HET) trucks in the American Army to move all its tanks around. Fortunately, several smaller alliance members from the Warsaw Pact had hundreds of such trucks available since they were no longer required by their former Russian masters in Europe. Czechoslovakia was instrumental in providing those transporters, a dependency we should not repeat in future conflicts. We ought to buy more trucks.

Special Operations Forces proved their worth in Desert Storm. We may never know the complete story of how they were employed; after all, their missions are deliberately cloaked in secrecy. But apparently these commandos convinced their greatest skeptic—General Schwarzkopf—of their worth prior to the battle. They evidently were employed in a doctrinal manner, conducting strategic reconnaissance deep behind enemy lines where only human eyes and ears could do. And they conducted "direct action" missions—meaning blowing things up and killing people—where it was necessary to do so clandestinely. The main impetus behind these successes was the maturity of the Special Operations Command (SOCOM) that was mandated by Congress in 1986. SOCOM gave such forces the bureaucratic and budgetary support they had always lacked in the past. And through their successes, they gained new respectability from their colleagues in the conventional forces, which largely had passed them off in the past as necessary but somewhat eccentric as well.

Finally, Desert Storm demonstrated a need to continue to develop technological advances in command, control, communications, and intelligence (C3I) systems. Two key capabilities available to the Allies were provided by high-tech airborne radar systems. The Airborne Warning and Control System (AWACS) had the skies over the KTO completely wired. Anything that flew was instantaneously detected and identified by AWACS, and Allied aircraft could respond much faster than the Iraqis ever knew. The equivalent for monitoring ground operations was the newly developed Joint Surveillance Target Attack System (JSTARS). JSTARS tracked vehicles moving on the ground and was particularly effective in locating mobile Scud launchers and tank forces preparing to attack. AWACS needs updating to account for newer emerging threats, and JSTARS has proven that it should be fully developed and deployed.

More important, with all this information now available, there is a growing need for a theater-wide information network that can distribute data in real time across the battlefield to those who need it. The current practice of having separate and unique down-link units from all these airborne and space-based sensors is already overwhelming commanders with an overabundance of ground stations. We must exploit information management technologies to reduce the numbers and varieties of such ground stations to a few common modules.

Our defense industrial base almost failed us in this conflict. To be sure, many patriotic defense companies voluntarily spent millions delivering requested items on short notice, without contractual authority and with only a promise of money to be paid later. In some cases they will not be paid. In others they delivered all of this year's production and will soon shut down due to lack of future orders. But in several areas the industry cracked. For example, the sole manufacturer of atropine nerve agent antidote autoinjectors was never able to produce sufficient quantities to issue the required two doses per individual. And the ammunition industry, formerly the bastion of the arsenal of democracy, nearly failed us totally. Had the ground war lasted another week, Army and Marine troops would have exhausted supplies of some kinds of ammunition, and the industry had no capacity to surge production. For some electronics components, the Defense Department found that its only sources were Japanese, and the Commerce Department had to negotiate with our erstwhile Asian trading partners for accelerated delivery of vital components. The defense industrial base will need a comprehensive policy overhaul for the 1990s.

It will not be easy to keep people, ideas, and things in balance in the future. The threats we face are not diminishing; they are only shifting. As underlying tensions around the globe come to the surface in the absence of an overriding superpower rivalry, conflicts are bound to increase. Where those conflicts threaten U.S. interests, America must be prepared to employ its armed forces to protect those interests.

Not every situation will be as demanding as Desert Storm, but some will. It is likely that one or two will require even more of us than did this war. And for sure we will not be able to assume that our next opponent will be as stupid as Saddam Hussein turned out to be. We must not become complacent. We must strive to build a force that will cause future Saddams to understand what can be brought to bear against them and not threaten our interests in the first place.

Prospects for the 1990s

The Middle East will continue to command our attention for the future. We have become the critical element of the military balance in the region, and we cannot now back out of that position without affecting that balance negatively. We will have to maintain the capability to bring military forces to bear in the region for the foreseeable future to protect our interests. U.S. interests in the Middle East include regional stability, reliable access to oil, strategic access to sea lines of communications, military access to the region, and the prevention of direct threats to the territory of the United States. These interests translate into a number of military objectives:

- ensure the survival of Israel
- promote the establishment of democratic governments
- encourage peaceful resolution of regional conflicts
- discourage proliferation of nuclear, chemical, and biological weapons
- encourage economic growth
- prevent a single actor from gaining control of oil

- prevent the formation of an oil cartel
- prevent the domination of resources by an extra-regional actor
- prevent a hostile regional actor from controlling key waterways
- prevent an extra-regional actor from gaining military facilities on key waterways
- preserve overflight rights in and to the region
- predeploy heavy equipment
- maintain some permanent air and naval facilities
- allow no extra-regional power to gain bases in the region
- promote the safety and security of U.S. citizens in the region
- discourage the proliferation of long-range ballistic missiles; and
- prevent terrorist threats to U.S. citizens and facilities worldwide

The arms race and the volatility of relationships among the states of the Middle East make the accomplishment of these objectives especially difficult.

The Military Balance

The military balance in the Middle East is not a balance at all, at least not in the sense of a stable equilibrium. The military situation is instead a very unstable solution that can be precipitated into a violent reaction with any number of catalysts. All states in the region are adding to their military arsenals both in terms of numbers and quality in an upward-spiraling arms race. No less than thirteen conflicts were ongoing and unresolved before the Persian Gulf War, according to March 1990 congressional testimony by U.S. Central Command Commander-in-Chief General H. Norman Schwarzkopf. It is, as former U.S. Ambassador to Saudi Arabia Robert Neuman put it at the CSIS conference on the Persian Gulf Crisis on January 4, 1991, more like nineteenth-century Europe than any other historical analogy. Indeed a classic balance of power system has developed in the Middle East.

There are four groups of military powers in the Middle East. The "Gullivers" include the major regional powers of Israel, Egypt, Turkey, Syria, Iran, and Iraq. By sheer weight of population, economy, and military manpower, these states collectively dominate the military situation in the region. Any conflict to which one of these is a party is a factor in the national security calculations of each of the others. And any conflict not involving a "Gulliver" state must consider the impact of potential entry by one of these countries, whether as a third party, an ally, or an ally of an opponent. If one of these states emerges as dominant, then the others will be driven to form a coalition in response.

The second group of states are the aspirants to regional power: Libya, Morocco, and Algeria. Each has defined for itself a unique role in the overall balance. Morocco has developed a strong military to deal with its internal security problem while Qaddafi's Libya has ambitions, perhaps vainglorious, of global Pan-Arab leadership. Algeria appears to be pursuing military strength in order to serve as a bridge between the West and the Arab world and thereby to increase its own relevance and power in both worlds. The "aspirant" states have large and powerful military establishments, but for their own reasons do not seek to be players in every power relationship among the "Gullivers" in the region.

At the third level of relative military strength are the "worriers." These smaller states are large enough that they must figure into the calculations of the larger "Gullivers" and "aspirants," but are not strong enough militarily to defend themselves without an alliance of several of the others. Thus Jordan, Saudi Arabia, Sudan, Tunisia, and the United Arab Emirates have substantial ground and air forces and must carefully consider each outbreak of conflict in the region and how it might get caught up in the conflict or how it might avoid involvement altogether.

Finally there are several "Lilliputian" states that are too small to defend themselves but that possess great influence because of their oil reserves. These potential "Sarajevos" include Bahrain, Kuwait, Qatar, and Oman. When they act in concert they can exert a substantial military power, as they did in the Persian Gulf War, but most of the time they will be influenced more by the military power and objectives of the others than by their own particular designs. Their single vital national interest is the preservation of their access to the international oil suppliers market, an interest that they are incapable of supporting through military power because of the small size of their population.

There are two special cases of national military power in the Middle East that do not fall neatly into any of the above categories. Lebanon is less a sovereign state and more a divided and occupied territory with no national military force. More than a decade of violent political rivalries among the sectarian groups of Lebanon, most with their own military arms, have resulted in a tearing asunder of Lebanon into separate Israeli and Syrian zones, with a chaotic Lebanese middle ground in between. Lebanon is not likely to be a major military power in the region for at least a decade.

The other special case is Yemen. With the unification of the Yemeni Arab Republic and the People's Democratic Republic of Yemen, a potentially powerful new state was born in the 1980s. With the military forces of the two countries unified there is the potential for the new Yemen to become a major military power of its own right in the region. It remains to be seen if the Yemenis can overcome the difficulties of unification during the 1990s, but if they do, they will have a military force potentially as powerful as Saudi Arabia's. The influence of a more united Yemen could be potentially greater than its population and economic strength because of its geostrategic location at the horn of the Arabian Peninsula spanning the Red Sea and the northern Indian Ocean approaches to the Persian Gulf, its oil reserves, and its mobile labor force that provides workers for much of the rest of the oil fields on the Arabian Peninsula.

A number of extra-regional actors have interests in the Middle East and will have reason to exert military influence over the region in the 1990s. These include the Soviet Union, the People's Republic of China, Western Europe, Japan, other OPEC states, and other Islamic states. Each will, of course, face constraints in their ability to gain from the influence their military power gives them but each will have some role to play. The U.S. must take them into account in its own calculations for the region.

The trend of military power in the Middle East is an ever-growing upward spiral. Each state has grown significantly in the 1980s, and despite several wars, each plans to continue its military growth in the 1990s. Every category of every weapon grew in numbers and technological advancement during the 1980s and the plans of most countries to continue to grow in the 1990s are largely well-known. The most dramatic buildups have been in Egypt and Syria, but both Iran and Iraq view their defeats in recent conflicts only as temporary setbacks in their longer-view plans for growth. Saudi plans for accelerated modernization in the wake of the Persian Gulf War will stimulate its Gulf Cooperation Council allies to do likewise, and this round of buildup will cause the "Gullivers" and the interested external powers to consider the impact on their own positions in the balance. Turkey has new security problems to deal with in the post–Cold War era that will cause it to be more concerned with its older Ottoman heritage than with its twentieth-century European identity. Thus Turkey may shift forces to its southern and eastern flanks both for external and internal security in the 1990s and may find it necessary to increase its military strength in these areas.

Contingencies

It is difficult to predict what contingencies might erupt in the Middle East region. Who would have predicted the particular alignment that came together, on both sides, during the Persian Gulf Crisis and War of 1990–1991? But certain possibilities suggest themselves and deserve attention for planning purposes in considering the role of military forces in America's strategic approach for the future.

The fundamental contingency is the underlying unresolved Arab-Israeli conflict. It is not likely to be permanently resolved in the 1990s so it must figure into the calculations of U.S. military force. If only two out of the five other "Gullivers" form a military coalition against Israel, the survival of the Jewish state will be threatened. This will require intervention by the United States, as it nearly did in 1973. Given the far greater potential destructive power of weapons in the arsenals of all the "Gullivers", the situation would be at least as dangerous in the 1990s as it was in the 1970s, even though the Soviets would be far less likely to be involved in the future than it was then.

The two "Gullivers" that have been devastated by war will rebuild. Iran has embarked on a recovery process that includes plans to reconstruct its military power. Already it has acquired 137 modern high-performance aircraft from Iraq to refurbish its once dominant air force. Iran is likely to exploit this windfall for its own defense. Iraq is broken but unbowed. Saddam Hussein has a resilience that should give us no cause for calm in the 1990s, and he still has a military force of some strength. He can be counted on to make every attempt to circumvent world sanctions designed to keep him in check.

If, however, the internal strife in Iraq eventually causes the downfall of the Saddam regime, the ensuing political chaos would likely result in a divided Iraq—Lebanon writ large. In this contingency, there is a real danger that Iran, Turkey, and Syria would move in for their share of the kill in the dismemberment of Iraq, each pursuing its own self-interest to preclude a threat on its border. This situation would create a cauldron of conflict at the very center of the Middle East, bordering on the world's most important oil supplies, that would be as much a threat to Western interests as a single dominant military power in the region.

A second type of threat to U.S. interests may come from extraregional actors seeking new strength in the Middle East. The Soviet Union demonstrated throughout the Persian Gulf crisis that while it may no longer be able to exert the military influence it once had over its clients in the region, it still considers the Middle East a vital interest of its own. A resurgent Soviet military policy might seek to build new clients in the 1990s through cheap military hardware sales for hard currency. While Western high technology was demonstrated to be extremely effective in the war with Iraq, the old Soviet approach of mass firepower was not disproved by Saddam's miscalculations. Several Middle East states may find Soviet, Chinese, Brazilian, or other offers of military assistance quite attractive.

Japan has been reluctant to exert its military force in the Persian Gulf, but it crossed an important divide when it deployed noncombatant military forces overseas for the first time in its history. Japan has the sixth largest military force in the world and it will continue to grow in the 1990s. It will by the end of the decade have some ability for power projection in its air and naval forces. If conflict in the Middle East threatens Japan's economic well-being, the Japanese will find it more useful, and less expensive, to send its own military contingent than to pay cash to exert influence over its interests in the Middle East in the 1990s.

Proliferation threats abound in the Middle East. The 1990s' round of the arms race promises to be the round of ballistic missiles and weapons of mass destruction. Many states have added tactical ballistic missiles to their arsenals. The Persian Gulf War demonstrated the political value of such weapons although the Scud did not do much for the reputation of such systems for military purposes. Other, more advanced systems will prove more useful not only to the "Gullivers," all of whom now have ballistic missiles, but also to the "aspirants" and the "worriers," as cheap balancers.

While chemical weapons were not employed by Iraq, as was feared, the utility of such instruments has been refined. While they have been disproved as the "poor man's atomic bomb," they have been used in anger in the Middle East. Military forces in the region that gain political authority to employ them will use them in situations where their opponents have no defense, as in the case of Iraqi use against Kurdish insurgents, or to break the momentum of an offensive assault, as employed by both Iran and Iraq in tactical situations during the eight-year war. Thus U.S. forces will have to continue to improve their chemical-defense capabilities. The proliferation of nuclear weapons will continue to be a problem of particular concern for the Middle East region.

Suggested Strategies

The United States cannot fight a war against every Saddam Hussein that might arise in the Middle East. More important, there will be too many potential military conflict situations arising out of the political tensions of the region for the U.S. to deploy military forces for combat every time. We cannot stand even the miraculously low casualty rates of Desert Storm if we have to repeat it several times. Moreover, by 1995, the U.S. will not be able to repeat the deployment feats of Desert Storm, given the scope of the military build-down that has been irrevocably set in motion by the Bush administration. We must thus rely on non-combat use of military force to support our overall strategy to achieve our objectives in the Middle East. Experience suggests a three-fold approach.

First, deterrence must aim to prevent regional conflict. The United States has won new credibility in the hearts and minds of the peoples of the Middle East. Never again can they assume that we will not be involved militarily; they will wonder for some time to come whether we will repeat our commitment demonstrated in the Persian Gulf War. This will have a lasting effect on the region that we can exploit to deter conflict. Moreover, it will not require as much in the way of military deployments to reinforce that deterrent threat, at least not on the scale required for conventional deterrence in Europe, since the positioning of a single cruise-missile-carrying ship within 700 miles of a target will remind everyone of those scenes from downtown Baghdad in January 1991. This is not to suggest a new form of "gunboat diplomacy," but it does mean that we can afford in the 1990s to "walk softly and carry a big stick." Ambiguous deployments and implied threats will have greater impact in the 1990s than they ever have in the past.

Because of the potentially devastating magnitude of conflict in the region, though, we must also pursue an arms control process that can at least try to manage the arms race. Part of the reason for attacking Iraq was not so much its possession of such a large military machine; after all, we have lived with the threat of annihilation from the Soviets for decades. The greater threat posed by Saddam Hussein's power was his demonstrated willingness to use force outside the bounds of accepted rules of the game. The most important of those rules is that weapons of mass destruction are never to be used; they can only deter. Saddam broke that rule in his use of chemical weapons and his incipient nuclear weapons program, which simply could not be tolerated by the rest of the world. An arms control process must replace the threat of military force to contain such proliferation pressures.

Finally, the U.S. must maintain a minimal forward presence for naval and air forces in the region. We cannot keep land combat forces there, but we must construct a network of relationships to permit the rapid introduction of substantial ground forces if needed. That network will have to build on the example set by the construction of the basing infrastructure in Saudi Arabia, although it is unlikely that we will be able to replicate that arrangement elsewhere. It will be important to secure alternatives to Saudi bases for the 1990s should those bases prove to be unavailable in a future crisis or too far away to make a difference.

We have won a great victory in the Persian Gulf. We have preserved our interests for the foreseeable future, but in the process we have unleashed new forces that will bring new pressures to bear on the region. We can have great confidence that our political leaders will work hard with others in the region to keep the peace and build a more democratic and prosperous Middle East. But we must remember that to keep the peace we must prepare for war. That old lesson is the greatest lesson of the Persian Gulf War.

INDEX